AL-ANDALUS REDISCOVERED

MARVINE HOWE

Al-Andalus Rediscovered

Iberia's New Muslims

Columbia University Press
New York

Columbia University Press
Publishers Since 1893
New York
cup.columbia.edu
© Marvine Howe, 2012
Library of Congress Cataloging-in-Publication Data

Howe, Marvine.
 Al-Andalus rediscovered : Iberia's new Muslims / Marvine Howe.
     p. cm.
 ISBN 978-0-231-70274-4 (alk. paper)
 1. Muslims—Spain. 2. Muslims—Portugal. 3. North Africans—Spain.
 4. North Africans—Portugal. 5. Immigrants—Spain. 6. Immigrants—Portugal.
 7. Spain—Emigration and immigration—Government policy. 8. Africa,
 North—Emigration and immigration. 9. Intercultural communication—Spain.
 10. Intercultural communication—Portugal. I. Title.

DP53.M87H68 2012
305.6'970946—dc23

                    2012003832

Columbia University Press books are printed on permanent and durable acid-free paper. This book is printed on paper with recycled content.
Printed in India

c 10 9 8 7 6 5 4 3 2 1

References to Internet Web sites (URLs) were accurate at the time of writing. Neither the author nor Columbia University Press is responsible for URLs that may have expired or changed since the manuscript was prepared.

CONTENTS

To

Dedee and Bertrand Bellaigue in appreciation of their encouragement and constructive criticism over the years.

1

GATE CRASHERS

Like some forbidden Eldorado, Spain's Costa del Sol beckons enticingly to Africa, barely a stone's throw away. The glittering beach resorts with golf courses and marinas, tropical haciendas, rows of luxury townhouses, super high-rise apartments and hillside holiday villages under construction exude promises of the good life. The entire coast has become a play-land for English, Germans, French, Americans, Scandinavians, and Arabian sheikhs and their retinues ... and a dream for African migrants. In fact, some Spanish like to say: Costa del Sol is full of wealthy Arabs and destitute Moors.

In recent years, countless undocumented Africans have braved the perilous waters of the Gibraltar Strait, only eight miles at its narrowest point, to reach southern Spain and the gateway to Europe. These uninvited visitors arrived by *pateras* (derelict wooden fishing boats), container ships, plastic rafts, jet-skis, water-motor-cycles, inner tubes, surf boards, or toy dinghies.

This is no triumphant return of the medieval Muslim armies to recover their lost paradise of Al Andalus, as some conservative Spanish circles suggest since Muslims have become more visible—and, ironically, some Al Qaeda leaders have threatened. From all accounts by social workers, journalists and undocumented migrants themselves, Moroccan migrants today come with one goal in mind: to find decent jobs and improve their living conditions and those of their families. And Moroccan authorities view immigration in general as a means to ease demographic strains but, above all, as the country's principal source of foreign exchange, even before tourism.

The tragedy is that many thousands of would-be immigrants never reach their destination, but lose their lives in the crossing. The Strait, particularly in winter, can be a treacherous place. Local residents remember the first *patera* wreck of 1 November 1988, and pictures of the dead body covered with dirt and seaweed, lying on the beach at Tarifa at the tip of Spain. The Guardia Civil found five drenched Moroccans nearby, who said they had sailed from Tangier the evening before. Their *patera* had been caught in a bad storm and capsized, and eighteen of their fellow passengers were lost at sea. Images of corpses floating along the shore and dehydrated boatpeople soon became a common sight along the Costa del Sol and in the Spanish press, disturbing even the most callous tourists. There are only piecemeal estimates of how many boatpeople have fallen victim to the cruel waters of the Mediterranean. Some 10,000 North African and African migrants lost their lives attempting to enter Spain from Morocco in the period between 1989–2002, according to CARIM (Consortium for Applied Research on International Migration), a European study group on migrations. Although it is impossible to confirm that grim toll, the number of immigrants lost at sea has increased with new security measures taken to seal off the peninsula from its unwanted southern neighbors. It is estimated that 7,000 people died trying to reach Spain in 2006 alone.[1]

It was the calamity of these desperate boatpeople, washed up on the shores of Spain's southern Andalucia region that awakened Iberians to the fact that, for the first time, they were faced with an immigration problem. And it was evident that most of these undocumented migrants were Muslim, thereby creating the confusion that the immigration problem was linked to the intractable question of the integration of new Muslim communities, like elsewhere in Europe.

Actually, the modern invasion of the Iberian Peninsula dates from 1991, when the European Union closed its doors to much of the world—110 countries, including all of Africa—under the Schengen Accord. The first boatpeople were Moroccans, Algerians and Tunisians, who had previously entered Spain without visas, under reciprocal accords with their countries. Inevitably, like the proverbial pressure cooker, when the lid was slammed shut, an explosion followed. In the first month after Schengen, some 17,000 Moroccans were turned away at the Spanish border. Thousands more were detained trying to enter the country illegally, and many already in Spain found themselves in illegal limbo. Shortly afterwards, there were reports that local drug traffickers, generally Spaniards and North Africans, had expanded their business to smuggling people. Their expertise, which came at a steep price for the migrants, accounted for the sudden and swift increase in numbers.

Early on, many Spaniards were moved by the plight of the boatpeople along the Costa del Sol, reminiscent of the Cuban refugees' struggle to get to the Florida coast. There are numerous tales of individual heroism, like the Franciscan priest from Algeciras who combed the beaches and nearby forests every night for foreigners *sin papeles* (without documentation) and gave them shelter. When the flood of boatpeople got out of hand, the local police called on the priest, Father Isidoro Macías, for help. Now Father Isidoro is known all over Africa as *Padre Pateras*. A national institution, he has appeared on numerous television shows in Spain and elsewhere in Europe. His compassionate work inspired the best-selling Spanish novel, *Luna Negra: La Luz del Padre Pateras*.[2]

The main task of providing emergency relief to the boatpeople has been assumed by the Spanish Red Cross. "At first, when a *patera* arrived, our volunteers would go to the beach with dry clothing and blankets and hot food because many boatpeople suffered from hypothermia; it was a question of humanity," María José Hernández Velázquez, a senior official of the Red Cross in Andalucia, told me in an interview at the provincial headquarters in Córdoba.[3] But with the waves of *pateras* multiplying, the Red Cross signed an accord of cooperation with the Spanish government in 2003. Today the Andalucian Red Cross has eight teams of volunteers working along the coast from the western port of Tarifa eastward to Almería. Besides initial assistance and screening for health problems, the Red Cross runs programs aimed at helping to integrate immigrants. Ten Offices for the Social Welfare of Immigrants (known by the Spanish acronym OASIS) provided more than 4,100 people with food aid, counsel and information, and Spanish classes in 2008. Volunteers also take first aid to the seasonal workers' camps in the area. In addition, the Red Cross operates three immigrant centers in the province.

"Our services change in accordance with the needs," Hernández said, noting that although the number of *pateras* reaching the Costa del Sol has dropped substantially, her services have more work than ever. "Many migrants are transferred here from the Canary Islands, and boatpeople are still heading towards the coast of Almería and end up with us," she explained. She recounted the tragic story of a twenty-nine-year-old Nigerian whose *patera* capsized off Almería on 8 July 2008. "He had to witness the drowning of his wife and their two children and it drove him mad," she said, adding that he was now getting psychiatric help. Hernández said that 90% of their funding comes from the central government and 10% from the provincial authorities. All the personnel are volunteers, except doctors and team leaders. The Red Cross never has problems finding volunteers for immigration projects. "Most Spaniards are sensitive to immigration questions," she stressed. "We all have family members who emigrated to Latin America over the years to make a better life, and more recently those who went to Germany and Switzerland to find work and had to live in slums."

Accompanied by Hernández, I visited the center at Baena, known as "the inn," which opened with twenty-eight beds in 2005 as an experiment for transient migrants. The atmosphere was more like a sports club than an institution. The residents were watching television, playing ping-pong and waiting for "the professor." They told me they had come to Spain by *cayucos* or large wooden fishing boats, from Guinea-Conakry, Ivory Coast, Mali, Senegal and Mauritania, via the Canary Islands. Some had been at the inn for two months, some longer, although theoretically a stay is limited to fifteen days. They were given room and board as well as Spanish classes, job training and contacts to official services. "This is not an internment center; the men are free to leave when they want," said Juan Manuel León de Toro, a public school teacher, who devotes his spare time to volunteer work as vice-president of the Red Cross at Baena. A large jovial man, León took us to meet his star protégé, a Mauritanian named Abou, who has been trying to obtain legal status for four years. Abou lives in a modest rehabilitated one-room flat donated to the Red Cross by a local family. He works on nearby olive plantations, does odd jobs for Spanish neighbors, and has become leader of the immigrant community in Baena. "Abou's case is difficult because there's an expulsion order against him, but he'll make it," León said confidently.

Other volunteer organizations connected to the Catholic Church, like Caritas, also give shelter, food and clothing to new arrivals. According to a report for 2009, Caritas' 300 centers in Spain provided help to 96,000 people, 62.81% of them immigrants. One of the most active non-governmental organizations is the network of *Acoges* or

Welcome Centers, set up by concerned citizens to provide immigrants with social care and legal assistance. In the winter of 1991–2, *Acoges* in Seville, Granada, Málaga and Almería formed the Andalucía *Acoge* Federation, which has become a key advocate of immigrants' rights and their integration into Spanish society.

Despite the good will of these charitable agencies, Spain wasn't ready for the onslaught of *pateras*. Police and port facilities were soon strained, and there was nowhere to put the unwanted guests, who had committed no crime except arriving without documents. Early in 1992, the government opened its first internment center at Tarifa, where many *pateras* landed. Meanwhile, Madrid reached an accord with the Moroccan government to accept repatriated citizens and step up the control of its own waters. For a while the flow of immigrants eased, but soon resumed at other sites along the coast.

Moroccan surveys at the time showed that most youths had a single ambition: to escape to Europe by any means and begin a new life. One of these young people was Aziz Darai, who lived on the streets in Casablanca and had tried four times to reach Europe as a stowaway on ferry boats. I first met Aziz in the comfortable living room of the Franciscan parish house at Algeciras in the summer of 2006. Slight of frame, dressed in worn jeans and a tee-shirt, he appeared much younger than his twenty-six years. Soberly and without embellishments, Aziz recounted his story. His parents had disappeared shortly after he was born, and he grew up in a Casablanca orphanage, which turned him out onto the street when he was nine. He found work as a handyman in a bakery, but there was no time for school.

"That was when my friends talked about Europe, how there were good opportunities and how all I had to do was to get there," Aziz told me.[4] He was fifteen when he first stowed away with a group of clandestine immigrants in a ship bound for Marseilles in 1995. After a month, he was arrested by the French police and dispatched back to Morocco, where he resumed his chores at the bakery. Over the next six years, Aziz picked up other trades—working as a freelance carpenter, electrician and bus driver. He made three more attempts to get to Europe, hiding in trucks on ferries that sailed from Tangier to Algeciras. Twice he was detained by Spanish authorities and sent packing. The last time, on arrival at Algeciras, he climbed down from his hideaway above the wheel of a truck, and was then hit by the truck. Aziz felt his back was broken, but he kept running to escape the police. A compatriot helped him get to the local mosque, where he and three other *sin papeles* were given food and a roof for the night. But Aziz could no longer move, and an ambulance took him to the hospital. In the emergency room, he learned he had a fractured pelvis and suffered from advanced kidney failure, among other problems. When the young Moroccan was released from hospital, he was taken to the Parish of San Pedro y San Francisco Javier, which agreed to keep him until a new kidney could be found. "Now I can only do easy tasks around here, like painting the fence, repairing motors or running errands," Aziz told me ruefully. His aim was to recover so that he could find a real job with a work contract and eventually go to Switzerland where he has close friends. When I returned to Algeciras two years later, I learned that Aziz had received his kidney implant and was doing well. He had settled in the Spanish port, married a Moroccan immigrant and had two babies. But he was still doing odd jobs as there was no steady work available because of the economic crisis.

The North African "candidates for immigration," as immigrant hopefuls are called, were soon followed by other migrants from warring, poverty-stricken regions of sub-Saharan Africa, lured by the economic development, social benefits and visions of the easy life in the European Union. At first, the Africans made their way overland through Algeria or by freighter to Morocco, where they camped out in the forests around Tangier and waited to make arrangements for crossing the Mediterranean. But the nature of the crossing progressively changed. What had begun as a makeshift shuttle of boatloads of Moroccan migrants hoping to find jobs in Europe soon turned into a big business which amounted to a revival of the African slave trade, only now the slaves appeared to be willing instruments. Drug dealers, involved in smuggling hashish to Europe from Morocco, one of the world's leading producers, suddenly found that human trafficking was more profitable.

"It seems like everybody wants to leave Africa," said Encarna Márquez, who runs Algeciras *Acoge* with a warm friendly manner towards every immigrant, whatever the problem. "Many Africans see television shows about Europe where everybody has automobiles, where dogs live more comfortably than most Africans, where people walk on money, and so they'll risk everything to get here," she said, pointing out that migrants often arrived as indentured servants bound to smuggling rings by huge debt. "Others come on their own to find work and to try to make a better life for their families—like my husband, Salif."[5] She did not give me his surname, although he has long since regularized his status.

Salif, thirty-six, had flown from Senegal to Morocco in 1992, with two sons aged twelve and fourteen from an earlier marriage, Márquez recounted. They made the crossing to Spain by *patera*. Detained on arrival, they were held in the Tarifa internment center, and then released with an order of expulsion. With help from Algeciras *Acoge*, Salif applied for political asylum but was refused. In those difficult times, he was helped by a sister living in La Linea and by the local Senegalese Association. At first he made a living by selling odds and ends, like belts and pocket knives, on the street. He had wanted to set up a business in horticulture but couldn't get the necessary financing. In June 1994, Márquez and Salif were married in a Muslim ceremony, followed by a civil marriage five months later. Salif worked in construction for a time, then served as an immigration consultant with the local city hall. After receiving training as a mediator, he worked with other NGOs in Madrid and Granada.

By the mid-1990s, Spanish construction and agricultural enterprises were urgently calling for labor, and migrants flocked to Spain from West and North Africa. Once again there were reports of shipwrecks and drownings off the Spanish coast and widespread detentions of illegal aliens. Morocco no longer applied the Readmission Agreement. Spain's Moroccan enclaves, Ceuta and Melilla, were overflowing with sub-Saharans determined to get to the mainland. Spanish attempts to curb the flow of Africans from these enclaves resulted in angry protests, mass detentions, clashes with the police and bad press. When the situation became untenable, Spain's conservative government declared an "extraordinary regularization" allowing most migrants in the enclaves to go to Spain proper with a one-year residence permit. The rest were herded into tents with no basic sanitary facilities at a military camp in Ceuta.

Actually, official statistics show that the African avalanche was not so menacing as portrayed by the media. Sub-Saharans represented only about 5% of the immigrant population. Large numbers of undocumented immigrants began to appear in Spain in 1997, mainly from Latin America, followed by East Europeans, mostly women from Poland, Romania, Bulgaria and Ukraine. Many had tourist visas or false documents and easily found employment, harvesting fruit and flowers, or serving as live-in domestics, babysitters and care-givers for the elderly. These Latino and European migrants came by "civilized" means, airplane, bus and train, and didn't rouse Spanish public opinion like the earlier scenes of Africans scaling the barbed wire fences of Ceuta and Melilla and *pateras* adrift off the Costa del Sol.

The brisk trade in boatpeople altered substantially in 2001–03, when Spain's Mediterranean patrols began to use a powerful radar system, known as the Integrated System of External Vigilance (or SIVE), originally set up to fight drug-trafficking in the area. By the spring of 2006, SIVE had effectively closed off much of Spain's Mediterranean coast. But this only meant a shift in the migrants' routes.

In the East Mediterranean, the island state of Malta and the Italian island of Lampedusa were in turn inundated with undocumented North Africans and sub-Saharan Africans, and soon declared their borders closed to boatpeople. With surveillance of the Mediterranean tighter, the immigrant-traffickers agilely moved their operations to the Atlantic. Spain's southernmost region of the Canary Islands, off former Spanish Sahara, became the new Mecca for migrants from all over Africa, alarming Madrid and the rest of the European Union.

Called "The Fortunate Islands," the Canary archipelago is a land of eternal spring and a popular holiday destination with northern Europeans, receiving some twelve million tourists a year. The cluster of thirteen volcanic islands is located barely seventy miles off Morocco's southern coast and has been an integral part of Spain since the fifteenth century. African boatpeople had tried to enter Europe through this southernmost gate since 1995, but by 2005 their numbers had dropped significantly because of Spain's accords with Morocco and Mauritania for the repatriation of their citizens. At this point the migrants' route shifted from the Mediterranean to the Atlantic. More than 33,000 boatpeople were detained in the waters off the Canary Islands in 2006, according to official sources, mostly Africans from Senegal, Mali, Gambia, Niger, Mauritania and Ivory Coast. This time, they did not come in flimsy *pateras* because the distances were much greater than in the Mediterranean, 900 miles from the northern coast of Senegal, and the journey more dangerous. They sailed in larger, sturdier *cayucos*, or wooden fishing boats, able to carry the necessary fuel and often chartered by the human traffickers. Despite the increase in coast guard patrols, *cayucos* carrying more than 100 migrants each reached the islands almost daily. The tragedies grew worse as the boats got larger.

In late August, the Mauritanian authorities recovered eighty-four bodies from the sea after their boat capsized en route from Senegal to the Canaries. It was a record for a single incident. By late summer of 2006, some 3,000 boatpeople had died from dehydration, hypothermia and drowning off the Canaries, according to the Red Cross.

That summer, the Spanish prime minister, José Luis Rodríguez Zapatero, interrupted his vacation in the Canaries to visit the internment camps and promised local authorities more aid to deal with the crisis. There he outlined his government's two-pronged immigration strategy: to reach repatriation agreements with more African states and increase development aid to Africa, ostensibly so the migrants would stay at home. The main trouble with this policy is that some African nations have been reluctant to accept repatriation. For one thing it makes them look like they are selling out their own citizens, but also they are heavily dependent on emigrant remittances.

The relentless waves of boatpeople trying to reach Spanish territory had a profoundly negative effect on Spanish public opinion. Official statistics show the dramatic change in attitudes over only a few months. In May 2006, only 27.7% of the people interviewed considered immigration to be the country's top problem. But by September that same year, the figure had changed to 59.2%.[6] Polls said that in 2006, the peak year for the arrival of boatpeople, or migrants trying to enter the country illegally by sea, Islamophobia reached its highest level, with 60% of Spaniards holding a negative opinion of Muslims, almost double the 37% in 2005.[7]

By fall of 2006, Spain's Socialist government, considered one of the most liberal in Europe, began to toughen its immigration policy after the arrival of more than 5,000 sub-Saharan boatpeople in the Canary Islands in barely a month's time. Immigration became a point of contention within the party, as the government called for more European cooperation to control the borders, proclaimed an end to mass legalizations and stepped up repatriations.

In view of the rising tension over immigration, FRONTEX (the European Union's border security agency) reported that nine members of the European Union had reached an accord to set up an Atlantic Patrol to combat traffickers dealing in human cargo. This meant that European naval and aircraft would keep watch for *cayucos* off the West African coast, as well as nearby Atlantic islands. Several months later, Spain announced it would give surveillance aircraft to Mauritania, Senegal and Cape Verde in exchange for continued cooperation from these African states with the European boat patrols. There were also reports that the Moroccan and Algerian authorities had stepped up action to discourage illegal emigration and were patrolling their own waters.

With the new security measures in the Atlantic, the pressure of boat-people around the Canaries let up somewhat, but the traffickers again turned their attention to the Mediterranean. In the spring of 2008, Italy proclaimed what was called an "immigration emergency." The right-wing government of the prime minister, Silvio Berlusconi, carried out widespread detentions of Africans and gypsies. At the same time, the Italian parliament passed harsh legislation making it a criminal offense merely to be in the country illegally.

Openly condemning Italy for its anti-immigration policy, Spain's deputy prime minister, María Teresa Fernández de la Vega, warned that the Berlusconi government's clampdown on immigrants could "incite violence, racism and xenophobia." She added: "We do not agree with a policy of expulsion that disregards the law and the rights [of immigrants.]"[8] It was clear that immigration was not only a major point of dissension in Iberia but also within the European Union, and no one seemed to have a solution.

When I returned to southern Spain in the summer of 2008, there were almost daily incidents involving *pateras* once more attempting to land along the coast from Alicante and Almería to Cádiz. During a twenty-four-hour period in mid-August, some 200 undocumented migrants from five *pateras* were detained in the waters off Tarifa. Wherever there was a gap in the security system, boatpeople tried to sneak through. Instead of taking the shortest route between Tangier and Tarifa, *pateras* now tended to sail from Morocco's wilder shores around Alhucemas and head for eastern Spain around Almería, a longer, riskier trip.

On that visit I finally met Father Isidoro Macías, the celebrated *Padre Pateras*, who no longer goes looking for hapless boatpeople, but still they come to him. "We have to receive them because after all Joseph, Mary and Jesus were immigrants," Father Isidoro told me, explaining why he gives help to undocumented migrants. "Like the holy family, today's immigrants come because they're fleeing dictators and wars, because they are hungry and needy."[9] But he acknowledged there were other causes for the persistent flow of *pateras*. Many people in the most remote corners of Africa have access to satellite television and mobile phones and are constantly tempted by visions of "the European paradise," the priest pointed out. This image is reinforced by vacationing immigrants, who return from Europe with big cars, bought on credit or second hand, and packed full of electrical appliances. Father Isidoro stressed there was also "the migrant mafia," unscrupulous traffickers who have found that trade in human beings is more lucrative than drugs and bleed the immigrants of their savings and even their future earnings.

We met at the office of the White Cross near the port of Algeciras, where the congenial sixty-two-year-old priest runs a home for the elderly. He had just given a final stir to a large pot of chicken soup, which he had prepared for the twenty-three residents. Father Isidoro, who also manages a home for immigrant mothers, said that most boat-people nowadays came from Nigeria overland to northern Morocco and then by *patera* to Spain. The African women tell tales of extreme hardship, starvation and sickness at home. But their accounts of the journey are even worse, the constant abuse from all sides, forced begging and prostitution to earn 2,000 euros to pay traffickers for their boat passage across the Mediterranean. Many boatwomen arrive pregnant or with newborn babies because they have been told this is the only way to gain residence in Spain, Father Isidoro explained. The padre takes them in, Christians, Muslims and non-believers alike, and tries to get them temporary work contracts or gives them train tickets to Madrid, where there are better job possibilities. "The big problem is there's almost no work now, just picking grapes and strawberries, and people generally prefer to hire Romanians and Poles to Africans," he commented sadly. "My main concern is that jobless immigrants are going to turn into delinquents."[10]

Encarna Márquez of *Algeciras Acoge* told me the situation on the ground had changed dramatically since our meeting two years before. "They're still coming from sub-Saharan Africa, maybe not in such large numbers, but there are now more undocumented women than men," she said, confirming what Father Isidoro had said about the influx of pregnant women.[11] "Immigrants believe in the myth that babies are the best passport to Spain," Márquez said wryly. The baby story got started in 2000 when the local authorities gave exceptional residence permits to African women with babies, she explained. Under Spanish law, however, babies born in Spain are not automatically accorded citizenship, but must remain in the country for at least a year and have one parent with legal status. Many women arrive after being raped by police officials or traffickers and end up in prostitution because they owe the smuggling ring between 35,000 and 45,000 euros for their passage from sub-Saharan Africa to Europe, Márquez recounted. And since the economic crisis, things have become worse for undocumented immigrants, she emphasized. Not only is it more difficult to find jobs, but police pressures have increased at the workplace and there are more deportations and restrictions on family reunion.

Yet by the summer of 2009, there was a significant slowdown in the arrival of *sin papeles* in Spanish waters. On both sides of the Strait, I heard that the clampdown on migrants in Morocco and increased surveillance of the coastal waters was having an effect. But above all, it was the global economic crisis, particularly in Spain, that had slowed the flow of migrants. Word had got out that there were no jobs in Europe.

Early in 2010, Spain's interior minister, Alfredo Pérez Rubalcaba, presented mixed news at a press conference. Security forces had intercepted 7,285 boatpeople in 2009, or 45.7% fewer than the year before and 81.4% fewer than in 2006, when nearly 40,000 undocumented immigrants tried to enter Spain by sea. He also stressed that the current economic crisis had reduced the number of undocumented immigrants from Latin America. But he went on to assert: "We can't let our guard down." Pointing out that while there had been a dramatic decrease in *cayucos* trying to reach the Canary Islands, the minister disclosed that the number of African boatpeople arriving along the mainland coast and the Balearic Islands was on the rise.[12]

* * *

The flood of African migrants to the Canary Islands in 2006 raised concerns in Lisbon, which had remained relatively unaffected by the influx of boatpeople on Spain's Costa del Sol. Portugal's former colony, the Cape Verde Islands, located south of the Canaries and 300 miles from the Senegalese coast, was cited as the next possible transit point on the African route to Europe. At the request of the Cape Verde government, a Portuguese Navy patrol boat with FRONTEX began to help the local coast guard control the waters around the islands. The Portuguese were also keeping a wary eye on their Madeira archipelago,

400 miles off the coast of Morocco and 550 miles southwest of Lisbon. The Atlantic resort has regular air connections to mainland Portugal, and is another gateway to Europe.

It seemed inevitable that Portugal, like Spain, would come under assault by boatpeople sooner or later. Remarkably, however, the invaders have not yet set their sights on Portugal's southern coast, the tourist region of the Algarve, even though it is located next to Spain's Bay of Cádiz, a popular destination for *pateras* before the enforcement of Spanish coastal patrols.

When questioned why Portugal has not been a target of boatpeople, the Portuguese invariably point to the dangers of their Atlantic shores. The northeasterly winds that have always plagued navigators and fishermen and the strong currents and rocky coast are powerful deterrents. There is also the distance; the Algarve is located at least 660 miles from the sub-Saharan coast, which is now the main launching pad for *cayucos*. North African and African migrants tell a different story. They generally cite the economy as the main reason why boatpeople have not tried to penetrate the Portuguese coast. Every aspiring immigrant knows that the Portuguese minimum wage is half that of Spain.

In fact, boatpeople have now begun to arrive in Portugal with regular fishing boats and plans to move on to Spain or northern Europe. Would-be immigrants are sometimes caught trying to debark from freighters by passing themselves off as crew, but it is nothing like the number of boatpeople arriving in neighboring Spain. Portugal's Bureau for Foreigners and Borders (SEF), announced in the fall of 2006 that clandestine immigration by sea was increasing. The reason given was that fourteen of the country's twenty-four main ports and marinas have practically no form of border control. SEF reported that in 2005, some 18,700 boats had been checked for transporting undocumented aliens and that legal action had been brought against more than 100 of them for abetting illegal immigration.

"It's a mystery why we haven't received *pateras* on the Portuguese coast yet, but they're going to come for sure,"[13] predicted Fernando de la Vieter Nobre, an Angolan-born neurologist and founding president of the International Medical Assistance (AMI). Modeled after Doctors without Borders, AMI is a Lisbon-based medical aid foundation, which has sent missions to sixty-three countries and operates ten homeless centers in Portugal. "The 2006 wave of African migrants was only the tip of the iceberg," Dr. Nobre emphasized. "Africans will continue to flee as long as nothing is done to end the corruption, bad governance and lack of development in their countries. They have no choice not to move."

Spain's immigration crisis has already produced "secondary effects" in Portugal. In his book, *Passport to Heaven*, Portuguese journalist Paulo Moura movingly relates the saga of the boatpeople and their desperate attempts to flee from Morocco and reach southern Spain. He notes that some women from as far as Benin and Nigeria, who make the crossing to Spain by *pateras*, end up as prostitutes in Lisbon's Intendente Square.[14]

In the spring of 2008, the Portuguese weekly *Expresso* reported that Spanish non-governmental agencies were helping undocumented migrants who had received expulsion orders go to Portugal, France and Belgium. If the aliens have friends or family ready to receive them in neighboring countries they are provided with transportation, the newspaper said, citing sources from the Spanish Committee for Help to Refugees (CEAR) and the Red Cross. The majority of those who choose to come to Portugal are natives of former Portuguese Guinea, *Expresso* said, relating the story of Seiko Djalo. The Guinean began his year-long odyssey in 2005, traveling from Guinea-Bissau by bus to Senegal, then Mali, Nigeria, Algeria and Morocco and by *cayuco* to the Canary Islands and Spain. After forty days in an internment center, he opted to go the Lisbon suburb of Damaia where he has relatives rather than live clandestinely in Spain with expulsion hanging over him. The Portuguese NGO, *Solidariedade Imigrante*, said there were new cases like these every day.

The first *patera* arrived at Portugal's Algarve province in December 2007, as far as anybody knows. A score of would-be immigrants from Morocco were detained off the island of Culatra, which is linked to the mainland by ferry. Although there have been no more sightings of *pateras* in the waters of the Algarve, a flurry of reports on hashish traffic in the area has caused mounting concern. In southern Spain, traffickers use the same routes and sometimes the same equipment to smuggle hashish and humans. The Portuguese have braced themselves for future incursions.

* * *

By 2010, the migrants' route had moved further eastward. Boatpeople were seeking new ways to get into Europe. *Pateras* with hundreds of

North Africans and sub-Saharans were still being intercepted in Spanish waters off Murcia, Almería, Alicante and Mallorca, even in the dangerous winter season. But generally fewer migrants were crossing the Mediterranean. The United Nations High Commission for Refugees reported "a steep decline" in the number of boats trying to land on the shores of Malta and Italy, as well as fewer attempts to reach Spain and France.[15] Turkey was now the main source for migrants pushing into Europe mostly overland. These newcomers were mostly Afghans, Somalis and Eritreans, again many of them Muslims. Turkish authorities arrested 70,000 undocumented immigrants in 2009 and reportedly even more in 2010.

Naturally the refugee route would shift again with the popular upheavals across North Africa early in 2011. This time the Italian government was first to raise a cry of alarm that Lampedusa was being overwhelmed by boatpeople from Tunisia. Some 5,000 North Africans arrived on the shores of the island across from Sicily in a five-day period, according to press reports, which also noted a number of missing persons. When the Tunisian dictator fell, security forces guarding the coastline vanished and there was a rush of young people trying to get to Europe. Also some police officials of the old regime, fearing for their lives, tried to escape. Declaring that the new invasion of boatpeople was a Mediterranean problem, Italian authorities called for help from the European Union. The foreign minister, Franco Frattini, went so far as to urge the EU to order FRONTEX to blockade Tunisian ports.

Spaniards warily watched events on the southern shores of the Mediterranean and waited for the next round. While Spain shares with Italy the frontline in the struggle against boatpeople, Madrid pointedly reminded the European Union of one of its core principles: compassion toward asylum seekers. "Europe historically has been a region of asylum and refuge, and we are not going to close the doors to those who come to Europe because of persecution in their countries," Spain's stalwart deputy prime minister and minister of interior, Alfredo Pérez Rubalcaba, told the press.[16] Expressing solidarity with Italy confronted by the sudden arrival of more than six thousand Tunisians, Rubalcaba also warned that Europe "will not tolerate" attempts by "mafias" to make a fortune from illegal immigrants. Later Rubalcaba announced agreement on a common European Union policy to aid Egypt and Tunisia, already grappling with "humanitarian crises" as refugees from Libya poured over their borders. "We cannot applaud democracy on the one hand and, on the other, forget the consequences, which require our aid," Rubalcaba said.[17]

It was clearly premature to suggest the possibility that with the seeds of democracy being sown across the region, the *patera* people could in time gain new hope and prefer to stay home.

2

MOORISH LEGACY

Like some stalwart sentinel out of the Arabian Nights, the palace of the Alhambra with its Moorish towers, marble courtyards, sculpted ceilings and exotic gardens stands watch over the modern city of Granada, and remains the most splendid jewel in the Spanish crown. Built in the fourteenth century by the Nasrids of Granada, the last ruling dynasty of Muslim Spain, the Alhambra is treasured by Spaniards as a monument to the Christian Reconquest of the peninsula. Yet the crimson fortress, as its name signifies in Arabic, is internationally viewed as a memorial to the glory that was Al Andalus and the single most popular monument of Spain, with thousands of adoring visitors each day from around the world.

The story of the Alhambra reflects Spaniards' mixed feelings about their Moorish legacy. After the Christian reconquest, the Alhambra was soon forsaken and left to fall into ruin—like many other architectural treasures built under Islamic rule. In the nineteenth century, a succession of prominent European visitors expressed shock over the deterioration of the medieval masterpiece. But it was New Yorker Washington Irving who is generally credited with saving what is considered the finest Muslim palace in Europe. His love song to "*The Alhambra*" stirred widespread concern for the fate of Granada's soaring citadel and apparently instigated the Spanish authorities to restore and preserve the landmark.

The myth of Al Andalus, Arabic for "land of the Vandals", has deeply divided Iberian specialists in modern times. For some, the Muslim reign in Al Andalus, which comprised much of what is today's

Spain and Portugal, constitutes a period of degradation; a cruel occupation overcome at great cost and now best forgotten. Others hail Al Andalus as a golden age of enlightenment, prosperity and the peaceful coexistence of Muslims, Christians and Jews. Ordinary Spaniards and Portuguese widely ignore their countries' Islamic past, or view its glorious monuments like the Alhambra and the Giralda as lucrative tourist attractions.

The basic facts of Muslim Iberia are not in dispute. In 711, a young Berber leader, Tariq ben Ziyad, crossed the Mediterranean with some 7,000 troops at the site that is named after him, Jebel Tariq, better known as Gibraltar, and defeated the unpopular Visigoth King Rodrigo. Berber and Arab forces, under various commanders, went on to capture the peninsula city by city—except for a mountainous fringe in the north—until they were halted by the Franks at the Battle of Tours in 732. The father of Al Andalus was an exiled Arabian prince, Abd al Rahman, of the Umayyad dynasty of Damascus, which had been overthrown in 750 by the rival Abbasids. With Arab and Berber followers, Abd al Rahman defeated the Emir of Córdoba in 756 and established Umayyad rule throughout most of Iberia, ushering in 250 years of prosperity, stability and interfaith harmony. In 929, Abd al Rahman III assumed the title of Caliph or Commander of the Faithful and proclaimed Córdoba as seat of the caliphate, or center of the Islamic world. In the end, the Umayyads succumbed not to the Christians but to internal strife and Berber forces from Morocco. The caliphate was abolished in 1009, and Al Andalus split up into numerous *taifa*, or petty kingdoms, ripe for the Christian reconquest.

While Christian leaders had progressively expanded their territories in the north, it was Afonso Henriques, son of King Alfonso VI, who led the reconquest of the northwest, known as Al Gharb Al Andalus, and was proclaimed the first King of Portugal in 1143. With help from Norman, English, Flemish and other crusaders, Afonso Henriques captured Lisbon in 1147, but the southern territories of the Alentejo and the Algarve remained under Muslim control until 1249. The turning point in the Reconquista in Spain occurred in 1212, when Christian forces, backed by European crusaders, defeated the local Muslim armies and their Moroccan allies in the battle of Las Navas de Tolosa, south of Toledo. In rapid succession, the Muslim kingdoms of Córdoba, Valencia and Seville fell to the army of King Ferdinand III of Castile. It would take another 244 years to conquer the last Muslim foothold in Iberia, the Kingdom of Granada. Finally on 2 January 1492, after a two-year siege, Queen Isabella of Castile and King Ferdinand of Aragón received the keys to the royal residence of the Alhambra from Muhammad XII. The last Muslim Prince of Al Andalus signed the Treaty of Capitulations to save his beloved Granada from certain destruction. That same year, Isabella and Ferdinand, known as the Catholic Monarchs, began their cleansing operation to rid the peninsula of unwanted Muslims and Jews through the Inquisition, mass expulsions and forced conversions. By the seventeenth century, the last *Moríscos* (Christianized Muslims) were expelled, and the Roman Catholic rulers believed they had resolved "the Muslim problem" once and for all.

Five centuries after the fall of the last Islamic bastion and the expulsion of all Muslims, Spaniards have yet to come to terms with their heritage from the Islamic occupation. One school of Spanish thought, dominant for a long period, holds that the Muslim rule was a blight on Spanish society and a major obstruction to modernization. For this sector of opinion, strongly influenced by the Roman Catholic Church, the history of Spain begins with the Christian reconquest. These Iberian nationalists include some of Spain's foremost thinkers. In his *Historia de los mozarabes de España*, nineteenth century Catholic historian Francisco Javier Simonet contends that the intellectual achievements of Al Andalus were essentially the work of Spaniards converted to Islam. Poet and novelist Miguel de Unamuno displayed his Arabophobia in a much quoted letter of 1912: "About the Arabs, I have nothing to say; I have a profound dislike for them, I hardly believe in what is called Arab civilization and I consider their passage through Spain to have been one of the greatest misfortunes we have ever suffered."[1] Even the prominent intellectual, José Ortega e Gasset, dismissed any positive influences from the Islamic occupation on Spanish culture in his book of essays, *Invertebrate Spain*.[2]

In the opposing camp, romantics, progressives and *afrancesados* (French-influenced scholars) exalted the glories of medieval Arabic poetry and the culture of Al Andalus. They blamed Spain's lag in science and technology and the warlike spirit of the conquistadors in Latin America on Catholicism and the expulsion of the Jews and Muslims. The best known apologist for Arab Spain was the aforementioned Washington Irving, who served as US minister to Spain. After poring over Spanish chronicles in the Jesuit Library of the University of Granada, Irving concluded: "The Arab invasion and conquest brought a higher civilization, and nobler style of thinking, into Gothic Spain. The Arabs were a quick-witted, sagacious, proud-spirited and poetical people, and were imbued with Oriental science and literature. Wherever they established a seat of power, it became a rallying place for the learned and ingenious, and they softened and reformed the people whom they conquered."[3]

The Spanish Arabist who inspired Irving was José Antonio Conde, director of the Escorial library and author of the first overall history of Islamic Spain, *Historia de la denominación de los Árabes en España*. But while Conde presented Arabic culture in a distinctly positive light, his work was flawed, containing basic errors and neglecting important sources. In the mid twentieth century, historian Américo Castro brought out his groundbreaking work, *La realidad histórica de España*, which highlights the impact of Spain's multicultural heritage on the country's language, customs, religion, art and basic character.[4]

Henry Kamen, British authority on the Spanish Inquisition, favors Américo Castro's thesis that Jews and Arabs played "a vital and positive role" in the formation of Spain's cultural identity.[5] In *The Disinherited*, he writes: "The astonishing truth was that for over a generation Spanish essayists, writers and historians engaged in passionate polemics over the Jewish and Arab aspects of their nation's history when they knew no Hebrew or Arabic and had never done any research into what they were arguing over. On one side were the traditionalists, who clung to the image of Spain as an integral part of western civilization ... On the other were the handful of scholars in the early twentieth century, literature experts like Castro and philologists like the priest Miguel Asín Palacios (1871–1944), who took care to learn Arabic and attempted to integrate the seven Muslim centuries into the fabric of Hispanic civilization."[6]

Spain's Arabic studies acquired impetus in 1912, with the establishment of its protectorate over northern Morocco. The Ministry of Foreign Affairs and the army began to promote North African studies in line with colonial policy. In 1937, an Institute for the study of Moroccan Arabic and Berber was established in Spanish Morocco and an Institute for African Studies in Madrid. Spanish attraction for Moroccan studies declined noticeably after the North African kingdom regained its independence in 1956.

Nevertheless, Franco's Spain, which had remained neutral during World War II, sought to end its diplomatic isolation by developing an active Arab Policy. In 1954, the Hispano-Arab Institute of Culture was established under the direction of Arabist Emilio García Gómez, an eminent poet and translator. This institute organized seminars on contemporary Arab culture, trained teachers in Arabic and Islamic studies for Spanish universities and published translations of Arab literature.

As a result of these official efforts, a new generation of Spanish Arabists was "to enlarge the scope of study of Arabism," according to Miguel Hernando de Larramendi and Bárbara Azaola, professors at the University of Castilla-La Mancha in their recent authoritative report on the development of Arabic studies in Spain.[7] They stress that Pedro Martínez Montávez, head of the Department of Arab and Islamic Studies and Oriental Studies at Madrid's Autonomous University from 1972–1994, succeeded in "extracting Arab studies from their 'engrossment in Andalusia' and bringing them closer to the political and social reality of the time."[8] Professors Larramendi and Azaola note the increase in doctoral dissertations on Arab and particularly North African subjects, the rise in the number of official schools teaching the Arabic language and the growth of institutes dealing with the Arab World and Mediterranean area.[9]

In an attempt to fathom where the controversy over Spain's Islamic heritage stands today, I went to see Bernabé López García, a prominent Arabist and scholar on North Africa. In line with Spain's new interest in its Mediterranean neighbors, the Autonomous University of Madrid revived North African studies and in 1992 set up the Workshop of International Mediterranean Studies, headed by López García. Through this program, the university has funded Arab research, provided grants for Arab students and begun training a new school of Arabists (Spaniards, Moroccans and other foreigners).

Professor Bernabé, as he is known by his students, received me in the book-lined living room of his apartment in the Hay Magdalena section of Madrid which he calls "the heart of Madrid's casbah." The Spanish academic is a keen observer of the Muslim world—past and present—and not a romantic Orientalist nor an angry denigrator. He told me that the surge of Moroccan immigration had awakened "old prejudices" in Spanish public opinion. Also, terrorist attacks by Muslim extremists since 9/11, particularly the assault on Spanish and Jewish targets in Casablanca in 2003 and the Madrid train bombings in 2004, have stirred "latent sentiments of hostility" among Spaniards. "Naturally these incidents have projected a negative image of Muslims, which is bound to affect the ongoing debate on the role of Islamic culture in Spain," Professor Bernabé noted. He said a number of Spanish historians still portray Muslims as "violent barbarians" and "systematically demonized Moroccans" in particular.[10]

A leading critic of Muslim Spain today is Serafín Fanjul, Professor *Catedrático* of Arabic Literature at the Autonomous University of Madrid, whose writings appear to be a direct rebuttal of the work of Américo Castro. In his book, *Al Andalus contra l'España*, Fanjul clearly aims to destroy "the myth" of Al Andalus as a flowering, lost paradise of intellectual tolerance and discovery. Summing up his views of the Islamic legacy in an interview in 2004, the scholar says: "Al Andalus, like all the medieval societies, was extremely brutal and unbearable, in light of our present day concepts of life."[11]

Another fervent naysayer is Gustavo de Arístegui, author of a controversial work *The Jihad in Spain*. The Spanish diplomat writes that Spaniards were the first people to suffer from radical Islam in the Middle Ages. He describes the Almoravid and Almohad invaders from Morocco as "the embryo of the oppressive radical Islamist regimes" that have since reigned in some countries.[12]

The most eloquent defender of Al Andalus in recent years is Cuban-born American medieval scholar María Rosa Menocal, who presents a vivid portrait of "the culture of tolerance" in her political history, *Ornament of the World*. "It was there that the profoundly Arabized Jews rediscovered and reinvented Hebrew; there that Christians embraced nearly every aspect of Arabic style—from the intellectual style of philosophy to the architectural style of mosques—not only while living in Islamic dominions but especially after wresting political control from them; there that men of unshakable faith, like Abelard and Maimonides and Averroes, saw no contradiction in pursuing the truth, whether philosophical or scientific or religious, across confessional lines."[13]

Haizam Amirah Fernández, a senior analyst at the Royal Elcano Institute for International and Strategic Studies, told me that in spite of Franco's pro-Arab policy, "there are today few Spanish academics knowledgeable in Arabic and Al Andalus studies." Son of a Jordanian physician, Amirah is a graduate of the University of Barcelona with an MA in Arabic Studies from Georgetown. He deplores "the lack of competent scholarship" in Arab studies in Spain today. Not many Spaniards are attracted to studies of Islamic religion and culture because of the current radicalism, he said ruefully. "Above all, students see no prospect for employment in Arabic studies, and think it's more important to study English or French."

With increasing recognition that Muslims are today part of the Iberian fabric, some Spanish scholars are calling for a new examination of the myths of Al Andalus and the Reconquista. In her introduction to a recent work on *Muslims in Spain*, Gema Martín Muñoz, director of the Casa Árabe, writes: "A proper understanding of the contribution of *al-Andalus* to Hispanic personality, without idealizing or devaluing its importance, is perhaps the best way to acquire a more impartial understanding of the integration of Muslims into modern Spanish society."[14]

* * *

The Portuguese, who ousted their Muslim rulers much earlier than their Spanish neighbors, have not engaged in the same wrenching debate over their Islamic heritage. For one thing, they are not confronted by the need to explain grandiose Islamic monuments like the Alhambra or the Great Mosque of Córdoba. Called Lusitania by the Romans and Al Gharb (the West) under Muslim rule, Portugal was a kind of backwater in the Middle Ages, with few cities of note and sparsely populated. Most Arab accounts of the conquest and settlement of Al Gharb have disappeared. There were few voices to counter the Christian version of events.

Portuguese schoolbooks generally portray the defeat of the Moors in 1139 at the Battle of Ourique as the major event leading to the creation of the Portuguese nation. These accounts make no attempt to hide their bias in favor of the Christian forces, who progressively recovered the peninsula. The forced conversion of Muslims and mass expulsion of "new Christians" in the seventeenth century did not arouse public reprobation. Like Spaniards, the Portuguese had been imbued with the Roman Catholic vision that Muslims were "infidels" and "the enemy." Only in the mid nineteenth century did a few historians, led by Alexandre Herculano, acknowledge the important contributions of Muslims to the nation's history.

Where Portugal's vision of the Islamic legacy was at variance with Spain's was in colonial policy. As far back as the sixteenth century, Portuguese rulers had decided that the only way their small nation could hold onto its far-flung commercial empire was through a deliberate policy of miscegenation and assimilation of the locals. Portuguese dictator António de Oliveira Salazar, an ardent Roman Catholic, viewed Portugal's colonial policy as a gradual process of assimilation through which natives would be inculcated with Portuguese values.

As the winds of nationalism swept across India and Africa, Portugal adopted the ideology of *Luso-Tropicalism*, conceived by Brazilian anthropologist Gilberto Freyre, who contended that the Portuguese were different from other European colonizers, more adaptable to tropical climes. "Our aim was to create new Brazils in Africa," states Adriano Moreira, the minister of overseas territories under Salazar and now head of the Portuguese Academy of Sciences.[15]

It is, however, the theory of the common origin of the peoples of Iberia and North Africa that is gaining credence among Portuguese academics. A leading historian, António Henrique Rodrigo de Oliveira Marques, argued that with the arrival of the Berber occupiers, Iberians recalled old customs, forgotten under centralized Roman and Visigoth rule. He noted in particular the similar social structures, shared wealth and kinship of languages of the mountain tribes on both sides of the Mediterranean.[16]

The Portuguese scholar also pointed out that many Muslim mosques in Portugal were later "disguised" or transformed into churches. He assured that most castles and walls built in the eleventh to thirteenth centuries south of the Mondego and Tagus rivers were "products of Moslem masonry and military science," but were later believed to be Christian works, he asserts.[17] He described in detail other Muslim contributions: agricultural techniques and plants, like Moorish wheat, rice, oranges and saffron; new skills in navigation, shipbuilding, long-distance fishing and maritime trade; and the trades of carpentry, masonry, tailoring, shoe making and pottery. Muslims also left their imprint on city planning and decoration. Finally the historian noted that while the structure of the Portuguese language is Latin, many expressions migrated from Arabic into Portuguese like words for clothing, agricultural implements and scientific devices.[18]

"The Portuguese don't have the same hang-ups over the Moors as Spaniards, who cannot forget losing 50–60,000 soldiers in the Battle of Annoual in the 1921 Rif War," according to António Dias Farinha, head of the Department of Modern History and professor of Arabic at Lisbon University. Professor Dias Farinha told me that Portuguese historians have generally held a romantic view of Al Gharb. "One of our problems is that so few Portuguese understand Arabic," said the scholar. Prior to 11 September 2001, there were no more than twenty to thirty students studying Arabic, he said. But since then there has been a surge of interest, with as many as eighty-two students in a class with a capacity of fifty.[19]

"It wouldn't have been possible to have the European renaissance as we know it without the Arab–Islamic legacy of Al Andalus," a leading Portuguese Arabist, José Adalberto Alves, declared, underlining "the extraordinary contribution of that civilization to every branch of science and the arts."[20] In an interview, Alves stressed that the Portuguese do not share the "the anti-Arabism" found in some Spanish circles, but "tend to glorify the golden age of tolerance of Al Andalus." A poet himself, Alves has made a significant contribution to the revival of the Arab-Islamic culture in Portugal through his translations of Arabic poetry and legends. He is currently working on a dictionary of Arabic words in Portuguese, estimated to be around 3,000.

Claudio Torres, in his mid-sixties, is not an Arabist but has a doctorate in medieval Art. And this self-taught archaeologist has probably done more than anyone to inform the Portuguese about the Muslim occupation of Al Gharb. Through his archaeological investigations, Torres has gathered evidence supporting the theory that "there was the same civilization on the northern and southern shores of the Mediterranean: the Berber civilization." Villagers in the Iberian mountains had the same social patterns, occupations and types of dwellings as the inhabitants of the Rif and Kabylie in North Africa.[21]

Like many young Communists, Torres opposed Salazar's colonial wars and completed his studies in exile in Prague and Paris. Returning to Portugal after the 1974 revolution, he interrupted an academic career at Lisbon University in 1978 to do archaeological research at the forgotten border town of Mértola, once a major trading-post on the Guadiana River.

Torres' Mértola today is an enchanting museum town which attracts visitors from around the country and abroad. Separate sites constitute a vivid timeline of Portuguese history including a Paleo-Christian Basilica, a Roman Museum, a Museum of Sacred Art and weavers' and blacksmiths' workshops. But Mértola is essentially a Muslim town, resembling a *casbah*, dominated by a thirteenth century castle with Moorish walls. The parish church has been restored as a mosque (non-functioning), with twelve Moorish columns and *mihrab* or prayer niche. The Islamic Museum is said to be the first such institution in Europe and contains a rich collection of ceramic water jugs and tiles. Torres' main achievement was getting Mértola and its county (6,500 inhabitants) declared the Natural Park of the Guadiana, with government support for continued excavations. His latest restoration project is a large white-washed building with arcades, opened in 2007 as a branch of the University of Algarve, offering a master's degree in economic development and expanded in 2008 to include the country's first Center of Islamic Studies with a doctoral program.

* * *

While Spanish scholars are still wrestling with the Islamic legacy and Portuguese academics are discovering their Moorish roots, many local authorities and business people have already decided that Islam is beautiful. Across the southern swath of the peninsula, where the Muslim penetration lasted longest, municipalities have decided that Arab castles are prime tourist attractions and have repaired crumbling walls, turning them into museums or inns or settings for concerts and plays.

Tourism, in fact, has had a significant impact on the revival of Iberia's Islamic past although excavations and rehabilitation have been slow. For example, works began in 1914 to resurrect Medina al Zahra near Córdoba, the splendid tenth century walled capital that Abd-Rahman III built for his beloved wife, which was laid to waste by Berber troops a century later. Only the royal palace has been excavated up to now, although the museum received the Aga Khan Prize in Architecture in 2010 for its harmonious integration into the landscape. Little remains of Arab Madrid, founded by the Emir of Córdoba in 852, and major digs in the capital would be next to impossible. The Royal Palace was built on the ruins of the Arab *alcázar*, and fragments of the ancient city walls have been integrated into the structure of the burgeoning new city. In the spring of 2006, however, Madrid's city hall announced plans to recover some of the eleventh century ramparts by expropriating ninety properties and demolishing three buildings. The aim is to create two new medieval walking tours along remaining stretches of the nine-meter-high brick wall. But this will take time.

Meanwhile, Spanish Arabist Jesús Riosalido has brought out a travel book on Islamic Iberia, entitled *Guía de Al-Andalus*. Former director general of the now defunct Hispanic-Arab Institute of Culture, Riosalido notes that in his travels through Muslim and Jewish Spain, he found the usual guidebooks only gave a few lines to the most important monuments "completely ignoring the rest." It was his intention to make up for these omissions with this guide book.[22]

In Portugal, the discoveries of Islamic, Roman and early Christian remains at Mértola, and their incorporation into museums, have transformed the dying town into a new travel destination. But archeological works on other Islamic sites in the Algarve have been halted for lack of funds. Even in the capital, Lisbon, excavations begun in 1990 on the remains of the twelfth century Grand Mosque, located inside the gothic cloisters of the cathedral, have been painfully slow. In the early 1990s, builders ran into vestiges of Islamic ruins when they began construction on a parking lot and picnic area inside the walls of São Jorge Castle in the heart of Lisbon. The castle was closed off to traffic and works were stopped for four years while the city decided what to do. A team of archeologists and art historians determined that the recent discoveries were the most important Islamic remains in any west European capital. Finally at the end of 2008, Lisbon's Mayor António Costa announced the opening of an Islamic archeological park at São Jorge Castle. A new museum in the walls shows various objects from the excavation site such as Middle Eastern amphora, a grave stone with Kufic inscriptions, a stone mould to make Korans and other instruments.

With foreign travelers in mind, Spaniards and Portuguese are increasingly using their Islamic monuments for cultural events. Seville holds exhibits at the Royal Alcázar and concerts in the palace gardens. In Granada, concerts are held in the Arrayanes courtyard of the Alhambra, and classic and modern ballet in the gardens of the Generalife. Córdoba opens the gates to its Moorish mansions and their flowering courtyards in its Festival de Los Patios, which is becoming an annual tradition.

The spirit of Al Andalus, however, is perhaps best conveyed by what is likely to become a permanent exhibit in Córdoba's fouteenth century Calahorra Tower, built on an Arab fortress next to the Roman Bridge. This is no ordinary museum but seeks to recreate the city's "golden centuries" from the ninth to the thirteenth, where "East was not separated from West, nor was Muslim from Jew or Christian."[23] The main feature is a dramatic audio-visual presentation on "The Meaning of Life in Al Andalus," according to Córdoba's native sons, Arab scientist Ibn Roshd, better known as Averroes, the Jewish physician-philosopher Moses Maimonides and the thirteenth century Catholic ruler, Alfonso the Wise.

In Seville, the Foundation for Three Cultures is working to revive the spirit of Al Andalus. In 1999, Andalucia's regional government and the Kingdom of Morocco established the foundation in a spectacular Arabian Nights building with fountains and archways, originally built as the Moroccan pavilion at Expo 92, the world exposition. "This is a center for peace and tolerance, democracy and dialogue," said Darío Marimón García, head of the Educational Programs.[24] Among the wide range of activities, he mentioned a cycle of talks on Palestinian women, a meeting of Palestinian and Israeli poets, encounters between the late Palestinian-American author Edward Said and Argentine conductor Daniel Barenboim, a conference on international conflicts, a seminar on immigration to Europe and Arabic courses.

Notwithstanding the efforts of organizations like the Foundation for Three Cultures and the Casa Árabe, more public conscience-raising needs to be done to counter centuries of hostility toward Moors. For some observers, it is disconcerting to find that towns and villages in southern Spain still reenact the medieval Reconquista, portraying the Christian conquerors in heroic terms and Muslims as the enemy. In the sixteenth century, the royal court promoted mock battles between *Cristianos y Moros* as a form of public entertainment, and these reenactments have became part of the folk culture. In the province of Valencia, the most elaborate costumed battles take place at Alcoy near Alicante, featuring the struggle of Muslim and Christian forces to seize the castle and culminating in a victory parade with fireworks. But while the Christians always win the combats, the Moors are often portrayed as valiant, worthy enemies. It is said that nearly 100 towns and villages celebrate the Reconquista with their own version of the Christian struggle against Muslim rule.

In the fall of 2006, Félix Herrero, former president of one of the country's two main Islamic federations, called for the elimination of the *Cristianos y Moros* festivals. But several prominent Muslim leaders from the Valencia area contended that the festivals should be preserved as evidence of Muslim presence in Spanish history.[25] Herrero backed down and urged only a modification of certain insulting aspects, such as the explosion of an image of the Prophet Mohammed's head. The following year, it was reported that the village of Bocairent, which had burned an effigy of Mohammed for the past 147 years, had changed the tradition "not to offend Muslims."[26]

In Portugal, reenactments are diplomatically labeled medieval Festivals and there is less emphasis on the Christian victory. I attended a medieval festival in the fall of 2006 at the central Portuguese city of Santarém, an important Arab trading post in the twelfth century. Sponsored by the city hall, the festival was advertised as "An Encounter of Cultures,"not as the Reconquista. Christian and Muslim military tents were set up in the city center, with displays of weaponry, costumes and pastimes. "Our aim is to demonstrate medieval values," explained Alexandre Cabrita, one of forty Portuguese volunteers taking part in the festival. They all belong to the Order of the Chivalry of Sacred Portugal, founded in 1991, which participates in medieval tournaments, fairs and other reenactments all year round. Cabrita appeared biased in favor of the Moors, praising their superior skills in tent-making, armor and horsemanship. In a Muslim market on the square nearby, Moroccan and Algerian merchants offered couscous and kebabs, almond cakes and mint tea, calligraphy and craftwork. Organizers of the market and the cultural part of the festival belonged to the Granada-based Islamic Community of Spain. For three days, there were lectures, plays, music and a Muslim and Christian show of arms. The event culminated in a *Dhikr*—a night of Arabic poetry and Sufi chants in praise of the Prophet.

Without doubt the most important event linked to the Christian Reconquista is the pilgrimage of Santiago de Compostela, dedicated to the apostle Saint James, who came to be known as "the Moor-killer." Christian legend has it that Saint James visited northern Hispania to bring the word of Christianity in 44 AD, although some scholars question the claim. At any rate, in 813, when Christians sorely needed help against the Muslim occupation, a peasant was said to have discovered the grave of Saint James in a field in northwestern Galicia. King Alfonso II built a church on the spot, and this very quickly became a pilgrimage site for Christians from all over Europe. Inspired by Saint James and backed by European crusaders, Iberian Christians intensified their struggle against the Moors. Al Mansur's destruction of the shrine of Santiago in 997 served to fuel the Christian Reconquista. Adding insult to devastation, Al Mansur stole the bells of Santiago and converted them into lamps for the mosque at Córdoba (they were returned to Santiago after the fall of Córdoba in 1236). These incidents gave rise to Christian tales of a vengeful Saint James leading Christian crusaders against the Moorish forces, and hence his title of *Matam-*

oros. A handsome baroque cathedral was built on the site of Saint James' tomb in the eleventh century, and remained a popular pilgrim site until the end of the sixteenth century. When England defeated the Spanish fleet off La Coruña, the church hid Saint James' relics for safe-keeping. At the end of the nineteenth century, the apostle's remains were restored to their place in the cathedral, and Santiago again became one of Christianity's most revered cities, along with Rome and Jerusalem.

In recent years, the pilgrimage of Santiago seems to have mellowed and lost its militant anti-Islam quality. Pilgrims told me they noted few signs of the original crusade spirit on the Way to Santiago. Instead it has become a spiritual, ecumenical journey of reconciliation, and one of the world's great travel experiences. The saint is no longer called "the Moor-killer" by pilgrimage organizers, but goes by the more politically correct title, "Santiago el Caballero," or the cavalier. This change occurred during the saint's jubilee year of 2004, just months after Muslim extremists attacked Madrid's commuter trains, killing 192 people and wounding nearly 2,000. Official sources in Santiago told me that the church had feared radical Muslims might take offense at the saint's popular epithet and carry out new attacks. Orders were given to hide the bodies of the dead Moors in paintings and on statues with piles of flowers or simply to remove any offensive artwork.

The recent affair of the *Moríscos* (Muslims forcibly converted to Christianity) is evidence of the Spanish ambivalence toward its Islamic past. According to historians, King Felipe III decreed on 9 April 1608, that all *Moríscos* would be expelled from Spain—about 300,000 people. The operation lasted until 1614, with many exiles seeking refuge in North Africa. These New Christians represented a significant percentage of the country's seven million inhabitants, and their departure was a blow to trade and agriculture. Although the reasons for the ethnic cleansing are not known, it has been suggested that Dom Felipe's court feared that the *Moríscos* would serve as a Fifth Column in support of Ottomans and Muslim pirates who threatened Spanish coasts.

In 1992, the King of Spain publicly demanded pardon for the expulsion of the Jews in 1492, but little was said of the mass expulsion of *Moríscos*. Then, early in 2009, the Andalucian Legacy Foundation, the Casa Árabe and several universities organized a series of events to mark the 400th anniversary of the exile of the *Moríscos*. Gema Martín of the Casa Árabe declared the need to create a new awareness of the experience of intolerance, fanaticism and racism "… to prevent such expulsions from happening again."[27] Conferences, concerts and exhibits about the tragedy of the *Moríscos* took place without much ado. But the ruling Socialist Party went further and introduced a bill calling for "the institutional recognition of the injustice committed by Spain towards *Moríscos*." The conservative press and blogosphere called the initiative laughable and unrealistic and suggested that, instead, Muslims should ask pardon for conquering Spain in the first place. The spokesperson for the opposing People's Party, Soraya Sáenz de Santamaría, declared that the Socialists "would do better to deal with the problems of millions of unemployed than what happened 400 years ago that nobody can change."[28] Spain was not yet ready for reconciliation.

3

THE EARLY NEWCOMERS

Iberia was a heartbreakingly beautiful land, largely shunned by its neighbors, when I first settled there in the early 1960s. Spain was still suffering from the moral devastation of the civil war, and Portugal was engaged in a costly military effort to cling to its African colonies. It was a depressed place of poor fishermen and farmers, a small coterie of wealthy landowners and colonial industrialists, and an educated elite, dwelling on past glories. Many intellectuals and political activists, who rebelled against the stifling dictatorial regimes, risked jail or found refuge in the former colonies of Latin America or in the United States. Young Spanish and Portuguese workers who sought a better life for their families often emigrated illegally to Europe—the peninsula was not considered part of the continent.

Portugal was essentially a third world country, dependent on emigrants' remittances and tourism revenue. Yet there were wealthy Portuguese with business interests in Portuguese Africa, particularly oil and diamond-rich Angola. And there was the Golden Triangle, Estoril-Cascais-Sintra, where Europe's exiled royalty and other foreigners had gathered because they could afford to live like kings. The Spanish economy had begun to pull out of the doldrums in the late 1950s, after the United States agreed to provide substantial aid in return for the right to establish military bases in Spain. Franco turned to a group of smart technocrats to rehabilitate the economy and promote tourism. Thus, large numbers of foreign excursionists discovered this long closed, affordable country, and British, German and Scandinavian retirees began to settle along the coast, seeking sun and a leisurely style of life.

At Franco's death in 1975, Spain's per capita income was $3,000. In 2011, it was estimated at $29,500, or comparable to that of France.

With their transition to democracy in the mid-1970s, Spain and Portugal began to attract large numbers of immigrants, mainly as a passage to greener pastures in western Europe, until European gates closed. Initially, North African immigrants flocked to Spain and sub-Saharan Africans to Portugal. It might be called reverse colonialism. The rebirth of Muslim communities in Iberia was intrinsically related to colonial experiences. As with other former European colonial powers, there was a special relationship between Spain and Portugal and their one-time colonial subjects, sentiments of shared history and culture and, in some cases, feelings of resentment and an outstanding debt.

With Moroccan independence, there was no great rush of Spanish colonials and their local allies to return to Spain, as would occur later with Portugal's African decolonization. Some Spanish civilian cadres stayed on in Morocco as technical advisers to the newly independent government or moved to the Spanish territories of Ceuta and Melilla. Moroccans were united behind the sultan and the nationalist movement, which preached national unity and discouraged the settling of accounts. I remember all the enthusiasm about building a new, independent and democratic Morocco. (The *pateras* would come only much later, when hope had evaporated.) Also, unlike France, Spain of the mid-1950s was no magnet for its former colonial subjects as the economy was still in shambles from the civil war.

The first Moroccan immigrants to arrive in Spain in the early 1960s were merely "passing through" en route to France, according to Spanish scholar, Bernabé López García, whose monumental *Atlas de Inmigración Magrebi* is the most comprehensive account of contemporary Moroccan immigration to Spain. In an interview, Professor Bernabé noted that after Moroccan independence, there were not enough jobs in Spain for Spanish workers, who themselves were emigrating by the thousands to France and other northern European countries.[1] North Africans began to emigrate to Spain during Franco's "developmentalist" phase from 1966–75, when Moroccans made their way to Cataluña, where there were jobs for the asking, according to Professor Bernabé. After France and Germany imposed restrictions on North Africans in the late 1980s, new concentrations of Moroccan immigrants appeared in northern Spain around Barcelona. Finally under the 1990, Schengen Treaty, visas were made obligatory for North Africans in most of Europe, which was the direct cause of the waves of illegal immigration from North Africa and later sub-Saharan Africa. "Moroccans led the way, fleeing the economic crisis at home," Professor Bernabé said. "They came as students and tourists and stayed, taking any kind of part time jobs they could find. It is this flux of immigrants that has stirred up old prejudices against Islam."

Some of those early Moroccan immigrants, who established new lives in Spain, were reluctant to break with their native land and now serve as a bridge between the two countries, like Abdeljalil Reklaoui. I first met this retired Arabic professor and newspaper publisher in his office at Algeciras in the summer of 2006, and have seen him several times since. Reklaoui describes himself as *Hispano-Maroquí*, commutes regularly between the two countries and feels at home in both.[2] The Reklaoui family comes from the Rif Mountains around Chauen in what was once Spanish Morocco. He now lives in Algeciras but goes to see family in Morocco every weekend. Reklaoui publishes *Al Manar: La Voz del Inmigrante*, a fortnightly newspaper in Spanish and Arabic. *Al Manar* aims to present "the true picture of immigrants and Islam" and denounces villains on all sides: the international human smuggling rings, Moroccan drug couriers, Spanish bosses who exploit Moroccan farm workers, Islamic fanatics and the media, prone to stereotype Muslims as "terrorists" since 11 September. The last time I saw the publisher in August 2008, he was unusually somber because of Spain's economic crisis. The boatpeople were still coming, he said, but Moroccans even with legal residence couldn't find jobs. Increasingly alienated young people were joining fundamentalist Islamic groups. He pointed out that Spaniards preferred to hire immigrants from their long lost empire in Latin America than people from their former protectorate of Morocco. "Moroccans should be given fair access to work," he said, adding that discrimination in the workplace was one cause of radicalization.[3]

Although immigration to Spain is recent, there is already a second generation of Moroccans, conscious of their rights. Mohamed Azaf, a social worker who works for Madrid city hall, resents the fast track for Latinos to obtain Spanish citizenship because of 'cultural links', meaning a two-year wait compared to ten years for Moroccans. "To be a policeman, a doctor, a politician, even a bus driver, you need Spanish nationality," he stressed. His father was a merchant from Tangier who settled in Madrid in 1966, and returned to Morocco for the birth of each of his five sons. "My brothers and I all live in Spain, but we generally go back to Morocco to get married," Azaf admitted.[4] Azaf told me the problem of most Moroccan immigrants is a sense of impermanence, forever planning to return home. "Our family had a dream: to earn enough money in Spain to build a house in Tangier. At twenty-five, I was still working for the house in Tangier. But we can't go home. We don't live in Morocco. We don't have any friends in Tangier. Our lives are here. What's more, I've discovered I'm not from Morocco or from Spain."

Some Moroccans who have married Spaniards—and there are more and more of them—seem well adjusted to their lives in Spain. Among these is the journalist Ali Lmrabet, whose family hails from former Spanish Morocco and has a long involvement with Spain that in many ways reflects the complex relationship between the two countries. Known as the *enfant terrible* of the Moroccan press, Lmrabet was publisher of *Demain*, an irreverent French language satirical weekly, and an Arabic counterpart, aimed at revealing scandals in high places. In May 2003, Lmrabet was sentenced to four years in prison for "insult to the king," with the publication of a cartoon depicting money bags going into the palace during an election. The following year, King Mohammed VI granted royal pardon to thirty-three political prisoners, among them Lmrabet. When the unrepentant publisher announced plans to open a new satirical magazine, he was banned from publishing in Morocco for ten years. Lmrabet went into self-imposed exile in Barcelona, where his wife, Laura Feliu, is engaged in research in the Arabic department of the University of Barcelona. I met them in their modest but comfortable apartment off the Rambla.

A large and burly figure, Lmrabet played gently with his fourteen-month-old son, as he told me the family story. "We come from the Rif Mountains in the former Spanish zone of Morocco. My grandfather fought for independence against Spain in the Rif War, from 1921–26. But when General Franco called for volunteers, my father marched with him, and after the civil war, he stayed in Spain although he would have received a commission in the Royal Moroccan Armed Forces. But he bought a house for the family in Tetuan. Like many Moroccan students, I lived in France from 1980–90 and studied history and business management at the Sorbonne. While I consider myself of the Left, I work for the conservative daily *El Mundo*, because they defended me when I was in prison and have given me freedom to write as I see fit. I am the only Moroccan journalist on the staff of a major Spanish newspaper. My wife is Catalán and we have a son, Elias, who is learning to speak *Darija* (Moroccan Arabic) and Catalán. My brother, Abdelwahid, was a civil servant in Tetuan and came here in 2000 to make a better life. He still can't find a proper job and sells odds and ends to tourists at Calella, a resort north of Barcelona. Even so, he makes more as a hawker in Cataluña than his civil service wages in Tetuan. Here, nobody dies of hunger."

Lmrabet gave the Spanish high marks for their approach to immigration. "Spain is the only country in Europe with a realistic immigration policy, much better than France. There is now a fourth generation of North Africans living in France and they're still not integrated. France's social housing has become ghettos. In Spain, immigrants are more spread out. The Spanish public has reacted to Islamic extremists better than other Europeans. The Dutch response to Theo Van Gogh's murder by a Moroccan was brutal. After the terrorist attacks on the Madrid train station, no mosques were attacked, no Moroccans killed. Generally Moroccans work better with Spaniards than with other westerners, and even now there's more *convivencia*."[5]

* * *

Portugal's decolonization took place much later than that of other European countries. Muslims who quit Portuguese Africa for the motherland were not of Arabo-Berber stock like most Muslims in Spain. Some were Africans from Portuguese Guinea, but the majority had their roots in India. Early in the twentieth century, Indians had emigrated from the Asian sub-continent to Africa, and Portuguese Mozambique in particular, where they became part of the educated elite. Well-to-do families from the colonies, including Muslims, sent their sons to Portuguese universities. But there was really no Islamic community in Portugal proper until after the revolution.

It is generally known as the Revolution of Carnations. On 25 April 1974, a group of Portuguese colonels and their followers, opposed to the costly, unending wars in Portuguese Africa, seized power with red carnations in their rifles and virtually no bloodshed. Within a year, Europe's last imperial power had granted independence to all five of its colonies in Africa. Portugal's closed, authoritarian police state metamorphosed into a chaotic free-for-all, succeeded by a Communist-inspired People's Republic, to become what it is today—a western-type social democracy. The sweeping transformations on mainland Portugal were accompanied by even greater upheavals in Portuguese Africa.

Abruptly granted independence in 1975, the colonies were ill prepared for self-government, lacking leadership and cadres of all kinds, infrastructure and financial resources. Bitter struggles for power ensued in impoverished Mozambique and Portuguese Guinea, along with a long, bloody civil war in Angola. In the chaos and uncertainty, Portuguese colonials—many of mixed African and Portuguese descent—panicked and fled to Portugal. Also taking flight were many ethnic Africans and Indians, who had served the colonial administration or fought in the colonial army, or were concerned about the lack of security in the newly independent nations. These refugees, whatever their ethnic origin, were called *retornados* (returnees) although many had never laid eyes on Portugal. It is said that more than a million people fled the African colonies and sought a haven in this modest country of nine million inhabitants, which could not in good conscience turn them away. Those *retornados* who had no relatives in the motherland were lodged in luxury hotels, schools, military barracks and holiday camps, until emergency housing could be built or third countries agreed to accept them.

Modern Portugal's first Muslim communities were born in this confusion. Predominantly Portuguese citizens of Indian origin from Mozambique—middle class merchants or bankers and their families—soon made themselves at home in Europe. The majority was Sunni Muslim, but there were also Ismailis, who belong to the Shiite branch of Islam. Other Muslims were Africans—Portuguese-educated students and colonial cadres from Portuguese Guinea, renamed Guinea-Bissau.

Today the head of Portugal's Islamic Community is Abdool Majid Vakil, a Sunni Muslim, former member of the colonial government in Mozambique, and a distinguished international banker. Vakil is the principal role model for Muslims in Portugal and someone whose opinion Portuguese governments of both the left and right value. After several attempts, I obtained an appointment with Vakil at the Lisbon office of his Engineering Financial Company Ltd., known by its Portuguese initials EFISA. Elegantly groomed, with graying hair, trim beard and moustache, and dark penetrating eyes, Vakil, sixty-seven, talked to me for nearly an hour, with only one interruption. It was an emergency call from the Papal Nuncio, anxious about the reaction of Portugal's Muslims to Pope Benedict XVI's controversial reference to the

Prophet Mohammed. Vakil listened attentively to the Vatican's representative, and said he would convey the clarification to the rest of the community's leadership. There was no rush to judgment, which is the way Portugal's Muslims have reacted on most controversial issues.

The Vakil family history is more than the classic rags to riches saga. It is a demonstration of resilience, adaptability to changing circumstances and determination to succeed, characteristics of many Portuguese Muslims. The banker's father left the Indian state of Gujarat for Mozambique in 1900 to seek new opportunities. Starting out as a peddler in the capital of Lourenço Marques, Vakil senior opened a general store in the 1930s, then a bigger shop, and in 1940 built the largest department store in the Portuguese colony. His son, Abdool Majid Vakil, first traveled to Portugal in 1956, at age seventeen, to study economics. Upon graduation, he worked as a research assistant in mathematics at Lisbon University's School of Economics. In 1961, he married a Portuguese Catholic, Rosaria, who converted to Islam, taking the name Jamila. Vakil had aspired to an academic career but soon found teaching in Portugal "not much of a challenge" and returned to Mozambique in 1968 with his wife and three children. He resumed teaching as professor of statistics at the University of Lourenço Marques. In 1972, he became a director of the *Banco Nacional Ultramarino* and the following year was named minister of planning and finance in the colonial government of Mozambique.

Portugal's revolution of 25 April 1974, came as a complete surprise to Vakil, who learned of it on the BBC. From the outset, the banker was invited to be an adviser to the minister of finance in Mozambique's new transitional government. But as factional fighting spread, Vakil's wife fled to Lisbon, where their children were in school. He followed when friends in Portugal's post-Salazar government said there was "a need for people like him" in the nationalized banking sector. By the time he arrived in Lisbon in early 1975, there had been a change of government and his job had disappeared, but he was soon offered several high level posts. After serving as economic consultant at the *Banco de Portugal*, he was named adviser to the minister of finance and Portugal's chief negotiator for foreign loans. The ambitious Vakil moved to London in 1979 to join Manufacturers Hanover Ltd., as an executive director, and later helped set up Gemini Financial Services, with support from S.G. Warburg. Finally, in 1988, he relocated to Portugal to establish EFISA, with financing from Warburg and Spanish, Portuguese and Kuwaiti groups, and became president of the board of one of the country's leading investment banks.

Parallel to his banking career, Vakil played an active role in Portugal's Muslim community. He recalls that in the late 1950s there were only half a dozen Muslim students from Mozambique in Portugal, and his home in the Lisbon suburb of Alvalade became the meeting place and prayer hall for the tiny group. There were no Muslim butchers and so they bought their meat from Kosher shops. In 1968, Vakil and a friend, Suleyman Valy Mamede, founded the Islamic Community of Lisbon, which began to attract a following in 1974, with the influx of Muslims from Portugal's colonies. Mamede, a university professor, writer and head of the Portuguese news agency, ANOP, served as the first president of the Muslim community until the opening of Lisbon's mosque in 1985. After a bitter struggle over Mamede's succession, Vakil was persuaded to assume the presidency in 1988, a post he has reluctantly held ever since. Named by the Portuguese minister of justice as the Muslim delegate to the national Commission on Religious Freedom in 2004, Vakil is increasingly asked to represent Portugal's Muslims.

"Most Portuguese Muslims do not feel like foreigners," Vakil told me, adding that he considers himself "Portuguese of Indian origin." He emphasized that half of Portugal's some 40,000 Muslims have Indo-Pakistani roots, via Mozambique. Most of the others are Africans from Guinea-Bissau, with some 3,000 North Africans, 3,000 Pakistanis and Bangladeshis, and 2,000 from the Middle East. It is this "texture" that makes Portugal's Muslims different, perhaps better integrated than Islamic communities in Spain and other European countries, Vakil suggested. But Portugal's Islamic community does have its problems, the banker acknowledged. The main difficulty is the general public's ignorance of Islamic practices and history. Historians are only now beginning to discover Portugal's Islamic heritage, and since 11 September, there have been a few incidents, insults and obscenities scrawled on the mosque walls. "The answer is education," Vakil stressed. "There is new interest in Islam; the proof is that many schools send classes to visit the Central Mosque and receive lectures on the faith. But religious studies in public schools should be improved, particularly in reference to Islam."[6]

Portugal's Ismailis, who belong to a Shiite branch of Islam and whose spiritual guide is the Aga Khan, followed much the same trajectory as the Sunnis, and have demonstrated similar drive and adaptability. They too left the Indian state of Gujarat in the early 1900s and settled in Mozambique, where the community prospered until the nationalist upheavals of the early 1970s. Concerned for the Ismailis' well-being in the new independent African state, the Aga Khan encouraged his followers to emigrate. A network was formed to organize the collective departure of some 7,000 Ismailis from Mozambique. Some emigrated to Canada and England, but the majority went to Portugal because many had Portuguese nationality and spoke the language. Lisbon is one of three main Ismaili centers, along with London and Toronto, for the world's fifteen million faithful.

The Ismailis have adjusted well to life in Portugal and maintain close friendly relations with the Sunni majority. Faranaz Keshavjee, a social anthropologist and journalist, smiles when she recalls arriving in Lisbon in 1974, at age five, with her mother and brother, as *retornados*. Now thirty-eight, tall with auburn hair and olive complexion, she says: "I realized then that I wasn't white, but I wasn't black; I was exotic, a *retornada*," she told me when we met over coffee at the Gulbenkian Foundation.[7] "We had to leave everything behind, and thirty of us from different families were crowded into one flat in the old Bairro Alto neighborhood of Lisbon," she recounted. Her father, who owned a furniture shop in Lourenço Marques, stayed to help members of the community transfer what funds they could to Portugal. Gradually things settled. The Ismailis took over Avenida Almirante Reis, a broad commercial boulevard leading to Lisbon's airport, opening all kinds of shops—dry goods, furniture, foodstuffs and clothing. By working hard, many were able to send their children to the best schools in England and the United States. Faranaz went to the French *lycée* in Lisbon and graduated from Lisbon University in social anthropology with a master's degree in social psychology. She attended the Ismaili Institute for Islamic Studies and Humanities in London and took her PhD at Cambridge with a thesis on "Muslim adolescents, gender representation and identity." She married a cousin, who has an information technology business in Angola, and they have two children, who go to a Catholic school in Lisbon. Currently, she writes a regular column, "Chronicles of a Muslim Woman," for Portugal's leading weekly, *Expresso*.

"Why did we come to Portugal?" asked Faranaz, who has clearly given a good deal of thought to the question. "For one thing, the Portuguese are more receptive to immigrant communities than other Europeans. Our relations with the Sunnis are fraternal because we grew up together in Mozambique, My father and Vakil's brother were school-mates. We respect each other's views and do our best to bridge the dif-ferences, not make them a source of conflict." She pointed out, however, that blacks have a harder time of it "My cousin, who is dark, is punished all the time. Some people insult her by calling her *preta* (black) and are reluctant to sit next to her on the bus or hire her to look after their kids." And even in Portugal, Muslims are seen as for-eigners, Faranaz emphasized. While there have been few incidents of Islamophobia here, international events have necessarily had an impact on the Muslim community. "People make you aware that you are dif-ferent for simply being Muslim," she said. "In school, children ask if my three-year-old son is Portuguese. In university, I am always con-scious of my Muslim identity. Colleagues ask: what do you have to say about a certain *fatwa* or some act of violence? How do you explain why kids become suicide bombers?" Like Vakil, Faranaz deplored the lack of Islamic studies in Portugal. "How can we have a pluralist soci-ety when there is such a profound ignorance of one another?"

Ethnic Africans who fled former Portuguese Guinea were Christians and Muslims, students, civil servants and opponents of the ruling Afri-can Party for the Independence of Guinea and Cape Verde (PAIGC). Some were labeled as collaborators and fled to Portugal with the idea that "the Portuguese owe us...." Some have ended up on welfare or in jail for petty crimes. Others learned to adapt to life in Portugal like José Amara Queta, a former Portuguese civil servant, who had to begin all over again.[8]

Queta now runs his own stationery store and is president of the Neighborhood Association and administrator of the local mosque. He proudly showed me his neighborhood, Quinta do Mocho, one of the better examples of social housing, built in 2001 to replace a shanty-town in the industrial zone of Sacavém, northeast of Lisbon. The com-plex of four-storey buildings is painted canary yellow and includes a church and a mosque. Some 3,000 people live in Quinta do Mocho, about 95% Africans and the majority Christian. A large outgoing man in his early sixties, Queta was the son of a Muslim tribal chief in rural Portuguese Guinea and, as a boy, studied the Koran at night over a wood fire. A family friend persuaded his father to send him to a Roman Catholic school in the capital of Bissau. The school obliged him to take a Portuguese name. Upon graduation, José Queta got a job with the Portuguese Guinea Airline. He went to Portugal for additional studies in 1971, and on his return home was offered a senior civil service position in the Department of Education. After the Portuguese revolution in 1974, Guinea became independent, and Queta was fired. In 1977, he was arrested as a collaborator and spent three and a half years in jail. On his release, he was promised an executive position in the Guinean Ministry of Education. But he had little confidence in the government and, in 1982, joined his brother, who was working in the hotel industry in Lisbon.

While Queta recalls Portuguese colonial rule with mixed feelings, he holds Guinea's nationalist leaders responsible for the violence and instability that has reigned since independence. "If the Guinean leadership had been smart, they would have kept the cadres on and let us teach the new generation, but they said we were traitors." Like many Guinean refugees, Queta started life in Portugal as a sub-contractor in the construction industry. In 1984, he obtained Portuguese nationality and was able to send for his wife and five children, and two years later he received his retirement pension from the Portuguese state. After taking a course in the hotel business, he worked as chief of stewards at Lisbon's Hotel Ritz. When the new development opened at Quinta do Mocho, he was given an apartment and space for his stationery shop. "Young people are our biggest concern; parents are afraid of their kids," Queta said. "They drop out of school and can't find jobs and end up doing drugs and mugging strangers." He was speaking as head of the Neighborhood Association and not as a parent, because his children are grown up and have their own families. He said the town hall has given them space for a soccer field, but they need a youth center so kids can spend their time on computers and other activities.

* * *

Iberia's economic explosion got underway at the beginning of the 1990s, with generous aid from the European Union. In Spain, there were preparations for celebrations of the 500th anniversary of Columbus' discovery of the Americas in 1492, which also marked the end of the Islamic empire in Al Andalus. Seville undertook elaborate works for the 1992 World's Fair. In Barcelona, major projects had been engaged for the Summer Olympics that year. Madrid had been named Europe's Cultural Capital. In Toledo, Spaniards and Jews celebrated their common history with the reopening of the School of Translators.

On the outskirts of Lisbon, a whole new city was going up for Expo 1998, to be followed by the construction or rehabilitation of ten stadiums around Portugal for the 2004 European Soccer Cup.

The aging Iberian societies needed workers for all these ambitious projects. Word got out that there were jobs around the peninsula and immigrants were welcome, even those without proper documentation. So they came, from the former colonies in Africa and long-lost possessions in Latin America, but also from non-Spanish or Portuguese-speaking countries like India, Pakistan and Bangladesh, as well as Eastern Europe; Ukraine, Romania and Moldova. Many stayed, even when times were not so good.

Actually, North Africans were drawn to Cataluña in the late 1980s after France and Germany closed their borders. Abdel Almountazir, forty-seven, now a successful actor, was one of these early migrants from Morocco. A Spanish friend introduced us and we met in a café on the Rambla in downtown Barcelona. He grew up in the Berber village of Ait Atta in the Atlas Mountains, where there were no roads, no modern conveniences and. it was a three-mile hike to school, he recounted.[9] His father, a leader of the Moroccan Liberation Army and a militant in the socialist opposition, was forced to go into exile with his family in neighboring Algeria in 1969. The young Almountazir went to France in 1984 on a student visa and enrolled at the *Institut des Hautes Etudes Sociales* in Paris. He admits he was "too busy with politics to go to class." The French authorities refused to give him a residence permit and the Moroccan consulate would only give him a *laissez passer* for Morocco. Friends advised him to take the travel permit and stopover in Spain where it was easier to get residence.

Arriving in Barcelona in March 1988, Almountazir soon became involved in the local North African Workers Association, the Catalán Labor Union and SOS Racism, and gave lessons in classical Arabic to support his activism. Eventually he went to work for the Federation of Immigrant Associations while holding down a restaurant job. But the uncertainty of his life was too much and he suffered "a crisis," living on the streets for fifteen months. His life began to turn around with Spain's 1991 immigrant regularization. The Catalán authorities gave him a residence permit and the Moroccan consulate a new passport. Once legalized, he took a training course in construction and immediately got a job. Shortly afterwards, he was hired to appear in a documentary on construction workers. The film, *En Construction*, won a prize at the San Sebastian Festival in 2001 and the Goya Prize in 2002. The "accidental actor" was recruited for another documentary on the 2001 mass attacks on immigrant workers at El Ejido, which came out in 2002 with the title *Poniente*. His career was launched.

"The worst problem for immigrants is that jobs are precarious and now there's lots of unemployment," said Almountazir. "If the migrant is lucky and finds work in construction or agriculture he can send money home, but he's exhausted all the time and can't do anything to improve his life. Then there's racism; El Ejido was about collective vengeance against *los moros*. Moroccans are used to racism and continue to come illegally anyway. Now more and more street kids from dislocated families are showing up and invariably end up in petty crime."

Later, I took a comfortable bus from Madrid to Almería, one of the main centers of migrant labor and off the Costa del Sol tourist circuit. There seems to be a battle for space going on between the builders of holiday villas and apartments along the sea and the plastic greenhouses snaking through the interior valleys and up the hills. At Motril, the plastic has taken over, blanketing the rocky terrain at the base of the mountain and the hilly terraces. In the distance, patches of plastic appear like glaciers on the naked hillsides. Along the road, there are endless signs announcing Export-Import Vegetables, Tropical Green Vegetables or a certain cooperative or greenhouse.

Almería is a quiet prosperous-looking modern city, whose main attractions are the ancient Arab palace on the hill and a lovely new archeology museum. I had been forewarned that July was off-season for greenhouses because most workers had gone north to escape the heat. As it was a weekend and offices were closed, I visited the local newspaper, *La Voz de Almería*, to find out about migrants. Assistant director Ignacio Escolar and his staff spoke at length about them and the greenhouse business.

About 25% of Almería's 600,000 inhabitants are migrants, mostly Moroccans, according to the journalists. Agriculture is the province's number one source of revenue, followed by tourism and the merchant marine. There were occasional incidents involving migrants, but nothing like the tragedy of nearby town El Ejido. Here riots broke out, after a Palestinian immigrant murdered two Spanish farmers on 22 January 2000. Ten days later, a Moroccan stabbed a twenty-six-year-old woman in the market. Hundreds of townspeople armed with iron bars and sticks went on a rampage, beating up any *moros* they could find, cutting off streets and destroying cars, shops and homes of immigrants in what the Spanish press described as "an orgy of racist vandalism."[10] The remarkable part of the story is that, despite the rising number of immigrants and increased unemployment, there haven't been any more El Ejidos in Spain. But the day I left Almería, the local press reported yet another tragedy. A Moroccan migrant, who had not moved north with the other workers for the summer, died of hypothermia; it was said to be a constant 104 degrees under the plastic sheeting where he worked and lived.

Lepe, on the opposite side of Costa del Sol, is a burgeoning industrial area and agricultural center. There I met Abdel Rahman Essadi, a Moroccan who knows Spain better than most Spaniards. He has harvested tomatoes in the fields of Badajoz, potatoes at Vitoria, oranges at Valencia, olives at Jaén, strawberries at Huelva, pears and apples at Lerida … the migrant worker's tour of Spain. "I know what it's like to sleep in the streets without a roof or food, what it's like to prefer alcohol to bread because it helps you forget and keeps you warm," the burly forty-one-year-old Moroccan told me in his office at the southwestern port of Lepe. "I know what it's like to live in stifling plastic greenhouses, which are worse than the *bidonvilles* (shantytowns) at home."[11]

Essadi, a graduate in classical and modern Arabic and linguistics from the University of Al Jadida, first came to Spain in 1992 on a three-month student visa. The only employment he found was seasonal farm work at twelve euros for an eight-hour day, considerably below the minimum wage of eighteen euros. He was lucky because he had relatives at Zaragoza who gave him food. After a year, he returned to Morocco but was unable to find a decently paid job, so he returned to the grim life of a wetback in Europe. He also pursued his interest in social work. Back home, he had been secretary general of a volunteer agency, the Moroccan Association of Education for Young People. In 1992, Essadi joined the Spanish immigration network, *Acoge*, as a volunteer and rose in the ranks to become a trainer, social worker, educator, trainer of trainers and an expert in intercultural development. For the past three years, he has served as president of the Andalusian Federation of *Acoge* from his base at Lepe; the first Moroccan to achieve such a position.

Essadi said that the most serious problem facing migrant workers in Spain is "the awful living conditions." *Acoge* has launched an awareness campaign to get the general public and the authorities to do something about migrants' lodgings. For Moroccan migrants, there is also the problem of discrimination, which has worsened in recent years, according to Essadi. He noted that while the political leadership has tried to make a distinction between terrorists and the majority of law-abiding Moroccans, their image is generally negative since the 11 March 2004 terrorist attack in Madrid. "Employers prefer East European labor to Arabs, and they prefer women to men because women accept hard work, spending six hours on their knees harvesting strawberries, without protest," Essadi said.

Portuguese agriculture does not offer the same opportunities for seasonal labor as Spain. The main attraction for immigrants in the 1990s was the construction industry. Another important incentive for immigrants has been the relatively benign attitude of the Portuguese authorities toward undocumented aliens and the periodical regularizations.

Braima Djalo likes to say he has built modern Portugal, and in fact he has worked on construction projects around the country since he arrived in the late 1990s. I met the slight, thirty-five-year-old Guinean at a café on Lisbon's Rossio Square, where Africans usually congregate to have news of one another and from home. I had been given Djalo's name by the government's Immigration Center, which was handling his requests for family reunion.[12] Articulate in French and Portuguese, Djalo was born in Guinea Bissau near the Senegalese border, where his father was a trader in foodstuffs between the two countries. The young Djalo had led a privileged life, going to a French school in Senegal for ten years. He married a Senegalese woman, with whom he had two children, and opened his own food store in Casamance, Guinea. But in 1999, rebel militias invaded the province, destroying his shop and whatever they could get their hands on. "There was no stability in Guinea, and it wasn't safe to stay in the region," Djalo said, explaining why he had decided to emigrate. Leaving his family with his mother, he took a minibus for Mauritania, where he joined other migrants in a *patera* to the Canary Islands. They were arrested on arrival and put in the care of the Red Cross until they were flown to Madrid with an order of expulsion. Djalo had no money but soon found work on a fishing boat headed for Portugal.

The word in African circles was that Portugal was hospitable to people from its former colonies, and the chances for legalization were better than other places. When he reached Lisbon, Djalo went to the "labor market" near the military college and found work in construction. By 1 July 2001, he had obtained Portuguese residence. The construction firm gave him a contract and sent him on jobs around the country. The most difficult part was living in containers. In the spring of 2006, Djalo brought his wife, Assanatou, to Portugal, and they have completed the paperwork to get their children. They live in a comfortable two-room apartment in Venda Nova, a Lisbon suburb popular with Africans, and are proud owners of a secondhand Renault. Assanatou, who is pregnant, is studying Portuguese and hopes to find work, cleaning offices or homes. Djalo, who describes himself as "a moderate Muslim," attends Sheikh Boubaker's mosque nearby. He has counseled his wife that she might have a better chance of finding work if she doesn't wear her usual headscarf. He hopes to get out of the construction business and has taken a course in communications and obtained a taxi driver's license. His ambition is to find "stable work," meaning a job that enables him to live at home with his family instead of on building sites.

The center of immigrant life in Lisbon is Martim Moniz Plaza, in a working class neighborhood at the base of the Mouraria, the medieval Moorish quarter. In fact, Martim Moniz is a kind of timeline for immigration to Portugal. In the early 1970s, gypsies and Indians had turned the vast square into a permanent flea market. In a drive to clean up the city, officials evacuated the square and built two large, ungainly shopping centers on the plaza. As soon as the Martim Moniz Center opened, its sixty-eight shops were taken over by Indian shopkeepers from Mozambique. Then followed Africans and Bangladeshis, and soon the place was too small. In 1990, the new Mouraria Center's 156 shops were quickly occupied by Africans, Pakistanis, Bangladeshis, Brazilians and Chinese. Now both centers are dominated by Chinese, and have become the hub of the ethnic wholesale business.

When Taslim Rana arrived in Lisbon in 1990, there were only four other Bangladeshis in Portugal, three working in construction and one as a receptionist. Today Rana owns three shops in Martim Moniz and is a leader of the Bangladeshi community of some 4,000 people. The thirty-nine-year-old immigrant, with thinning hair, spoke to me over tea in a miniscule Bangladeshi restaurant near his dry goods store. Our conversation was interrupted by a message from a Lisbon judge who needed an interpreter, which he shrugged off.[13]

Born in Dacca, Rana completed his studies in political science and journalism in the Bangladeshi capital, and then set off to see the world.

His first port of call was Hong Kong, where he took up the import-export trade, which gave him the opportunity to travel. Arriving at Lisbon, he headed for the Central Mosque, where he met countrymen and other contacts. Although he missed the luxury and fast life of Hong Kong, Rana decided to remain in Portugal because he had heard it was easy to find work. He soon opened a shop in Martim Moniz and got a job as a sub-contractor in a construction firm. In 1993, Rana obtained a Portuguese residence permit and, the following year, he opened a gift shop at the beach resort of Caparica south of Lisbon. In 1995, the tireless entrepreneur embarked on a new career, that of interpreter-translator. As the foreign community grew, Portuguese courts, the official immigration agency and the police sought out the services of Rana, who is fluent in Bengali and Hindi, English and Portuguese, and understands Urdu. Empowered by his official contacts, Rana and some friends established a Bangladeshi association to help newcomers. Learning of a mass legalization program in 1996, some 400 Bangladeshis converged on Portugal from all over Europe. Many left because they couldn't find jobs; others lived by selling flowers or trinkets in Lisbon's many cafés and bars.

A devout Muslim, Rana was a prime mover behind the creation of the Bangladeshi mosque in a derelict building off Martim Moniz Square. The mosque grew so crowded—up to 300 people for special events—that it was a safety hazard. Finally at the close of Ramadan, 2006, the worshippers moved into a more spacious building across the street. Unlike Spain, there was no protest from the neighbors over the opening of a new mosque. In fact, Portuguese friends were invited to the inauguration. "Most Muslims in Portugal come from Africa and are kind, and don't take part in demonstrations," the Bangladeshi said, expressing hope that the community could escape the radicalization that was taking place in many parts of the world. "Our Muslims are working sixteen hours a day and don't even have time to go to funerals," he added, suggesting a work ethic akin to that of immigrants in the United States.

4

SPAIN'S 11 SEPTEMBER

The olive-green glass monolith rises next to Madrid's austere Atocha railway station, a shimmering tribute to the victims of the worst terrorist act in Spanish history. Inside a dark blue chamber in the heart of the monument, visitors can read the names of nearly 200 persons who lost their lives in the commuter train bombings of 11 March 2004. Inscribed on the sky-lit walls are personal messages from mourners, written in Spanish but also in English and Arabic. "Please leave us alone and let the happiness come to our hearts again," reads one appeal. And a protest: "Why is it that it's the innocent who always pay?" A somber memorial to the victims of that day, the crystal cylinder also stands as a stark reminder that Spain has become a target of Islamic extremists.

Recent threats by Islamist zealots "to recover Al Andalus" have caught Spaniards and Portuguese completely by surprise. Little attention was paid to Osama bin Laden when he first voiced his intention to regain all of the lost Muslim lands "from Palestine to Al Andalus" in a 1994 video-taped interview. But when he renewed his challenge shortly after the attacks on 11 September 2001, he was taken more seriously. Subsequently, various Al Qaeda leaders have designated Iberia as Europe's frontline, with repeated proclamations of their goal to take back all Muslim lands, including Al Andalus. Initially discounted as futile posturing, these warnings generated a certain unease on the Iberian Peninsula, particularly as they coincided with a dramatic increase in the number of Muslim immigrants from Africa and Asia. The assault by Islamic extremists against the United States stirred widespread sympathy across Iberia for the American victims and led to a new focus on Islam and its followers. But there was a general feeling that such a terrorist attack could not happen in present-day Spain or Portugal, whose governments have gone out of the way to maintain good relations with the Muslim world.

It was the shock of 11 March 2004—the Madrid train bombings—that brought the global war with radical Islamists close to home. During the early morning rush hour, ten bombs exploded on four crowded suburban trains on the outskirts of Madrid, killing 191 commuters and wounding more than 1,800. It was the first attack attributed to Al Qaeda sympathizers on European soil and, with national elections in Spain scheduled for a few days later, served as wake up call for Europe's governing circles who believed that Islamic extremism was essentially an American problem.

Though early evidence implicated Muslim extremists in the plot, Spain's conservative government promptly attributed the deadly attack to ETA, the Basque separatist organization with a long history of political violence. In fact there had been threats from the Basque separatists in the run-up to national legislative elections. The cover of the 8 March issue of the popular Spanish weekly, *Cambio 16*, showed the menacing picture of a hooded man with a pistol and the headline: "ETA Attack on Democracy." The next edition, on the stands at the time of the terrorist attack, featured an illustration of the so-called "Truce Bomb," which was a reference to ETA's offer to cease armed activity during the election campaign, but only in Cataluña, where there were said to be Basque sympathizers. When violence did explode in Madrid, the interior minister, Ángel Acebes, formally blamed ETA for the massacre, despite denials from the organization's political wing.

Yet various signs pointed away from ETA. The indiscriminate massacre without the usual advance warning, the use of sports bags packed with a different type of explosive and the precise coordination of the blasts did not follow the typical pattern of ETA violence. Evidence of a Muslim connection emerged with the discovery of a van, parked near the railway station, which contained explosives and detonators, together with an audiotape of verses from the Koran. Furthermore, three bombs which failed to explode, and a backpack with a cellphone and dynamite, provided more clues. A pre-paid phone card was traced to a telephone shop owned by a Moroccan immigrant, Jamal Zougam. Spanish investigators had earlier questioned Zougam in connection with the 11 September attacks but released him for lack of evidence. This time, Zougam was held and a search of his apartment turned up radical Islamic documents, videos of training camps, presumably in Afghanistan, and the telephone numbers of Al Qaeda suspects.

The ETA connection was further cast into doubt by a report in a pro-Islamic Arabic language newspaper in London, *Al-Quds al-Arabi*, the day after the Madrid attack. A group called the Abu Hafs Al-Masri Brigade declared that Al Qaeda was behind the train bombings, which were said to be aimed at settling accounts with Spain for its alliance with the United States in the war against Islam. Some foreign investigators questioned the statement because the little-known Al-Masri brigade, believed to oversee Al Qaeda's European operations, has made false claims in the past. The Muslim trail, however, was reinforced shortly after the bombing, when a videotape was found near the city's main mosque. It contained a declaration by Abu Dujan Al Afghani, described as Al Qaeda's military spokesman in Europe, who claimed responsibility for the assault, in response to crimes committed by the US and its allies, particularly in Iraq and Afghanistan.

On the eve of the national elections, more than a million *Madrileños* gathered in the rain-drenched streets of the capital in a sober demonstration. While the crowd was united in condemning terrorism, the brunt of its protest was directed against the prime minister, José María Aznar, for failure to disclose information about the attacks and for inciting Muslim antipathy by supporting the United States' war in Iraq. Though similar mass gatherings were held in other cities around the country, the elections took place as scheduled. Again, Spaniards expressed their disapproval of the Aznar government, voting heavily for the Socialist opposition, which early on had declared itself against the war in Iraq. The Socialist leader, José Luis Rodríguez Zapatero, a youthful forty-four, had pledged specifically to withdraw Spanish troops from the US-led coalition in Iraq by the following June, even if there were not a United Nations mandate to do so. The message was clear: Spaniards had voted for change and for removing Spanish troops from Iraq. Some voices in the losing camp suggested that Spanish voters had been intimidated by terrorists and the Socialists had profited from the broad revulsion over the bombings. Spanish public opinion, however, had long expressed hostility to Aznar's special relationship with the Bush administration. Spaniards were particularly angered by the 16 March summit meeting in Portugal's Azores Islands, during which Aznar had joined President Bush and the British prime minister, Tony Blair, in delivering an ultimatum to Saddam Hussein to comply with UN Security Council Resolution 1441 to disarm unconditionally within twenty-four hours or face "serious consequences."

The Madrid attacks raised widespread compassion around the world for Spain, particularly among its European partners. In response to the tragedy, the European Council, meeting in Brussels two weeks later, named a new EU counterterrorism coordinator, Dutch ambassador Gijs deVries. Conveying solidarity with the Spanish victims and their families, the European leaders approved a lengthy Declaration on Combating Terrorism. New measures, designed to correct failings in Europe's counterterrorism procedures, included improved border information, additional powers to arrest persons suspected of links to terrorism, judicial cooperation, visa information exchange and a common effort against money laundering. While the incoming prime minister, Zapatero, renewed his electoral pledge to recall Spain's small contingent of troops from Iraq, he reassured allies that the struggle against terrorism would be given priority. He also made it clear that Spanish troops would remain with NATO's mission in Afghanistan.

In Washington, a Senate hearing on the Madrid attacks resulted in expressions of sympathy and horror over the tragedy, but also concern about its influence on the Spanish elections. Several speakers lamented the loss of a key ally in the war in Iraq, suggested that Spaniards had voted for appeasement to terrorists and questioned whether Spain and Europe as a whole would remain firm in the war against terrorism. Addressing the hearing, J. Cofer Black, coordinator for counterterrorism at the US State Department, noted that the Madrid bombings have provided Europeans with "additional impetus for action" and that the EU summit had demonstrated "a new sense of urgency." Emphasizing that Spanish support in the war on terrorism had been "excellent" in the past, ambassador Black declared: "After the election, the Spanish have underscored to us their full acceptance that terrorism is an issue of great significance to them. They plan to engage it more closely, unilaterally as well as with their European partners."[1]

On 2 April the Spanish police announced the discovery of an unexploded bomb on the Madrid-Seville high-speed railroad tracks, which caused a new wave of alarm. Within days of the Madrid bombings, Spanish officials had implicated an underground Islamist organization, the Moroccan Islamic Combatant Group, known by its initials in

French as GICM, and arrested a score of Moroccans, including Zougam. Three weeks after the attack, the police traced cellphone numbers to a group of suspects in an apartment in the working class suburb of Leganés, south of Madrid, but before the fugitives could be detained they blew themselves up. Two of the seven suspects killed in the blast were identified as GICM leaders: Serhane Ben Abdelmajid Fakhet, a Tunisian real estate agent and assiduous mosque-goer married to a Moroccan, and Jamal Ahmidan, a Moroccan drug trafficker who had become jihadist during a stint in a jail in Tetuan. Fakhet was later purported to be the master-mind of the conspiracy.

The GICM had surfaced a year earlier in connection with the 16 May terrorist action against foreign and Jewish targets in Morocco. In the Casablanca attacks, twelve Moroccan Islamic extremists killed thirty-three Europeans and Moroccans and wounded 100, then blew themselves up. A senior Moroccan intelligence officer told me at the time that orders for the suicide bombings had come from leaders of the GICM, who allegedly had links with Osama bin Laden and operated out of Madrid and London. Moroccan officials had provided Spanish authorities with a list of GICM suspects believed to be active in Spain, including Jamal Zougam, but Madrid had disregarded a request for their extradition, according to the Moroccan sources. Likewise, London officials had refused the extradition of another GICM suspect. Following the 11 March terrorist attacks, the Moroccan government sent high level security officers to Madrid to assist in the investigation, and a Moroccan official told me that perhaps now the Spanish would take their warnings seriously.

After the collective suicide at Leganés, the Spanish interior minister, Acebes, announced that the terrorist cell behind the train bombings had been virtually dismantled. The Spanish press, however, was skeptical. *Cambio 16* reported there were "dozens of sleeper cells in immigrant neighborhoods waiting to receive orders."[2] The leading Spanish expert on global terrorism, Fernando Reinares, described the situation bluntly, declaring that Spain had become "one of the main bases of Al Qaeda in Europe."[3] Reinares, a professor of political sciences at the Juan Carlos I University, noted that traditionally Al Qaeda militants had used Spain as a logistics hub, refuge, command center and center for the transfer of funds, as well as a base from which to move terrorist cells to northern Europe.

Remarkably, there were no mass demonstrations against the Muslim community in the wake of the 11 March bombings, even when it became apparent that Islamic fanatics were behind the tragedy and that most of the suspects were Moroccan. "I didn't detect any anti-Muslim incidents in the aftermath of 11 March; the Spanish public didn't fall into the trap of equating Muslims with terrorists," Said Kirhlani, a Moroccan PhD student who lives in Madrid, told me.[4] He emphasized that the Spanish government had handled the disaster well, without passing any exceptional laws or closing a single prayer hall but with reiterated calls for calm. Spain's main Islamic groups swiftly condemned the terrorist action and also tried to tranquilize their followers. Speaking in the name of the Muslim community, the Islamic Cultural Center, which runs the principal mosque in Madrid, issued a communiqué expressing "profound repugnance" for the attack and denounced "any kind of terrorism wherever it comes from." Offering their deepest sorrow and condolences to families of the victims, the center's leadership said that all Muslims "shared the pain of the Spanish people at this difficult time" and prayed to Allah for help to overcome the country's misfortune.

The strongest denunciation of the train bombings was issued by Spain's Islamic Commission, which represents the main Muslim organizations in the country. On the first anniversary of the 2004 attacks, Mansur Escudero, co-secretary general of the commission, called on all imams of Spain to condemn terrorism in their Friday prayers and observe a special prayer for the victims of 11 March. Escudero also announced that the commission had issued a *fatwa*, condemning terrorism of any kind and declaring that Osama bin Laden and Al Qaeda should be considered as "apostates" and "outside of Islam."[5] Despite a general reprobation of the attacks, other Muslims in Spain appeared ambivalent about Bin Laden and his connection to the atrocity. Riay Tatari, co-leader of the Islamic Commission with Escudero, declared he had not been informed of the *fatwa* and stressed that the commission was not empowered to give juridical opinions. After considerable internal pressure, Escudero was forced to resign from the commission, but the *fatwa* against Bin Laden had spread around the world via the internet.

* * *

In an effort to piece together the background to the bloody aggression of 11 March, I talked with a number of experts who specialize in counterterrorism.[6] According to these experts, Spain has been used by radical Islamic groups as a strategic center for coordination, financing and recruitment for terrorist actions since before the 1990s in connection with the war against the Soviet Union in Afghanistan. During the Afghan jihad against Soviet occupation from 1982–1989, jihadi recruiters had focused on Muslims within the Syrian community in Spain. These Syrians had fled to Spain after a failed coup against the Damascus regime led to the brutal repression of the Islamic opposition in 1982. They were generally affiliated with the Muslim Brotherhood, an Islamic reform movement founded in Egypt in 1928 and committed to the creation of an Islamic state. Spain's Syrians formed a generally educated community estimated to number about 30,000, mostly professionals and business people. But among the well-integrated Muslims, a nucleus of Islamic militants would eventually join forces with Al Qaeda.

Counterterrorism experts usually identify Mustafa Setmariam Nasar, the Al Qaeda ideologue, as founder of the movement's cells in Spain. Setmariam is author of the jihadi classic, *The Call for a Global Islamic Resistance*, which first appeared under the pen-name of Abu Musab al Suri on radical Islamic websites in 2004. Born in Aleppo in 1959, Setmariam had studied engineering before taking part in the Muslim Brotherhood's unsuccessful attempt to overthrow former Syrian dictator Hafez al Assad in 1982. After fleeing Syria, Setmariam is said to have received training in explosives and guerrilla warfare in Jordan and Egypt before joining Syrian exiles in Spain in 1985. The dashing red-haired Syrian soon acquired Spanish nationality through marriage to a Spaniard, identified as Elena Morena, and they settled in the southern region of Andalucia.

Like Muslim activists around the world, Setmariam traveled to Afghanistan in 1985 to take part in the fight against the Soviet occupation. There, in Arab-Afghan camps, Setmariam trained elite fighters in military methodology and his own specialties: the fabrication of explosives, special operations and guerrilla warfare. The following year, the jihadist is quoted as saying that he was "honored by coming to know Sheikh Usama" and became a member of Al Qaeda.[7] In 1992, he was sent back to Spain with the mission to establish Al Qaeda cells in Europe, but little is known of his activities. Three years later, he moved to London, where he acted as a spokesperson for Bin Laden. Setmariam and his Spanish family returned to Afghanistan in 1998, where he set up the Al Ghuraba training camp.[8] After the United States invaded Afghanistan in 2001, Setmariam is said to have gone into hiding somewhere between Pakistan and Afghanistan, where he was arrested in the border town of Quetta in October 2005 and turned over to US intelligence operatives.

In the spring of 2006, Setmariam was profiled in a front page article in the *Washington Post* as the "Architect of a New War on the West." The *Post's* Madrid correspondent, Craig Whitlock, reported that the Al Qaeda strategist had written his "masterwork" from secret hideouts in South Asia. The 1,600 page tome, according to Whitlock, outlines "the strategy for a truly global conflict on as many fronts as possible and in the form of resistance by small cells or individuals, rather than traditional guerrilla warfare."[9] Citing official sources, the *Post* reporter identified Setmariam's theories behind several major terrorist attacks, including those that took place in Casablanca in 2003, Madrid in 2004 and London in 2005. "In each case," Whitlock wrote, "the perpetrators organized themselves into local, self-sustaining cells that acted on their own but also likely accepted guidance from visiting emissaries of the global movements."

The establishment of Syrian Islamists in Spain was followed by another injection of Islamic militants, this time from Algeria in 1993–4, according to the counterterrorism experts. In December 1991, Algeria's main opposition party, the Islamic Salvation Front, which called for the creation of an Islamic state, had won national elections but was barred from coming to power by the military, ushering in a long and bloody civil war. Most Algerian Islamists headed for France, but a hardcore group from the Armed Islamist Group, or GIA, settled in Spain, particularly in the regions of Barcelona and Marbella. At that time, Setmariam's small group of Syrian radicals formed an alliance with the Algerian Islamists, who had operational skills. At the end of the 1990s, a radical Moroccan group appeared in Spain, the GICM, which was said to be a motley mix of Moroccan fighters from Afghanistan, drug traffickers and immigrant smugglers. By 2003, there were various Moroccan jihadi organizations scattered around Spain, but there was no indication of links to Al Qaeda.

These shadowy groups drew the attention of Spain's ambitious investigating magistrate, Baltasar Garzón Real, who had explored the activities of Islamic radicals long before Al Qaeda won worldwide notoriety with the 11 September 2001, attacks on the United States. Garzón had gained national prominence in the late 1980s with his zealous investigations into terrorist activities of the Basque separatist movement ETA and anti-ETA death squads. The Spanish magistrate began looking into Islamic extremists in the early 1990s, and by 1996 he had uncovered a network of religious militants that raised money and campaigned for recruits to fight in Bosnia and Afghanistan. No arrests were made at the time, although several Islamists were kept under surveillance, like another Spaniard of Syrian origin, Imad Eddin Barakat Yarkas, forty-two, who used the alias of Abu Dahdah and worked as a used car salesman. Meanwhile Garzón acquired international renown in October 1998, with his campaign to extradite the former Chilean president, Augusto Pinochet, from Britain, where he was undergoing medical treatment, for crimes of torture and other human rights abuses against Spanish citizens. As a result of Garzón's efforts, the late dictator was put under house arrest until March 2000, when he was judged unfit for trial.

In the wake of 11 September the Spanish crusader embarked on another high profile case: the use of Spain as a staging ground for international acts of terrorism by radical Islamic groups. Barely two months later, Garzón ordered the arrest of Yarkas and two associates on suspicion of raising funds and recruiting on behalf of Al Qaeda within Spain, charges they denied. While Spain's 'Super Judge,' as he is often called, won kudos in western intelligence circles with this action, he was viewed by radical Islamists as having thrown down the gauntlet. Garzón plunged ahead to launch Europe's most ambitious legal proceeding against Al Qaeda, acting under a Spanish Law of Universal Justice, which states that crimes of terrorism, like crimes against humanity, can be tried in Spain regardless of where they are committed. In September 2003, the audacious examining magistrate issued a nearly 700-page indictment charging Osama bin Laden and forty other suspects of conspiring with an international terrorist organization to commit the deadly 11 September attacks. According to the document, Yarkas was Bin Laden's man in Madrid, and he had provided funds and logistics for the 9/11 attacks. The Spanish Syrian, who had contacts with Muslim Brothers in Hamburg, is said to have met twice in Spain with Mohammed Atta, the lead 9/11 suspect. Yarkas' last meeting with Atta and Al Qaeda coordinator Ramzi Bin-al-Shibh took place on 16 July at Tarragona, a resort south of Barcelona, and its purpose, according to the indictment, was to finalize plans for the attacks in the United States.

In June 2004, on the heels of the 11 March terrorist attacks, Garzón made public the results of his larger eight year long inquiry into Muslim extremist groups in Spain. The probe showed that the Hamburg cell had received logistic support from militants in Spain and that the country served as a platform for various terrorist actions. When Garzón's 9/11 case finally went to trial in Madrid in April 2005, however, it was clear that much of the evidence against suspected Al Qaeda operatives was circumstantial. While there was little doubt of the suspects' links to Al Qaeda, it was a leap to prove conspiracy to murder. On 26 September 2005, only twenty-four of the forty-one suspects appeared for sentencing—the rest were fugitives, mostly thought to be elsewhere in Europe and in Morocco or Algeria. The court convicted Yarkas of being the leader of a terrorist organization that had conspired with the plotters of 11 September and sentenced him to twenty-seven years prison, but there was insufficient evidence to convict him of the murder of the 3,000 victims of the terrorist attacks in the United States. It was the same for Yarkas' two co-defendants, who had been charged with conspiring mass murder. His Moroccan aide Driss Chebli, thirty-five, was sentenced to six years prison for collaborating with a terrorist organization, and Syrian-born Ghasoub al Abrash Ghalyoun, forty-one, accused of making videotapes of the World Trade Center in 1997 for the terrorist organization, was cleared of all charges. Syrian-born Spanish journalist Tayseer Alouni, who worked for the Arab TV network Al Jazeera, was accused of sending funds to Islamic militants in Afghanistan and sentenced to seven years prison. Another fifteen suspects received prison terms of eleven to seventeen years on terrorist-related charges not connected with 11 September, and five others were acquitted.

During the lengthy trial the Spanish, like other Europeans, discovered the difficulties of prosecuting Islamists accused of inspiring jihadists who belonged to small unstructured groups. The trial also clearly demonstrated Spain's needs for new anti-terror legislation. The present laws had been framed to meet the challenge from ETA, a unified and disciplined organization, and provided generally light sentences for armed bands, presumably to avoid filling the jails with Basque martyrs. Under these circumstances, it was hard to make a case stick against nebulous international terrorist groups. This weakness would again become apparent two years later during the 11 March trial.

* * *

While Garzón was investigating terrorist activities in Spain, the focus of his investigation remained on Al Qaeda's activities against the United States. Neither Spanish authorities nor the general public imagined that Islamic extremists would take action on Spanish soil. Yet, there had been warnings for those who would heed them.

One of these was Haizam Amirah Fernández, a senior analyst at the Elcano Royal Institute, a think tank for international and strategic studies. Amirah points to two public statements made by Al Qaeda, singling out Spain as a target months before the Madrid bombings. The first alert, according to a report by Amirah, was a forty-seven-page analysis of the political situation in Iraq, prepared by the Centre of Services for the Mujahidin, a hitherto unknown organization formed "in support of the Iraqi people" and published in Arabic on 3 September 2003, on Islamic websites. The document devotes six pages to foreign policy in Spain, which it describes as one of "the European appendages" of the United States, and states that "successive attacks against Spanish citizens would force the Popular [People's] Party government to withdraw Spain's troops from Iraq." If that does not take place, the document predicts that "the Socialist Party would come to power and would put in practice its electoral pledge to withdraw the troops."[10]

The second document referred to by Amirah is dated 3 December 2003, and was published online by the External Communications Department of the Mujahideen Center after the murder of seven Spanish intelligence agents in Iraq. This four-page "Message to the Spanish People" provides its own account of the suffering of Iraqis during the dictatorship of Saddam Hussein and also under American military occupation, placing blame on the countries that supported the United States and their leaders who 'lied [to their people] and dragged them into a war in which they had no interest."[11]

Amirah told me there were few Arab speakers in the police and nobody who can read Arabic. "This means the authorities don't know what's happening in the underground mosques, the call centers or on the jihadi websites."[12]

There are also few ethnic Arabs in the Spanish administration, aside from those in the enclaves of Ceuta and Melilla in Morocco. My friend Mohamed Azaf, employed by the Madrid municipality to work with the Arabic-speaking immigrant community, is a notable exception. "There's an urgent need for more Arab-speakers in positions of responsibility; almost nobody in the police speaks Arabic, no undercover agents, nobody in politics," Azaf stressed. Pointing out that North African immigration was a relatively new phenomenon, he noted that most Moroccans in Spain don't have the necessary education to get good government jobs. They usually drop out of school so they can work in construction or in agriculture to send money home to their families, he said. Those with advanced education don't stay long in Spain but go to the Middle East where they easily obtain well-paid work in hospitals, laboratories or industry."[13]

Latent hostility to North African immigrants, accused of flooding the country and stealing jobs, was enhanced by the fear of "Islamic terrorists." In headline-grabbing statements, Judge Garzón expressed the concerns of many Spaniards when he declared that "the biggest terrorist threat" facing Europe came from Morocco. The media-conscious magistrate was not directly involved in the investigations of the 11 March train bombings, but testified on 15 July 2004, as an expert on terrorism before a parliamentary commission examining the government's handling of the terrorist attacks. In his testimony, Garzón argued that Morocco was just a short ferry ride away and hosted some 100 terrorist cells, linked to Al Qaeda, which raised money smuggling hashish and people into Spain. He acknowledged that the previous Spanish government's support for the war in Iraq was probably one factor behind the terrorist attacks, but he stressed that Muslims in North Africa had also voiced a historic claim to Al Andalus.

Leaders of Spain's Muslim community lost no opportunity to condemn the deadly assaults on Madrid's commuters. Mohammed Saleh, secretary of Madrid's Islamic Center, told me: "People were shocked by the terrorist attacks. We explained that Islam is against terrorism. Fortunately Spaniards realized the difference, that Muslims are not all guilty, just like you can't condemn all Basques for ETA." Saleh, a Jordanian who has lived in Spain since 1980, said that following 11 March, the Islamic Center organized three campaigns to collect blood "as a sign of solidarity with the people of Madrid." The center has also taken part in anti-terrorism demonstrations and held several inter-religious conferences.[14] There was similar condemnation of terrorism from substitute Helal-Jamal Abboshi, secretary of the Abu Bakr Mosque in the working class Tetuan neighborhood of Madrid. "Our community denounced the 11 March attacks and offered to cooperate with the authorities," he said readily. A Palestinian who came to Spain in 1971 to study pharmacy, Abboshi emphasized that it was still not clear who was behind the terrorists or what was their aim. "But the action was against the existence of the Muslim community in Spain and our *convivencia* (good relations) with the Spanish."[15]

The police reacted swiftly and firmly to scattered anti-Islamic incidents, which increased noticeably after the 11 March terrorist attacks and offensive graffiti, such as swastikas and phrases like "*Moros* go home," appeared on walls of mosques and prayer halls in Madrid and towns of Cataluña and Valencia provinces, wherever there were numerous Muslim immigrants. Police attributed the slurs and threatening letters to skinheads and other right-wing extremists. Muslim leaders have generally played down the insults to avoid confrontation and called on the faithful to refrain from responding to provocations. Sheikh Moneir Mahmoud, the Egyptian imam of Madrid's largest mosque, has received a number of letters since 11 March with insults like "Muslims are equal to terrorists," which he has simply torn up and thrown into the trash.[16] After a popular Muslim shrine was burned down in the Spanish enclave of Ceuta in Morocco, the leaders of Spain's two largest Muslim federations called on the government to take measures against rising acts of xenophobia, but insults and vandalism directed against Muslims continued.

The new climate of suspicion towards Muslims has been aggravated by stepped up warnings from Al Qaeda that Al Andalus is in its sights. Claiming responsibility for a rash of terrorist attacks in Morocco and Algeria in April 2007, Al Qaeda's organization in North Africa swore "to liberate the land of Islam from Jerusalem to Al Andalus." Several months later, it was reported that Al Qaeda in North Africa was threatening to destroy Algeria's oil and gas pipelines. The news was particularly alarming for Spain, which depends on Algeria for one third of its gas supply. The threats were published on the terrorist organization's website, after four attacks against Algerian oil and gas facilities in which one Russian technician and two local security guards were killed. Moreover, on several occasions, Bin Laden's chief aide, Ayman al-Zawahri, appeared in videos calling for the liberation of all former Muslim territories "from Al Andalus to Iraq."

* * *

The M/11 trial, as the Madrid terrorist case came to be known, opened on 15 February 2007, in a heavily guarded courthouse built for the occasion on the outskirts of the Spanish capital. The legal action was intended to clarify once and for all who were the true authors of the tragedy, establish their motives, and render justice on behalf of the victims, their families and the shattered public. Despite all the evidence to the contrary, there lingered questions in the minds of many Spaniards about the possible involvement of Basque extremists, and many Muslims doubted the Al Qaeda connection. On the other hand, for Bruce Hoffman, a leading American counterterrorism expert, the facts were clear. The 11 March terrorist assault was "dramatic confirmation that after 11 September, Al Qaeda had opened a new frontline in Europe," he told a Congressional hearing in Washington DC.[17] Hoffman, professor in the security studies program at Georgetown University, expressed concern that the issue of terrorism had become "extremely politicized" in Spain. He acknowledged that initially Spanish investigators believed the attacks were the work of independent Islamic radicals but it was becoming clear that "Al Qaeda's participation was fundamental."

During five months of the proceedings, the court heard some 300 witnesses and nearly 100 experts and received 90,000 pages of evidence. In an effort to ensure transparency, the trial was televised live, providing some insight into the activities of the group before and after the attacks. All twenty-eight suspects on trial had pleaded not guilty to the charges of terrorism. Among the accused, there were the stereotype young hot-headed Islamic fanatics, but also an odd mix of seemingly devout ordinary Muslims and petty criminals, mostly in their thirties. Absent from the proceedings, of course, were the seven main suspects, who had blown themselves up when cornered by security officers in the Madrid suburb of Leganés three weeks after the attacks.

According to court testimony, the Madrid train bombing plot was hatched in the wake of Osama bin Laden's October 2003 appeal to Muslims everywhere to attack western interests, during which he had specifically mentioned Spain. The four core authors of the plot were said to be: Rabei Osman el Sayed, an Egyptian who fled to Italy after the train massacre and was serving a ten-year prison sentence for terrorist activities there; Serhane ben Abdelmajid Fakhet, one of the group who had committed suicide in Leganés; Youssef Belhadj, alleged head of Al Qaeda's military wing in Europe; and Hassan el Haski, described as chief of the clandestine Moroccan Islamic Combatant Group (GICM) in Spain. These "masterminds" were said to have recruited foot soldiers to carry out the train attacks at Madrid's two main mosques. While cellphones had been used to activate the blasts, they also played a key role in the investigation, their electronic footprints leading investigators to the murky world of Islamic extremists active within Spain, and their contacts overseas.

North Africans in Madrid reacted to the trial with widespread skepticism. Even the most politically astute observers remained unconvinced of the prosecution's contention that the bombings were the work of Muslim extremists, linked to Al Qaeda. Moroccans pointed to the opposition People's Party's continuing claims of an ETA involvement, a line that resonated with Muslims, who could not believe that devout Muslims would kill innocent people. "We still don't know who was really behind the train bombings," a Moroccan scholar told me, emphasizing that the arrests were "arbitrary and without sufficient proof" and the alleged ring-leaders had all "conveniently committed suicide."

Spanish observers, who followed the case closely, praised the three-judge panel for the "seriousness" and "neutrality" of the proceedings, but faulted the media for politicizing the case. "The Spanish press seemed to be covering two different trials, manipulating the testimony and evidence for their own purposes," a Spanish academic confided.

The much awaited M-11 verdict, announced at the end of October 2007, wound up in a disappointing draw, leaving basic questions unanswered: who was behind the attacks and what were their motives. Two Moroccan militants and a Spanish accomplice were convicted of murdering 191 persons and wounding more than 1800 others. The Moroccans, Jamal Zougam, thirty-four, and Otman el Gnaoui, thirty-two, were sentenced to more than 42,000 years in prison each for planting the backpack-bombs on the trains, along with the seven terrorists who had committed suicide in Leganés. It was established that Zougam owned the shop that had provided the phone-card detonators, but there was insufficient evidence to convict him of links to the shadowy Moroccan Islamic Combat Group. Gnaoui was also found guilty of transporting the explosives. Spaniard José Emilio Suarez Trashorras, thirty, a former miner from Asturias, who was said to have no previous connection with Islamic extremists, was sentenced to almost 35,000 years prison for supplying the explosives. The prison sentences were largely symbolic, however, since under Spanish law the maximum time a convict can serve is forty years. Two additional defendants, Hassan el Haski and Youssef Belhadj, were sentenced to fourteen years prison for belonging to a terrorist organization but acquitted of charges of organizing the train attacks. Eight Spanish citizens, accused of involvement in the transfer of explosives to the terrorists, were cleared of all charges. El Haski was extradited to Morocco in 2008 and tried for his role in the 2003 Casablanca attacks, and acquitted.

The tribunal ruled that an Islamist cell had been responsible for the attacks and cleared the Basque separatist group ETA of involvement. But the court failed to establish a connection between the terrorists and any international organization like Al Qaeda. In its most controversial ruling, the court acquitted Rabei Osman el Sayed Ahmed, thirty-five, who was accused of being one of the main instigators of the bombings. A suspected Al Qaeda operative based in Spain, Ahmed claimed to be a chauffeur by profession and a "normal" practicing Muslim, "not an extremist." In June 2004, he had fled to Milan, where he was put under police surveillance after a tip from Spanish investigators. During a wire tapped phone conversation, Ahmed was heard bragging that the Madrid bombing was "my project." Subsequently he was sentenced to serve ten years in prison in Milan, for conspiracy to participate in international terrorism.

Each of the families of the victims was awarded 900,000 euros indemnity and the wounded were to receive between 30,000 and 1.5 million euros in compensation. But the verdict seemed to satisfy no one. Some expressed anger that the main suspects behind the attacks had either committed suicide or been acquitted, while the lengthy and inconclusive M/11 proceedings confirmed what antiterrorism experts had been saying all along. The existing laws in Spain, like those in most European countries, were simply not prepared to address the challenges of international terrorism.

* * *

Until 11 March 2004, the Portuguese had little reason to believe their modest country on Europe's periphery could be a target of international terrorism. Nevertheless, organizers of the much-anticipated 2004 Euro Cup soccer championship, which was to open several months after the Madrid attacks, had previously warned their Portuguese hosts that the games could become a magnet not only for the usual bands of hooligans but also for emboldened terrorists. The games were scheduled to take place over a three-week period starting

12 July, in ten flashy new or renovated stadiums around the country, and were expected to draw more than a million fans. Lisbon officials had boasted at the beginning of the year that there had been no specific terrorist threats linked to the games and that appropriate measures had been taken to deal with the usual rowdiness. Authorities had banned 2,000 fans from England with violent records, canceled police leave during the event, and purchased new anti-riot equipment, including water canon trucks. They believed everything was under control.

After the 11 March attacks in Madrid, the games' organizers provided an additional two million euros for the security budget. Lisbon announced the mobilization of 60,000 police, firefighters, emergency medical officers and reinforced border patrols, while NATO was asked to help patrol the skies. Portuguese authorities showed new zeal in screening visitors from North Africa. At the end of April, it was reported that Portugal had refused visas to two well known Moroccan painters, who had been invited to attend the inauguration of an exhibit on contemporary Moroccan art in the ancient Arab capital of Silves, on the pretext that the artists had been refused visas to Spain and France.

Before the tournament, a group of Neo-Nazis who threatened trouble was taken into custody. Police raided their hideaway, where they found stockpiles of weapons, and the threat was over in twenty-four hours. Several days after the start of the matches, it was reported that fifteen North Africans had been arrested in the northern city of Oporto on suspicion of links to Al Qaeda. Later, eight of them were released and all but one deported on immigration violations. In the end, the Euro Cup games went off smoothly. The only serious casualty was the stabbing of an English fan, who died from his wound. A Ukrainian pickpocket was arrested in connection with the crime.

The Portuguese interior minister, António Costa, spoke proudly of "the Portuguese security model" developed for Euro Cup 2004. "There were no major problems," Costa said in an interview, explaining that the Portuguese had adopted antiterrorist prevention and detection measures from authorities in Belgium and Holland. Since the event went off successfully, Portugal was asked to share its expertise with the Germans for the World Soccer Cup in 2006 and the Chinese in preparation for the Olympics in Beijing in 2008, he added. "Of course 11 March could happen here," he acknowledged, saying that he had no illusions that Portugal could escape the global risks. "All of us in Europe feel threatened since the Madrid massacre."[18]

While there is a heightened wariness towards Muslims in general in the wake of the Madrid attacks, most Portuguese contend that their Muslims are "different." For one thing, the Islamic community is much smaller and more cohesive than that in Spain, goes the argument. A majority of new immigrants comes from former Portuguese territories like Brazil and the Cape Verde Islands, and are Christian not Muslim. Then too, unlike elsewhere in Europe, there have been virtually no religious conflicts in Portugal. The authorities have made no move to ban headscarves or other religious garb and there has been little public opposition to the establishment of Muslim places of worship. Muslims live not in isolated ghettos but interspersed with the Christian majority, even in the largely ethnic African communities.

Likewise, Muslims in Portugal generally insist that their community is relatively insulated from the radical currents sweeping other parts of the world, even after Islamic extremists were implicated in the 2004 train bombings in neighboring Spain. But the 7 July 2005, attacks on the London Underground shocked Lisbon's Muslims. The suspects in London were like the majority of Portugal's Muslims of Asian origin, from Pakistan, Bangladesh and India. Portugal's Muslim leaders, who have contacts with Muslim communities in England, admit that radicals could easily enter the country and expressed concern over their potential influence on the growing number of alienated young people.

"Our mosques are open, our imams are men of moderation and we don't have any radical groups in our community," Sheikh David Munir, imam of Lisbon's Central Mosque told me in an interview. "But we can't control the outsiders."[19]

5

IBERIAN OUTREACH

It seemed the Portuguese were seeing the Senegalese, Nigerians, Pakistanis, Bangladeshis, Russians and Ukrainians around them for the first time that spring of 2006. Portuguese society had grown accustomed to the presence of immigrants from their former colonies, but it came as a surprise to discover all the other newcomers in *Os Lisboetas* (The Lisboners), a prize-winning documentary by French-Portuguese director Sérgio Tréfaut. I cannot recall any other documentary that attracted so much media attention in Portugal, most of it favorable.

Os Lisboetas is not a romantic panegyric to downtrodden migrants, or a diatribe against a heartless bureaucracy that doesn't know how to cope with the mass of foreigners begging to stay. It is a human portrait of foreigners who have chosen to settle in Portugal, bringing with them their religions and languages. It is the story of the difficulties encountered along the way and occasional joys. Tréfaut's immigrants endure endless lines and bureaucratic hurdles at the Bureau for Foreigners and Borders, complain of language and education problems, and experience repeated disappointments at labor "auctions." There are also heart-warming scenes of long distance telephone calls home, worshippers in a Muslim prayer hall, a Sikh temple and Pentecostal church, and children playing in city fountains or on nearby beaches. Through his film, Tréfaut has shaken up the Portuguese and made them see the reality of immigration, people who are not transitory figurants but have come to live, work and raise families.

"I suppose if there is a message from *Os Lisboetas* it's to show the Portuguese that the country is enriched by immigrants and more can be done to help solve their problems," said Tréfaut, whom I have known many years.[1] A boyish forty-two, Tréfaut understands the life of migrants because he himself was born in exile, son of a Portuguese Communist journalist and his French wife, who fled to Brazil during the Salazar dictatorship, and only returned to Portugal with the restoration of democracy. We got together at Tréfaut's office next to the eighteenth century Magdalena Church in Lisbon's ancient Arab quarter of the Alfama, whose time-scarred buildings now house many immigrants. On a tour of the neighborhood, we encountered several of his film's African "stars," who greeted him as one of them and told him the latest news. At his favorite Pakistani eating nook, the owner willingly shared his life story and travails as an undocumented immigrant. At the Bengali prayer hall, several worshippers welcomed Tréfaut warmly like a fellow believer. They told him so many faithful were coming for prayers that they feared the building would collapse and were looking for a new locale. It was another lesson of *Os Lisboetas*; the immigrants were here, waiting for people to listen to their stories.

Another groundbreaking work is the book *Muslims in Portugal*, published in Portuguese by a leading newspaper, *Público*. For one year, from Ramadan (the Muslim month of fasting) 2003 to Ramadan 2004, two Portuguese journalists, Middle East expert Alexandra Prado Coelho and photographer Daniel Rocha, immersed themselves in the life of the new Muslim communities. The result is this intimate reportage on Muslims—their associations, young people and women, religious leaders, and their traditions and festivities—all stunningly photographed in black and white. "We took on this project because people in Portugal know so very little about Muslims and Islam," Prado Coelho explained, when I saw her at *Público*'s office in downtown Lisbon. "In the end we found that there is no Muslim problem here but problems of blacks and poverty."[2]

The man in charge of Portugal's immigration commission told me pretty much the same thing. "There is no Islamic question in Portugal. The majority of the Muslims come from our former colonies; it's a small community and well integrated," Rui Marques, high commissioner for immigration and ethnic minorities asserted.[3] He admitted, however, that there were signs of new public hostility toward African immigrants, whose image was increasingly associated with criminal activity. The high commissioner spoke to me during a seminar on "Descendants of Immigrants: Among Three Worlds." The two-day conference was organized by one of the country's main think tanks, the Orient Foundation, and held in the Arrábida Monastery, on the wooded peninsula south of Lisbon. Spanish and Portuguese scholars and representatives of foreign communities discussed immigrant-related issues like preserving ties with countries of origin and forming new ties in the host country. Pointing out that Portugal's immigration policy is in flux, Marques said that France's assimilation policy had clearly not worked and suggested that Canada's diversity in unity could be a good model.

Several speakers acknowledged integration problems with the second generation. Rosa Aparicio Gómez, professor at Madrid's Comillas University, said her 2003 study of the Moroccan, Dominican and Peruvian communities in Spain showed that children of immigrants were better educated than their parents and found slightly better jobs. A surprising aspect of her research was that second generation Moroccans in Spain were better adjusted than either the Dominicans or Peruvians. "We concluded that the main reason was because the Moroccan children came from stable families, whereas the Latin Americans were often from single parent homes," Professor Aparicio told the seminar. But she noted that Moroccans suffer from discrimination. Spanish opinion polls give Moroccans a very low rating, just above gypsies. Dominicans are also victims of racism. "They discover they are colored in Spain," the Spanish academic pointed out. She noted that Peruvian immigrants are mostly single mothers and their offspring are often *niños llaves* (latchkey children) because the parents are never there.[4] Anabela Rodrigues, head of a Portuguese volunteer agency called Windmill of Youth, whose family comes from the former Portuguese colony of Cape Verde, spoke for many second generation immigrants, Christian as well as Muslim, when she asked: "We don't identify with Portugal or with Cape Verde; what are we?"[5]

I left the conference with the basic question: what were Portugal and Spain doing to integrate the new waves of immigrants? To find out, I took up the high commissioner's offer to continue our conversation at his office in Lisbon. The headquarters of ACIME, as the High Commission for Immigration and Ethnic Minorities was known by its initials in Portuguese, is appropriately located in the immigrant neighborhood of Martim Moniz and across from the Anjos Church, where immigrants often congregate. During ACIME's office hours there's usually a long line of people waiting for help with a variety of problems: legal advice on residence permits; access to social services; information about the job market; aid with housing and procedures for family reunion.

Rui Marques, forty-four, was named high commissioner of Portugal's immigration agency in 2005, with masters' degrees in medicine and in communications and a long career in social work. Emphasizing that there was no common European policy on immigration, he told me that Portugal had opted for the "humanist approach."[6] He noted that the new nationality law, which went into effect at the end of 2006, is considered the most generous law of its kind in Europe. Henceforth, foreigners could acquire Portuguese citizenship after six years of legal residence, compared to eight years previously, and ten years for non-Latinos in Spain. "The whole nationalization process has become more flexible, more humane and more adequate to meet the needs of the labor market," Marques said. The high commissioner also showed a benevolent attitude towards undocumented aliens. Foreigners who come to Portugal with tourist visas and let their visas lapse are here illegally and subject to expulsion if arrested for a crime, he said, emphasizing: "but they still have human rights." He pointed out that all children of immigrants, regardless of the legal status of their parents, have the right to free health care and education.

The main mission of ACIME is to ensure that immigrants understand their rights and facilitate their integration, according to Marques. The agency acts as a kind of intermediary with other governmental departments like the ministries of education, health and labor. ACIME has two operational branches in Lisbon and Oporto known as National Support Centers for Immigrants. The Lisbon center receives between 400 and 500 people a day and has six jurists on hand to provide free legal advice, according to Francesca Teixeira, a cheerful, outgoing woman of forty-three and head of the Lisbon Center.[7]

"We work with many immigrants who are here irregularly, most of them from Brazil," Teixeira said, noting that the majority of her staff were immigrants themselves, and so could deal with visitors in their languages. Besides attending immigrants personally, the center operates an SOS telephone service which provides information in various languages and receives complaints of discrimination. In addition there is a free translation service in some fifty languages. Another program, called "Choices," is aimed at children of immigrants and ethnic minorities, particularly in the poorer neighborhoods. Working with local civic groups, "Choices" sponsors more than eighty dance and theater groups, sports and cooking clubs, after school study programs and computer classes. "What we're trying to do is combat social and cultural exclusion and create a new generation of community leaders," Teixeira said.

After observing ACIME's different services first hand, I concluded that its leadership has already achieved something quite remarkable: the image of an immigrant-friendly government agency acting on behalf of newcomers. This is not the usual Immigration Service that stirs fear and resentment in the hearts of immigrants. That role has been left to SEF, the Bureau for Foreigners and Borders, which serves as the enforcement arm of immigration policy. In fact, ACIME often acts as the immigrants' advocate with the general public as well as with other government departments. Its widely distributed brochures debunk common myths: that immigrants are invading Portugal, that they have come to steal Portuguese jobs and lower wages, that they are criminals, bring diseases, and threaten Portuguese culture and traditions. Emphasizing that Portugal was always an emigrant country and needs immigrants because of low birth rates and an aging population, ACIME points out that for every immigrant in Portugal, there are ten Portuguese emigrants around the world.

ACIME is also a conduit to non-governmental organizations who deal with immigrants and sometimes co-sponsors programs with them. Many associations are connected to the Catholic Church, which helped relocate refugees from former Portuguese Africa after independence in the mid-1970s. Now these organizations have opened their doors to other immigrants, from Brazil to Bangladesh.

The Bairro 6 de Maio is one of greater Lisbon's "problem neighborhoods," known as a haunt of drug traffickers, thieves and other criminals. Taxis usually refuse to go near the place. I persuaded a friend to drive me to the entrance of the neighborhood, where the social center is located. Sister Mafalda, who runs the center with three other Dominican nuns, laughed heartily when I asked if she were afraid to work in such a dangerous neighborhood. "The people of the *bairro* protect us; they are our alarm system and nobody dares rob us," she said, inviting me to take a tour of the neighborhood with her.[8] Wherever we went, young and old alike greeted the diminutive nun warmly and occasionally raised personal problems. Although the houses of crumbling concrete and pieces of tin and wood were small and cramped and the dirt alleys so narrow you couldn't open an umbrella, the *bairro* was impeccably clean, with no sign of the refuse so prevalent in "better" neighborhoods. "Last week we mobilized the young people to take part in a clean-up campaign," Sister Mafalda explained, adding that currently she was organizing a movement to fight clandestine pit bull betting, which was a common scourge.

The *bairro* dates back to the late 1960s when many Portuguese emigrated to better-paying jobs in France and Germany, and workers were needed for Portuguese agriculture and industry, Sister Mafalda recounted. Laborers were imported from the colonies, mainly the Cape Verde Islands and Portuguese Guinea, and they settled in makeshift shantytowns like Bairro 6 de Maio in the dormitory town of Amadora. To help integrate the migrants, the Dominican Sisters of Rosário built the social center in 1983 on municipal land with financial help from the European Union. Then in the 1990s, many Guineans arrived, fleeing civil war and followed by their families. There was also an influx of gypsies in the area and, most recently, East Europeans.

With the recent economic slump, the numbers of school dropouts and jobless persons have risen, providing fertile ground for the spread of drug trafficking, youth gangs and violence, Sister Mafalda told me. Undaunted, the nuns stuck it out and feel they are making headway, with many immigrants relocating and integrating into the broader community. They currently serve 700 families in the *bairro* with a variety of programs, including pre-school social development, leisure activities for adolescents, school coaching, adult literacy classes, vacation camps, and music and dance groups. Sister Mafalda stressed that there are no special problems between the Christian and Muslim migrants. In fact, she said, they have organized Christians and Muslims for Peace meetings at the social center and a nearby mosque, and Sheikh Munir of Lisbon's central mosque has visited the center and talked about Islam.

Another dynamic Portuguese woman devoted to the cause of immigrants is anthropologist Rosário Farmhouse, who inherited her fair complexion and surname from an Irish grandfather. When I first met her, she headed the Jesuit Refugee Service (JRS) in Portugal (she would later succeed Rui Marques as director of the national immigration agency). Farmhouse conceded that Portugal grants few requests for asylum, only 102 in 2005, but she stressed that JRS also works with other immigrants, including those without proper documentation. "We don't ask people what is their religion," Farmhouse said, pointing out that many Guineans she works with are Muslim. She told me of Ibrahim, a blind boy from Guinea with tuberculosis, who had one lung removed and was still under treatment. He lives with a cousin, but JRS gives him food and Portuguese language classes. Portugal has agreements with its former colonies to provide major medical care but that does not cover recuperation. Thus a number of patients in recovery are living on the streets or in shelters and need help from private organizations like JRS.[9]

Farmhouse showed me around the spacious Jesuit compound at Lumiar on the outskirts of Lisbon. Here migrants from Russia, Ukraine, Romania and Moldova attend Portuguese language classes, while other migrants from Eastern Europe, Portuguese-speaking Africa and Brazil meet at the Jesuits' Employment Club to learn about the job market and its requirements. Farmhouse spoke enthusiastically about the programs for immigrant doctors and nurses sponsored by JRS and the Gulbenkian Foundation. Since Portugal badly needs doctors and there are many highly qualified doctors from Eastern Europe in non-medical jobs, a special program was launched to help the immigrants meet Portuguese requirements to practice medicine. By 2006, she said, 105 doctors from Eastern Europe, Cuba and Africa had obtained equivalent diplomas and were practicing their profession in Portugal. At the request of the Portuguese Ministry of Health, another 150 doctors have enrolled in this program. Some sixty nurses have completed a similar program and are working around the country.

Farmhouse urged me to visit Portugal's two new internment centers for refugees awaiting asylum and homeless migrants, in Lisbon and Oporto. I welcomed her invitation, especially because Spanish internment centers were closed to the media and even social workers. The Bobadela Reception Center (a much more hospitable name than internment center) is located in an industrial suburb of Lisbon. Teresa Mendes, the director, proudly showed me about the complex, which could have passed for a luxury boarding school, with a modern kitchen and laundry and a children's playground. At the time there were thirty-three residents, from Iraq, Afghanistan, Georgia, Colombia, Somalia and other African countries, mostly single men but also several families. When I asked to speak to a refugee family, Mendes said it would have to be arranged in advance because of security considerations. Then she suggested I talk to the reception clerk, a Palestinian refugee from Syria, who had been granted asylum and Portuguese residence.

The stocky, balding, sixty-one-year-old Muslim refugee asked me not to disclose his name as he still has relatives in Syria. His family comes from Safad, now part of Israel, and fled to Syria in 1948. Growing up in Damascus, he was the leader of a student group opposed to the dictatorial regime of the late president, Hafez al Assad. When the young Palestinian refused to join the Syrian army, he was arrested and accused of being a spy for Israel. For his militancy, he spent a total of thirty-five years in prison without trial. On his release, he seized the first opportunity to flee the country on a ship that happened to be headed for Portugal. "I arrived in Lisbon in February 2005, without any documents, only my story," he recalled. "People believed me and were very good to me. It was like being reborn as a human being."

Numerous private Portuguese volunteer associations serve as lobbies for immigrant rights. The most vociferous and effective group is Solidaridade Imigrante, better known by its acronym SOLIM, which campaigns for decent housing for immigrants, family reunification and legal status. "Our aim is for immigrants to be treated as equals," said Timoteo Macedo, a Portuguese professor of design from Angola, who founded SOLIM in 2001. The soft-spoken director said it now has 8,200 members from eighty-six countries, with the largest contingents from Guinea and Brazil. Immigrants pay 2.5 euros a month in dues; "that way they feel they belong and we have financial autonomy," Macedo said.[10] SOLIM's office is located in a dilapidated building in the heart of old Lisbon. The first time I visited the association, the main room was abuzz with small clusters of Africans discussing their problems with members of the staff. In an adjacent room, migrants from Kazakhstan, Senegal, Guinea and Ukraine were seated at computers, taking a course on information technology. All immigrants were treated alike, with no distinction of religion or ethnic origin.

Macedo said the new immigration law was an improvement over past legislation. Previously there had been five different kinds of residence authorizations, which are now unified. Also the renewal of permits is done by municipalities and no longer handled by the police. He emphasized that the main flaw in the legislation was that it does not provide any way for more than 150,000 immigrants, in Portugal illegally, to regularize their status.

Another problem, according to Macedo, is that since 11 September, immigration issues have been infused with security considerations. Immigrants, particularly those from Muslim countries, are treated by some officials with suspicion, as potential criminals. Family reunions particularly have been penalized. "We need approximation, not talk of terrorists," the immigration advocate said. He told me that Portuguese embassies in Islamabad and New Delhi were arbitrarily rejecting requests for visas for children of Muslims on the grounds that papers had been falsified. Although officials are not saying so publicly, other immigration experts confirm that Muslim applications for family reunification are facing increased scrutiny by Portuguese authorities "for security reasons."

In addition to their work as a pressure group and watchdog, SOLIM's staff often appear in the trenches, alongside slum dwellers, mostly immigrants and gypsies, who are threatened with eviction and demolition. Macedo emphasized that there are many ghettos in the Lisbon area, such as Azinhaga dos Besouros, the scene of bitter confrontations in the summer of 2006. "We are fighting alongside neighborhood associations through the courts and by direct action for dignified social housing," he said, warning that if something were not done soon, Portugal risked a social explosion like France in 2005.

SOS Racismo is another non-governmental group which has denounced the proliferation of slums and forced dislocations without alternative housing. Dedicated to the creation of a "just, egalitarian, multicultural society without racism and xenophobia," SOS Racismo was set up by a group of Portuguese volunteers in 1990, inspired by the French model, with the goal of establishing a European-wide anti-racist network. Increasingly the Portuguese association has become a spokesperson for immigrants, speaking out against landlords who turn away African tenants because of their color or employers who reject Muslim women wearing headscarves, seen by some as a symbol of radical Islam.

It was SOS Racismo that called on Diana Andringa, head of the Portuguese Journalists Union, to investigate the 2005 *arrastão* (literally dragnet) that the Portuguese media claimed to be the worst race riots in Portugal's modern history. News of an *arrastão* caused widespread shock in Portugal. After all, most Portuguese prided themselves on being non-racist, and were under the illusion that they should be given high marks for absorbing the new ethnic communities. According to the media reports, organized gangs of more than 500 African youths had invaded the beach of Carcavelos over the 10 June national holiday, attacking, wounding and robbing a number of beachgoers. Profiting from the reports on youth gangs and urban violence, right-wing politicians pushed their message of hate against Africans and immigrants in general. Even the police spoke of "hundreds of assailants." Andringa filmed interviews with many people who had been on Carcavelos beach that day and testified that there had been no *arrastão*. The alleged attacks were based on the accounts of two witnesses and a photograph of a group of Africans running from the police. According to Andringa's findings, the trouble began with two separate incidents: a Brazilian couple was heard engaged in a loud argument, and an East European man stole a gold chain from a Portuguese woman. The police arrived on the scene, firing in the air and beating anyone within reach, and the African beachgoers—some fifty not 500—ran to get out of the way. Overreacting, the mayor called for more police, and the government sent reinforcements to the main beaches around the country. The far right National Renovation Party organized a demonstration against crime and immigration the following week. After a few days, the Lisbon police issued a denial, admitting that there had been no *arrastão* and spoke of "police error." A newspaper published a report on "the *arrastão* that never happened." Nevertheless, the damage had been done. "We put our film on the internet, but how do you combat a wave of racism based on false news?" Andringa said, adding that six months later, in a debate on racism, she was shocked to find people still believed in the *arrastão*.[11]

Finally, on the first anniversary of the *arrastão*, the High Commission for Immigration and Ethnic Minorities formally asked the pardon of the immigrant community for "the moral damage caused by the false reports of the pseudo-*arrastão*." On its website, ACIME stressed that the majority of Portuguese were persuaded that there had been an *arrastão* because the media had failed to publicize the denials. "The consequences of the false reports were very harmful for the entire community of African immigrants and their descendants, who found themselves accused of a crime that never occurred," ACIME declared. "There has been a rise in distrust and hostility towards this community that has reinforced the stigma linking immigration to criminality."

* * *

It is hardly surprising that there is no central immigration agency in decentralized Spain, but rather a host of official and non-governmental organizations grappling with the problems stemming from the recent flood of immigrants. In broad terms, the Ministry of Labor and Social Affairs works with provincial authorities and unions to help immigrants with housing, job training and language instruction. On the other hand, the Ministry of Justice supports projects by religious minorities that promote integration. At the same time, the autonomous regions share much of the responsibility for the integration of immigrants through health, education and other social programs. Numerous volunteer associations give legal and social assistance to newcomers, often including undocumented aliens. They also have programs to help with integration, such as language instruction, information on employment and housing, classes in civic education. I can only brush the surface, referring to some of the most active agencies I have encountered, with apologies to other deserving groups omitted because of lack of space.

Madrid possesses no equivalent of ACIME, Portugal's High Commission for Immigration and Ethnic Minorities. Instead, a secretariat of state for immigration and emigration was set up under the Spanish Ministry of Labor and Social Affairs in 2004, charged with the government's alien and migration policy. Previously immigration matters had been handled by different departments of the Ministry of Interior and the Foreign Ministry.

César Mogo Zaro, director of the immigration secretariat and a Socialist Party stalwart, gave me a rundown on Spain's new comprehensive immigration program, whose title alone indicates the progressive spirit in which it was drafted. "The Strategic Plan for Citizenship and Integration, 2007–2010, is based on the principles of equality, intercultural diversity, and social cohesion," Mogo said.[12] He stressed that the philosophy of the plan was contrary to the policy of assimilation as conducted in France. Adapting a holistic approach, Spain's Strategic Plan emphasizes that public policies in education, employment, social services, health and housing must be adapted to meet the needs of the new immigrant population. The plan also stipulates that immigrants should be given access to public services in equal conditions to that of the indigenous population.

A key chapter of the Strategic Plan deals with employment. Among the main objectives is the improvement of migration management in accordance with the functioning of the Spanish labor market. This is being done through collective contracts in specific countries with which

Spain has agreements with countries like Morocco, though Mogo admitted that there have been problems with fraudulent contracts. Another aim is to adapt immigrants' skills to the needs and opportunities of the Spanish labor market, through training and new career paths. The Spanish official highlighted the importance of the Catalogue of Difficult to Cover Occupations—those open to immigrants. "Spaniards don't want to be barbers anymore," he said, pointing out that workers in this profession were much in demand. Other areas listed in the catalogue include services like child care, senior care, construction and fishing. The Strategic Plan also underscores the government's fight against the use of underground labor and discriminatory practices involving immigrants. Mogo said sanctions are already imposed on businesses employing undocumented workers. "But there's such a rapid growth in services, we don't have enough control," he admitted.

The Labor official emphasized that the new plan talks about participation rather than integration, and the need to support immigrants' associations and their interaction with the broader population. It aims to raise immigrants' participation in mainstream organizations such as neighborhood associations, as well as school, sports, leisure, trade union, business and professional groups. Finally, it calls for the expansion of immigrants' political participation in local public affairs.

Although it may seem a stretch, the Ministry of Justice is the government agency directly in contact with the Muslim communities and charged with promoting their integration into Spanish society. Mercedes Rico Carabias, director general of the ministry's department of religious affairs, recalled that 1992 was "a momentous year for Spain," not only because of commemorations for Christopher Columbus but also for the accords that marked the end of 500 years of the expulsion of Muslims and Jews. She pointed out that in 1992, the agreements with the religious minorities could be considered largely symbolic because the communities were so tiny. "But now," she added, "with all the new immigrants, the accords provide a useful structure for a society with religious pluralism."

During a lengthy interview in her somber office at the ministry in central Madrid, Rico, a career diplomat, said the government aimed to cooperate with the main minority faiths (Islam, Judaism and Protestantism) as it does with the Catholic Church. "Specifically, we want to help Muslims retain their identity while achieving normal relations with the society around them ... that is real integration, not multiculturalism or ghettoization."[13]

A lot of time has been lost in relations with the Muslim communities, the Spanish official conceded. The main problem, she explained, was divergences among the Muslims themselves and their failure to get together in a single representative body, like the Protestant and Jewish communities have done. Rico recognized that the present situation was not satisfactory; the government has an agreement with the Islamic Commission of Spain, comprised of two Muslim federations, which does not represent the majority of the Muslim population. "We hoped they would form one national Islamic organization, but there are an increasing number of independent federations, and so perhaps the solution will be a regional one, and typically Spanish," she remarked ruefully. Another obstacle to implementing the religious accords was the conservative Peoples' Party which came to power in 1996 and "blocked everything," Ms. Rico said candidly, noting that little had been done about religious education for minorities in public schools until the Socialists returned to government in 2004. Then, of course, it was very difficult to promote Islamic studies in the aftermath of the 11 March terrorist attacks "when public opinion could easily see Muslims as threatening," Rico pursued. Nevertheless, progress has been made, she said, pointing out that Spain and Austria were pioneers in Europe in teaching Islam in public schools. "Muslims have the right to religious education but their teachers must observe Spanish law," she said, admitting there have been delays because the municipalities—many led by the opposition—are in charge of school programs. On the other hand, she emphasized, the program establishing Muslim chaplains has proved to be a success. Now the Ministry of Interior selects Muslims to provide religious assistance to Muslim prisoners, whereas previously prison directors chose chaplains among the most pious inmates, who often turned out to be the most radical.

Initially the Socialist government ran into stonewalling from its own parliamentarians, who insisted that the secular state could not fund religions, Rico acknowledged. Thus, at the end of 2004, the government established a private agency called the Foundation for Pluralism and Coexistence whose mission is to provide financial support to religious minorities "for cultural and social activities."

Several days later, I met the director of the Pluralism Foundation, José María Contreras Mazarío, who echoed Ms. Rico's complaint about difficulties working with Muslims because of their disunity. "We should have signed the accords with one federation for Muslims, like we did with Jews and Protestants; instead we have more than 400 Muslim communities officially registered, and many of them do not belong to the two Muslim federations that signed the 1992 accords," Contreras lamented, adding; "it's an administrative problem, not religious."

Despite these difficulties, the foundation more than doubled its financial support to the three main religious minorities to 2.5 million euros in 2007 from one million euros in 2005, according to director Contreras. Contributions went to 487 projects of 434 religious communities in 2007, compared to 174 projects of 148 communities in 2005. The Muslim communities, he stressed, which are much more numerous than the Jewish and Protestants, were granted about half the total funds. Among the programs for Muslims that receive official funding are courses on Spanish and Islamic culture and Spanish and Arabic language, scholarships in Islamic culture and civilization and Islamic radio broadcasts and websites, according to Contreras. He was particularly proud of the first textbook on Islam in Spanish for primary schools, published in 2006 at the request of the Union of Islamic Communities of Spain. *Descubrir el Islam* describes in Spanish Islam's core beliefs, basic prayers and obligations and holidays, with colorful photographs and drawings.

Contreras went on to say that projects of the Jewish Federation supported by the foundation include: the creation of two new communities in Alicante and Murcia, works on the Jewish museum in Salamanca and the opening of a museum in the Madrid synagogue, the expansion of the community's Radio Sefarad, and the Week of Jewish Books and Sefardi Culture in Madrid. The Protestant Federation receives funding for projects like anti-drug activities, the creation of a library and archives of Spanish Protestantism, and the training of teachers in evangelical education.

In the autonomous regions of Spain, municipal governments are increasingly involved in outreach to their immigrant communities. The Madrid municipality has set up the Centro Hispano Marroquí, which provides immigrants with language courses, and also runs an active bicultural program, with Spanish-Moroccan debates and exhibits. At a special program for Ramadan, Moroccan community leaders explained the meaning and customs of the Muslim month of fasting but also discussed the rise of Islamophobia in Spain. During the main Muslim feast, the Aid el Kebir, the center organized a fiesta for people in the immigrant neighborhood of Lavapiés with Moroccan foods, music and films. Another association supported by the Madrid municipality, city hall and the Ministry of Culture is the Foundation of Islamic Culture, which promotes a Euro-Islamic dialogue through exhibits and meetings. In Barcelona, Seville, Valenica and other cities with substantial Muslim communities, municipal authorities increasingly sponsor intercultural programs with local Muslim groups.

But it is the world of NGOs who are essentially responsible for carrying out the government's immigration policies, providing basic necessities and legal services and links to government departments. As we have seen earlier, the Red Cross is the primary agency that receives boatpeople and other undocumented migrants, transfers them to internment centers and offers temporary emergency assistance to those in need. Like Portugal, the Catholic Church and related agencies such as Caritas play an important role in channeling aid to needy immigrants, including legal assistance.

One of the most active volunteer organizations working with immigrants in Spain is the *Acoge* network, founded by a group of Catholics, mentioned earlier in this work. The *Acoge* offices help immigrants, often undocumented foreigners, with immediate needs like lodgings, food and clothing, family contacts, general information on Spanish laws and referrals to other private and public agencies. Programs for long-term needs include legal help with visas, work permits and family reunion, contacts with health and education services, and help with employment.

At the headquarters of Andalucía *Acoge* in Seville, José Miguel Morales, a spokesman for the non-profit agency, told me that Spain had given little thought to immigration issues until the early 1990s, when the economy took off thanks to European Union subsidies for infrastructure and agriculture. "After the soaring economic growth, there was an urgent need for labor, and a long-term immigration policy," Morales stressed. But by 1998, the conservative government had hardened its stand on immigration. There was a growing "immigration-phobia," as people blamed the rising delinquency on immigration. And so the *Acoges* worked with the regional Junta of Andalucía, which pursued a policy of assistance to all immigrants, whatever their legal status. A registry was set up in the municipalities, paving the way for all immigrant children to have access to public health and education services. The situation improved in 2004 with the new Socialist government willing to invest more in immigration policy. "We don't criticize the authorities for reinforcing the borders," Morales stressed. "What we are asking for is more facilities for immigrants who are already here, like employment centers and improved access to legalization."[14]

I encountered other active volunteer groups working with immigrants at Valencia, ancient trading and industrial center on Spain's eastern coast, which has become a showcase for modern architecture, thanks to native son Santiago de Calatrava. "Valencia is not a traditional destination for asylum seekers, but the number of immigrants is rising," Sara Verdú Vila, coordinator of the Valencia branch of the Spanish Commission for Help to Refugees, told me in an interview at her office.[15] Madrid-based CEAR, as it is generally known, has seven branches around the country and is funded by both public and private contributions. It was founded in 1979 to handle the wave of Latin American refugees, fleeing repression from the continent's rightwing military dictatorships. In the 1980s, refugees arrived from Russia and other countries of the Soviet Union, followed in the early 1990s by victims from the turmoil in Bosnia; the first Muslims to request asylum. Now refugees come from Colombia and Russia, but also Algeria and Nigeria. Most refugees arrive by air at Madrid's Barrajas airport, according to Verdú. From there, they are distributed to different cities around the country, to be settled temporarily pending the outcome of their requests for asylum. Verdú, who completed law studies, said many more immigrants could benefit from the status of refugee but are afraid to apply because they know few people are accorded asylum nowadays—only 2.3% of the applications. If a petition is rejected, the applicant is expelled and cannot return to Spain for five years. CEAR also tries to help undocumented aliens obtain residence and working papers, said Verdú, acknowledging, though, that it was difficult. But what CEAR can do is encourage those without papers to register with the municipal authorities so that their children can benefit from health and school facilities.

Some volunteer agencies are dedicated to helping young unaccompanied immigrants, an increasingly serious problem. Francisco Javier Edo Ausach is a professor of anthropology at Valencia University and heads the Valencian Association of Assistance to Refugees, commonly called by its acronym AVAR. "We believe in immigration as a human right, but not for young kids on their own, because they don't have the money to pay the immigration traffickers and can easily fall under the influence of gangs," Edo explained in an interview at AVAR's busy downtown office. AVAR works with immigrants between the ages of fourteen and twenty years old—mostly from Morocco and Ghana—helping them obtain refugee status or residence permits, offering language and cultural courses and finding them jobs once they are sixteen. "When unaccompanied minors arrive in the province of Valencia, the municipal authorities try to contact their families. If no family member can be located, it becomes a problem for Spain," the anthropologist said.[16]

The northern region of Cataluña and its dynamic capital of Barcelona have been the main magnets for migrant workers since Franco's time, but in those days they were Spaniards from impoverished Andalucia, whereas today they are North Africans, Latin Americans and East Europeans. Having heard that the Catalán unions were in the forefront of the fight for the rights of immigrant workers, I visited the department of immigration of the National Workers Commission of Cataluna (CCOO), the leading union, in Barcelona. Ghassan Saliba Zeghondi, secretary of immigration for the CCOO, runs forty-three information centers, which help immigrants with documentation, employment, language instruction and vocational training. The centers also find housing and schools for immigrants' families and put them on the road to citizenship.

"Spain needs workers, unskilled and skilled, but the government hasn't understood we need people with skills," said Saliba, who came to Spain from Lebanon in 1980 to complete pharmaceutical studies and has been working with immigrants since 1987.[17] In an interview at union headquarters, Saliba said the Immigration Commission for Jobs in Public Service surveys the employment situation every three months and has found there was at that time a 20% deficit in highly skilled jobs like doctors, engineers and technicians in Cataluña. Moroccans were the first immigrants to settle in Cataluña and know their rights, according to Saliba. They make up 30% of the union's 170,000 immigrant members, elect their own delegates, and work in construction, hotels and other services and agriculture. Ecuadorians are now a close second, followed by Colombians and Romanians. Thirty percent of immigrant women work, mostly as domestics. Saliba said that the union's immigration department also organizes actions against any kind of discrimination and abuse of immigrants at the workplace, such as absence of contracts and unequal opportunity. He noted that while there is diversity in the work centers, no immigrants are active in the neighborhood associations. Spaniards are becoming increasingly anti-

immigrant—all immigrants—the unionist acknowledged. Negative stereotypes involve Moroccans and other Muslims, who are often linked
to terrorism in public opinion. But the media has also contributed to
immigrant-bashing by associating East Europeans with criminal gangs
and Latin Americans with drug trafficking, he stressed.

And with the severe economic crisis, the situation has only worsened
since I carried out these interviews. It is clear that despite continued
efforts at outreach by government agencies, Spain and Portugal have
yet to enact a comprehensive policy to integrate their new immigrant
communities, especially Muslims. Increasingly, as the governments
have come under increasing pressures at home and from their European partners to observe more restrictive immigration policies, the role
of non-governmental agencies has assumed new importance. It is
through the public-volunteer partnerships, often linked to religious
groups, that Iberians have managed to preserve their humane approach
to immigration.

6

MUSLIM SOLIDARITY

On Madrid's venerable seventeenth century Plaza Mayor, white robed drummers cast their hypnotic spell outside an immense Berber tent. Inside, visitors were transported to an exotic realm of multi-colored carpets and wall-hangings, sparkling copper, fine leather and textiles, bathed in the pungent aroma of mint tea and spices. And in a crowded hall nearby, Spanish and Moroccan academics talked frankly about many centuries of shared history, personal ties and the recent rise of Morophobia. It was the first ever Hispano-Moroccan Festival, organized by private Moroccan associations and businesses in May of 2006. For ten days, Moroccans opened a broad window on their national culture, from the typical Moroccan wedding rites to the henna tattooing ceremony and couscous-tasting. There were caftan fashion parades, concerts of sufi music, *gnawa* drummers and traditional Andalucian *malhoun* ballads, as well as athletics, children's games and craftwork. An alien display, but friendly and non-threatening.

Clearly the goal of the festival was to reach out to a reticent Spanish public, battered by reports of a relentless invasion of migrants from North Africa and sub-Saharan Africa. It was, above all, an attempt to counter the pervasive image of Moroccans as terrorists, ever since the train bombings of 11 March 2004. Although no one said so explicitly, the festival was also an affirmation by Moroccan civil society of an identity outside the mosque. It was an important statement of coexistence with the Spanish public, who find it increasingly difficult to distinguish between the average practicing Muslim and their more radical brothers. Like new immigrants everywhere, Moroccans, one of the largest foreign groups in Spain, have set up professional, social and cultural organizations to help one another get established and resolve outstanding problems with their hosts.

"We want them to get to know us and see that we're like them," said Hanan Taibi, a member of the Moroccan University Students Association of Spain, a sponsor of the festival. Part of the reception committee, Taibi was trained as a geologist but is working as a baby sitter in a Spanish family. She looks Mediterranean, with thick dark hair and honey-colored skin, and says that personally she has never had any problems with Spaniards. She notes, however, that friends who wear headscarves complain they are the butt of jokes and insults. Taibi does resent anti-Moroccan slurs in the Spanish press, which she said was quick to denounce a Moroccan thief, but generally omits the nationality when referring to Latin American or East European gangs.

Another festival hostess and member of the students' association, Saida Diouri, said the Spanish public has an increasingly negative image of "*los Moros*" as thieves, tramps and illegal immigrants. Diouri has lived in Spain for eight years, completed pharmaceutical studies and earns her living by teaching French. Fair complexioned, Diouri says Spaniards generally react with disbelief when they learn she is Moroccan. But that still doesn't help her get ahead, she remarked, not hiding a certain bitterness. Both young women said it was necessary to be Spanish to get a decent job in their professions, and complained about the "discriminatory" nationality laws. It was a complaint I was to hear many times; Latin American immigrants can obtain Spanish nationality after two years' residence, while it takes ten years or more for North Africans. This discrimination carries over to academia, the Moroccan women pointed out, emphasizing that in competitive situations someone with Spanish nationality, even if less qualified, would be favored over a foreigner. And it was the same with scholarships, they added.[1]

The theme of the festival was "Consolidating *la Convivencia*" (usually translated as coexistence but implying a sense of harmony). The organizers were small private groups, working with almost no publicity and little funding. They had won some support from the Madrid Community and the Moroccan Consulate General, several Spanish and Moroccan banks and Royal Air Maroc. But noteworthy was the absence of religious associations in the organizing committee. A majority of Moroccan organizations in Spain are Islamic-inspired, often linked to mosques and recipients of Spanish government subsidies. In fact, the religious organizations have generally monopolized the discourse with Spanish society. Here was the opportunity to establish contacts with representatives of Madrid's budding Moroccan civil society. Over the next few months I came to know a number of these community leaders, who are working within the Spanish system to improve the lot of their fellow immigrants. They are Moroccans who don't fall into the usual stereotypes of either religious militants or delinquents, but are the natural partners of the socially conscious members of Spanish society.

"Our aim was to show that peaceful coexistence is possible, even after the tragedy of 11 March," said Khalid Shakroun, one of the festival organizers, who heads a small volunteer agency called El Atlas, which works with immigrant children.[2] We met at the Madrid branch of a Moroccan bank where Shakroun, forty-one, is a senior officer. He was unsure whether the festival could be classified as a success because despite the good crowds, the organization still had unpaid debts, and would not be able to make a repeat performance in the near future.

Shakroun, whose father was a poor imam in Fez, is the first member of his family to go to university. After obtaining a master's degree in English literature, he went to Madrid to pursue his studies. Benefiting from the 1991 immigrant legalization program, he settled in Spain and married a Moroccan immigrant, with whom he has a son. In 1993–94, Shakroun worked for Madrid's institute of the family and minors, where he became familiar with the problems of street children. Expressing deep concern over the rising number of Moroccan minors coming to Spain illegally without their families, Shakroun said he understands why.

"Since 1990, young people in Morocco are full of pessimism. They see college graduates demonstrating in the streets because they can't find jobs. Those who find work, hear their neighbors in nearby Spain earn three times their salary. Through internet and satellite TV, they learn that people in Europe have comprehensive health care and a better life in general ... And so they come to Spain to find work. The big problem is that most are illiterate even in their own language, and are easily exploited. Soon they are swallowed by a milieu of drugs, sex and petty crime. Now there's another problem; jobs are not so easy to come by as they were in the 1990s. Even my younger brother, who has a college degree, can't find work in Spain."

Over the past few years, Shakroun has tackled the question of immigrant minors at the source. Through El Atlas, he has introduced consciousness-raising programs to volunteer agencies in Fez and Tangier, from where many immigrant children come. He is also working with the Solidarity Association for the Social and Occupational Integration of Immigrants (ASISI), another Madrid-based Moroccan volunteer organization, which runs a course for the vocational training of young immigrants, among other programs.

Hassan el Arabi heads ASISI. I first met him during the festival, when he moderated a roundtable discussion on "The Legacy of Andalucía Yesterday and Today." Asked about Al Qaeda's ambitions to recover Al Andalus, El Arabi stressed that most Moroccan immigrants were "indifferent" to the Alhambra and the glories of Muslim Spain. "They come to Spain to work, not resurrect the past," he told the largely Spanish audience. I saw El Arabi again several month later at ASISI's modest office in a heavily immigrant neighborhood of Madrid. ASISI boasts a computer section, a counseling room, the director's office and a working staff of eight people. El Arabi, thirty-nine, comes from a poor farming family in the central Moroccan town of Berkane. He started out as a waiter in a Madrid restaurant and worked his way through school, obtaining his doctorate in Spanish philology in 1998, and is now employed as a civil servant in the Spanish Ministry of Interior.[3]

Acutely aware of the problems of fellow immigrants, El Arabi established ASISI in 1999 to promote their integration in Spanish society and particularly the job market. His first priority was to set up Spanish language classes for immigrants. "In the beginning, they don't know the language and are lost without their families," he pointed out. "They can do anything just to survive. Moroccan men usually fend for themselves, but women aren't used to being on their own and can get into trouble." With help from the Madrid Municipality and the National Savings Bank, ASISI offers Spanish as a second language classes for foreigners, a counseling service for immigrant women and cultural programs for foreign minors. Another of its important tasks is to provide immigrants with reliable legal aid referrals for residence and employment papers. ASISI also runs a vocational program with subsidies from the European Union. A member of the Observatory against Racism and Xenophobia, El Arabi noted that Islamophobia, intolerance and racism are on the ascent in Spanish society. He and members of his staff regularly take part in intercultural dialogues in schools and public forums to counter the increasingly unfavorable image of North Africans.

The oldest and perhaps the most influential Moroccan organization not affiliated with any mosque is the Association of Moroccan Workers and Immigrants in Spain, known by its Spanish initials, ATIME. On the walls of the spacious reception room are posters from various ATIME events and evidence of the organization's militancy. "No to exclusion; support the march of Moroccan immigrants," declares one poster in Spanish. Another says: "Immigrants are also citizens." A beach scene evokes boatpeople and implores, "Bet on life; no more deaths."

Kamal Rahmouni, the thirty-four-year-old leader of ATIME, has the makings of a politician: tall, good looking, articulate and ambitious. Originally from Tetuan, Rahmouni came to Spain in 1992 to complete studies in physics, and put himself through school by working in hotels and restaurants. Rahmouni recalled that many immigrants at the time had been obliged to pay off public officials in Morocco to obtain a passport. ATIME had been set up by a group of Moroccan immigrants in 1989, to help their compatriots obtain legal status. The association refused to be beholden to Moroccan authorities, and even now does not ask them for funding, Rahmouni emphasized. ATIME, however, does receive financial support from Spanish municipal authorities for Spanish language classes and from the Ministry of Labor for vocational training courses. In 2005, Rahmouni was elected president of ATIME, which has a staff of fifty-three full time lawyers, social workers, psychologists, teachers, mediators and translators as well as a number of part time professionals. He said the association serves mainly as a "mediator" between the Moroccan immigrant community and official Spanish departments like health, education and labor.

"Our aim is to obtain full citizenship with the right to vote for Moroccan immigrants after five years' residence—not the present ten years or more—even if it's necessary to change the Spanish constitution," the ATIME leader told me resolutely in an interview. "Immigration is in Spain to stay, but we must find our own way. The French model has not worked. North Africans do not identify with the French; they feel they are not wanted and have no future in France. We are in time in Spain; we can still avoid the alienation of immigrants. Spanish society must be prepared for assimilation, which means a combined effort by politicians, the press, official institutions and NGOs."[4] Asked what could be done to avoid a repetition of the 11 March terrorist attacks, Rahmouni stated unambiguously: "Full integration is the way to avoid radicalization." Noting that the Spanish public has been able to distinguish between moderate Muslims and terrorists, he expressed the conviction that the "real cause" of the terrorist attacks was the Spanish government's backing of the war in Iraq and US policy in the Middle East. The Moroccan leader stressed that the former prime minister, Aznar, had decided to support President Bush against Spanish public opinion, which was united in its opposition to the war. As for Al Qaeda's discourse about "the recovery of Al Andalus," Rahmouni laughed, saying, "It's foolishness—in today's age of globalization."

Spain's best known North African community leader outside religious circles is Mohammed Chaib. A pharmacist by profession, Chaib is the first and only Muslim elected deputy to the parliament of Cataluña on the Socialist ticket in 2003. He is also a member of the Forum for Social Integration of Immigrants of Spain, under the Ministry of Labor and Social Affairs. His power base is the Ibn Batuta Socio-Cultural Association, the most influential private Moroccan social service organization in Cataluña. In the Barcelona region, whenever newcomers seek legal help, job opportunities, instruction in Spanish and Catalán languages and culture, they invariably wind up at Ibn Batuta, which was established in 1994 by Chaib.

I met the busy deputy at the sprawling parliament in Barcelona's Parc de la Ciutadella. His time was limited, but he would see me again the next day to complete the interview. Slight and youthful at forty-five, Chaib is perfectly bilingual—actually trilingual, including Catalán. Born in Tangier, he went to Spain at age four with his family, where his father was working in a restaurant. One of eight children, Chaib's childhood was divided between Spain and Morocco, and he spoke Spanish and Catalán better than he did Arabic. His father eventually returned to Tangier where he had built a house and opened a cafeteria. After completing his baccalaureate in Tangier, Chaib graduated from the University of Barcelona with a master's degree in pharmacy and went to work for a Swiss pharmaceutical firm in Spain. He is married to a Catalán educator and they have two young children.[5]

Chaib told me that Moroccan immigrants have been flocking to Cataluña since the development surge of the early 1990s, but there was no Moroccan agency to help them with multiple social and legal problems. To fill the vacuum, he founded Ibn Batuta, geared to Moroccans, the main immigrant community, but open to other nationalities. With support from the Barcelona Municipality and a staff of fifteen Moroccans and Catalán and numerous volunteers, the association deals with everything from the regularization of undocumented workers to generational conflicts within families and general problems of integration. Although he claims no ties to the Moroccan consulate, Chaib is frequently called on as informal representative of the local immigrant community. For example, he helped broker an accord between the Catalán *Generalitat*, or government, and Morocco's Hassan II Foundation to provide fifteen Arabic teachers for public schools with a substantial Moroccan enrolment. He has also taken part in various commissions on immigrant education. At the conclusion of our conversation, Chaib arranged for me to visit Ibn Batuta and speak with one of his chief aides, a Catalán woman named Mercés Amor. The Moroccan association is centrally located across from the Barcelona Library. It's a cheerful, compact space with various meeting rooms, painted yellow with blue trim and decorated with numerous trophies won by Ibn Batuta's sports teams.

"We go to schools and civic centers with a heavy immigrant population and explain Catalán customs, holidays and food specialties," Mercés said, adding that sometimes the immigrant women reciprocate with tea and pastries. She said that in some small towns there is a lot of tension and immigrant children suffer from de facto segregation in public schools. "What's missing is communication," Mercés said, pointing out that neither Spaniards nor Africans know much about each other's civilization. And so Ibn Batuta organizes intercultural activities, from lectures, story telling, exhibits and games to workshops on Islam and calligraphy. There are special programs for young people, including Arabic classes, internet workshops, theater and sports, as well as literacy classes for women and help for minors in the Catalán and Spanish languages.[6]

On a later visit to Barcelona, I met Dr. Huma Jamshed, president of the Cultural, Educational, Social Operating Association of Pakistani Women, familiarly known as ACESOP, with 300 members including several Cataláns. In 1997, the Karachi-born professor of physical chemistry accompanied her husband to Spain, where he was named financial director of the Madrid office of Pakistan International Airlines. While caring for their two young children, she studied Spanish, enrolled in the Complutense University's Department of Chemical Engineering, and obtained her doctorate on polymeric membranes in 2001. That year, her husband was moved to Barcelona, and she had to learn Catalán. Soon she was giving lectures on Asian culture at the

University of Barcelona and to Catalán and immigrant organizations. In May 2005, the scientist created ACESOP in her spacious apartment, and it has taken over her life.

"I found that immigrant women were generally unhappy, confused and worried about their children and their culture," Dr. Jamshed explained. "The children feel Spanish and parents have difficulty accepting this and don't want their children to lose the good things in their own culture. We started by educating the young people about their own culture, language and religion. One of the most difficult tasks was to persuade Pakistani men to let their wives and daughters attend our classes and multicultural festivals and learn to enjoy life outside the home. Then I showed the parents they must respect Spanish culture and participate in Spanish life whenever they get the chance. I make them go to the PTA, the neighborhood associations, and take part in local events at every level, their building, street, neighborhood and city. Now the fire brigade, clinics, hospitals and municipal sports teams ask us to come to their social activities. There was prejudice against Muslims at first, but it has changed."[7]

Although ACESOP deals essentially with social and cultural issues it is also concerned with religious problems facing the Muslim community. Adding to the clamor of Muslim leaders asking for a proper mosque in Barcelona, some thirty ACESOP activists have publicly asked for "the right to a decent place" in which families can worship. They pointed out that most of the Muslim prayer halls in Cataluña were very small and located in garages, storefronts or bars, "with no space for women."[8]

In Madrid, I met another impressive female Muslim leader. Laure Rodríguez Quiroga describes herself as a Basque Muslim feminist, which sounds like a contradiction in terms. But there's no ambivalence about the president of the first Union for Muslim Women in Spain. Rodríguez is thirty-five with loosely coiffed dark hair—"no headscarf for me"—and knows what she wants and how to get it. "Our objective is empowerment and the way to do it is through alliances."[9]

I met the flamboyant Muslim convert at her husband's Riad Café, a dimly lit, exotic coffee house located near Madrid's Convent of the Royal Barefoot Nuns. Over numerous glasses of mint tea, Rodríguez told me about her life and ambitions. Born in Paris, daughter of Galician immigrants, she grew up in Irún and obtained a master's degree in intercultural studies from the University of the Basque Country at

San Sebastián. She began her career in social work with street children in Nicaragua and Costa Rica, returning home in 1998 to join the Red Cross and work with mostly Moroccan minors. She also fell in love with a Moroccan restaurant owner, attended Koranic courses at the main mosque in Madrid and read the works of leading Muslim women writers. In 2002, Rodríguez and her partner went to Rabat, where he ran a catering business and she worked in the Spanish embassy. She converted to Islam in 2004 and, at the same time, she broke off from her partner. Returning to Madrid, she assumed the post of director at the Torre de Babel, a social and intercultural consulting firm. She founded the Association of Young Muslim Women in 2006 and, two years later, she formed the Union for Muslim Women in Spain.

The Muslim Union is led by a group of fifteen activists—Latin Americans, Spanish, Filipinos and Africans—and groups together a number of Muslim women's associations around the country. The head office is located next to the Estrecho Mosque, and the imam, Sheikh Moneir, gives regular Koranic lessons to the members, who are mostly married to Moroccans and don't know the Koran very well. The union is also building alliances with like-minded organizations, according to Rodríguez, who is herself secretary of gender issues of the Muslim Federation of Spain—one of the main Muslim groups in the country. Another leader of the Muslim Union is Ndeye Andujar, vice president of the Islamic Junta in Cataluña. A partner is the feminist organization, the Platform of Women Artists against Gender Violence. The Muslim Union shares with other feminist groups the aim of getting Spaniards to implement the Law of Equality, which is one of the most advanced in Europe. For example, the Muslim Union has demanded a place for women in the Islamic Commission of Spain, the nationwide group which is supposed to represent all Muslim communities in contact with the authorities.

One specific objective of the Union is to change the image of Muslim women in general, according to Rodríguez. "Muslim women are generally viewed as submissive victims of male aggressors, crying over their fate, whether in Palestine, Iraq or Western Sahara. Or they are thought of as immigrants who don't speak Spanish and don't have time to go to language classes. Most first generation Muslim immigrants aren't used to volunteer work, but their daughters have another mentality. And there are an increasing number of Spanish Muslims who are not immigrants."

As the country saw more and more outbursts of anti-Muslim feelings during the winter of 2009–10, the Muslim Union was called on to present courses on Islamic issues at several city halls in Cataluña. Rodríguez was asked almost daily to make statements on burqas and headscarves and Islamic radicals. Whereas most Muslim leaders hesitate to denounce the Salafists or fundamentalists, Rodríguez has no problem in speaking out against Islamic radicals. However, she defended the right to wear the hijab or headscarf as an individual act of faith. Noting that the burqa was not part of Islam but merely a tradition in Afghanistan, she stressed there was no need to ban the full-body covering in Spain since there were virtually none in the country. "There are so many more important issues to be concerned about, like trafficking in women, prostitution, abuse of minors and drug addiction," she pointed out repeatedly.

* * *

Portugal's Muslim community is generally seen as being well adjusted to life on the peninsula, certainly more so than Muslims elsewhere in Europe. Observers point to the homogeneity and stability of the Muslim leadership, the adaptability of the community and the absence of polemics around emotional topics like the veil and underground prayer halls. The primary concern of the Muslim leaders is the future of the second generation and those young people who have lost their parents' identity without acquiring a new one. Like their counterparts in Spain, Muslim immigrants in Portugal have set up associations to defend their rights and help with integration. But most of these organizations have links to mosques or prayer halls.

The most influential Muslim association is the Islamic Community in Lisbon (known by its initials, CIL) founded in 1968 by a group of a dozen students from Mozambique. Since there had been no Muslim community in Portugal in modern times, CIL had to start from scratch and organize everything from prayer halls to sources for halal meat, which is similar to kosher in its dietary laws, to a place where Muslims could bury their dead. In the 1970s, CIL arranged through the Jewish Community to obtain meat from Jewish butchers, which had been ritually slaughtered in the presence of a rabbi. By the 1990s, several Muslim butchers had set up shop in Lisbon and the suburbs, and today halal meat products are available in many supermarkets. In the beginning, Muslims, even those who were Portuguese citizens, had to be buried in the International Cemetery at Estoril because they were not accepted in the Catholic cemeteries. In 1976, CIL was able to negotiate space for Muslims in Lisbon's main cemetery of Alto de São João and several suburban burial grounds.

In fact, CIL was the driving force behind the construction of Lisbon's Central Mosque, which opened in 1985 and is the seat for community activities. These include Islamic instruction for children, aid for recent converts to Islam, support for the Islamic school at Palmela, participation in national charity and blood drives, and outreach to the Portuguese public, namely through programs on the state television.

"It can be said that the birth of CIL was the establishment of the first religious association representing the Muslims in Portugal, thus institutionalizing the return of an Islamic presence in our country after about 400 years," declared Abdool Majid Vakil, president of CIL, during commemorations for the organization's 40th anniversary. (Vakil is the international banker whom I introduced in an earlier chapter.) The ceremony was attended by the president of Portugal, the minister of justice and the mayor of Lisbon, as well as representatives of the Christian, Jewish, Hindu, Shiite and other religious communities, evidence of the stature that CIL has gained in this Roman Catholic country. Vakil, one of CIL's founders, recalled that the original aim was simply to find a place where Muslims could say their prayers and celebrate religious holidays. As more Muslims flocked to Portugal after the independence of Portuguese Africa in 1975, CIL was called on to meet new needs; to provide space for weddings and Koranic classes. Later there was a need to help integrate young Muslims into the European society and establish a "place of intercultural and interreligious dialogue and concord," Vakil said.[10]

One of the most prestigious Muslim organizations is the Aga Khan Foundation, which started out as a philanthropic institution for needy Ismailis (Shiites) and now has an international outreach. It was the Aga Khan himself who decided that Lisbon should be home to one of the main Ismaili centers. The Lisbon center, located in the Laranjeiras district, oversees the foundation's programs for the Iberian Peninsula, Mozambique and the rest of Portuguese-speaking Africa. Nazir Sacoor, an Ismaili born in Mozambique, is CEO of the Aga Khan Foundation's Development Network in Portugal, which includes sections for health, education, economic development, micro-finance, culture and humanitarian assistance. Currently present in sixteen countries with 130 programs, the network receives funding from the Aga Khan Foundation and government grants, as well as contributions from the private sector and the Ismaili community.

The Aga Khan Foundation was established in Portugal in 1983 to help Ismaili refugees from Mozambique to settle in their new homeland, Sacoor told me in a lengthy interview. The foundation has continued to provide support for the community's elderly and its young people, offering after school tutoring and education opportunities abroad. The Ismaili community in Portugal today is "highly integrated and largely self-sufficient," the CEO stressed. Almost from the outset, the foundation's programs included the broader Portuguese society. For the first two decades, the Lisbon office worked with the Portuguese authorities and non-governmental organizations giving grants for short-term projects, principally in education and training. "The foundation eventually came to be seen as a super-fireman, which could be counted on for help in times of crisis," Sacoor pointed out.[11] It has provided humanitarian and technical assistance for a broad range of problems from forest fires and earthquakes to the preservation of bees. Then at the end of 2005, the foundation signed a protocol with the Portuguese government to introduce its parent-based program for early childhood development. Adapting a rural model to urban conditions, the foundation, working with the Ministry of Labor, has initiated projects in the Lisbon and Sintra municipalities. Launched in early 2007, the program involves 9,344 direct beneficiaries. It was hoped that in time this model could be introduced to other areas of the country.

"Our primary goal is to improve the quality of life of marginalized communities and help people help themselves," Sacoor said. He stressed that, in line with the Aga Khan's views, the foundation's development activity was "deeply rooted in social principles ... non-denominational, independent of religion and race." Asked about the impact of 11 September and other terrorist attacks by Muslim extremists on the foundation's activities, Sacoor quoted the Aga Khan as saying that it was a time of "tremendous educational opportunity" and the chance for Christians and Muslims to get to know one another.

It's generally acknowledged that Portugal's Muslims of African origin have had a harder time integrating into the new multicultural society than their Asian counterparts. For one thing, most sub-Saharan Africans were poor and unskilled on arrival in Europe. And there was no African Aga Khan in the wings ready to give them a boost. Sheikh Munir, who presides over Lisbon's Central Mosque, has repeatedly declared that the sanctuary "belongs to all Muslims" of different origins and different schools of thought, and he has created a Commission of Muslims from Guinea Bissau. But there is no denying that the leadership of the Islamic Community of Lisbon remains overwhelmingly ethnic Indian.

Although the West Africans flock to the Central Mosque for Friday prayers and Islamic Feast days, they felt the need to create their own associations and prayer halls and meeting places. It was the Guineans—including many veterans who had fought for Portugal in the colonial wars—who "occupied" the space in front of the National Theater on Rossio Square in the mid-1970s. To this day, Rossio is an African forum where people receive news from home, see friends, make business contacts and do their essential networking. It has also gained the reputation as a popular drug market, which has not helped the African image.

Manso Baldé, from former Portuguese Guinea, created the Association of Muslims from Guinea-Bissau in the early 1990s, to meet the needs of the new wave of African immigrants, attracted by Portugal's construction boom. Initially, the association helped newcomers find jobs and regularize their status. Today the organization is located in a windowless cellar of a storefront in downtown Lisbon, and claims thousands of members from Guinea-Bissau and also from the former French territories of Guinea: Conakry and Senegal. The main problem now is family reunification, according to Baldé. Conditions have become increasingly strict for immigrants in general and Muslims in particular. Many of the men work in construction and live on the sites or rent a bed in an apartment with other workers. The association helps them find a place to live and provides the necessary guarantee to rent lodgings.

One of the most active African-Muslim community organizations is the Portuguese Research Center of Arabic-Pulaar and Islamic Culture. Located on the second floor of a modern office building in the multi-ethnic working class maze of Amadora on the outskirts of Lisbon, the center includes a small mosque, a classroom and a library. The leader of the center is Sheikh Bubacar Baldé, thirty-six, from Portuguese Guinea—no relation to Manso Baldé—who studied Arabic language and Islamic culture in Senegal and then Cairo. Reluctant to return to Guinea because of the authoritarian regime, Sheikh Bubacar went to

Lisbon in 1994 on a transit visa and soon became an illegal. At first the only kind of work he could do was construction; he likes to say "I built the Colombo Shopping Mall," referring to a huge modern emporium on the outskirts of Lisbon. In 1996, he obtained a residence permit under one of Portugal's mass regularization programs, and resumed his theological work. He served as second imam at the Central Mosque for two years and then felt ready to realize an old dream; opening his own institute to teach children about Islam. He had put money aside from teaching at the Lusophone University's summer school and also got help from friends in the Islamic Community. In 2002, he opened the center at Amadora, and now provides courses in Portuguese, Arabic, the Koran and the Hadiths (sayings of or about the Prophet) to fifty African students.[12]

When I first visited the center, Sheikh Bubacar and his staff were feverishly making last minute arrangements for the First International Conference on the Culture of the Fulas and Pulaar (the Fula Language) in Portugal, to be held in Amadora that weekend, with the support of the municipality and the high commission for immigration and ethnic minorities. Emphasizing that 80% of the Muslims in Portugal come from black Africa, the sheikh said that 4,000 to 5,000 of them are ethnic Fulas. The International Fula Association, he added, is based in Paris with branches in eight countries and aims to preserve and develop the Fula culture. Sheikh Bubacar made it clear that the conference would not be confined to Fula semantics but rather would focus on problems facing African immigrants in Europe and particularly illegal immigration, "a new and very dangerous phenomenon." At the close of the conference, Sheikh Bubacar told me that some 170 Fula delegates from France, Spain, Italy and Portugal had endorsed his appeal for a campaign against illegal immigration. Also, the Portuguese government had implicitly recognized the Portuguese Center for Arabic-Pulaar Studies and Islamic Culture as a partner in its efforts to improve the integration of African immigrants.

"I don't see any religious problem in Portugal," Sheikh Bubacar said, when I asked him if there had been any repercussions from the incidents involving Muslim extremists in other European countries. "Our job is to teach children non-violence and how to live together without concern for color. Guineans don't feel like foreigners here. We feel both Guinean and Portuguese; after all, the Portuguese occupied our country for 500 years." The main problem for immigrants in Portugal is lack of jobs, according to the sheikh. But he stressed that despite the current economic crisis and difficulty in finding work, life is better than in Africa. West Africans are continuing to come, even from non-Portuguese-speaking areas, he noted. "A couple of years ago, there were only a score of immigrants from Guinea-Conakry here, now there are hundreds."[13]

A few African Muslims who started out as community activists are now engaged in human rights advocacy on the national scene, like Mamadou Ba, a thirty-three-year-old Muslim from Senegal. Ba emphasizes that there is not the same Islamophobia in Portugal as in Spain and France, but rather "prejudice against blacks and the poor." Ba's father was a merchant from Guinea-Conakry, who had close ties with the nationalist leadership in former Portuguese Guinea. One of seventeen children, Ba was born in Senegal, studied Portuguese in Dakar, and was active in the Senegalese student movement. When he arrived in Portugal in 1997 on a scholarship, he organized the migrants from French-speaking Africa into the Luso-Senegalese Association with 500 members. Then he moved on and set up the Association of Residents and Friends of Guinea-Conakry with nearly a thousand members.[14]

"West Africans were a minority in the minority, and so we had an even tougher fight for our rights," Ba recalls. "We had to get organized." In 1999 he joined the Portuguese branch of SOS Racismo and was named delegate to the European Network against Racism. Their aim, he said, is to provide immigrants with equal opportunity in employment, training, health and political rights. At the same time, Ba was invited to enter Portuguese politics as an adviser to the Leftist Bloc in Lisbon city hall. He notes that Portugal has an advantage over its European neighbors in that most of its Muslims came from sub-Saharan Africa and were generally opposed to radicalism. Also, he added, the community leaders are generally well integrated—people like Vakil, who is seen as a symbol of success and modernity. "But there are practically no sub-Saharan Africans in Portuguese political life; this must change for a healthy democracy," Ba stressed. He pointed out that unlike other European countries, there have been no open racial conflicts in Portugal, but there is a rise in juvenile delinquency in immigrant communities and a new "Salafist current" among Muslim students. "The industrial belt south of Lisbon in the Seixal area is on the brink of explosion," he warned.

Other Muslim leaders acknowledge concern for the future of the second generation, particularly those whose parents came from sub-Saharan Africa. In Lisbon's industrial suburbs, where most immigrants live, there is a youth problem among Muslims and non-Muslims alike. Community activists complain of a high rate of school dropouts among immigrant children. Young people from African families are having trouble finding jobs and an increasing number are turning to drugs and robberies, a relatively new phenomenon in Portugal. "It's got so bad that parents are afraid of their own sons," the Guinean administrator of a Muslim prayer hall in an industrial suburb of Lisbon, told me.

On the other hand, the North African minority, so numerous and active in neighboring Spain, is barely visible in Portugal. The only time I saw a large crowd of Moroccans was at the embassy's garden party in honor of the tenth anniversary of the reign of King Mohammed VI. It was a spectacular event with women in traditional caftans, men in white robes, dancers and musicians from the Sahara whose drums echoed through the quiet diplomatic neighborhood of Restelo. Ambassador Karima Benyaïch told me there are only about 3,500 Moroccan residents in Portugal; businessmen, retired soccer players, academics and some seasonal workers. It seemed that most of them were at the celebration. The ambassador, who has actively promoted Morocco's bids to host the World Soccer Championship, spoke enthusiastically of "Mundialinho," a Portuguese program for the integration of immigrants through soccer, "even though the Moroccan team lost its first match to the Brazilians."[15]

The Moroccan embassy helped me contact members of the community. There are those Moroccans married to Portuguese women who seem fully integrated, like Karim Rzini. An associate professor in the Faculty of Sciences at the University of the Algarve, Rzini is head of the Fisheries, Biodiversity and Conservation Group, which is part of the research center for ocean sciences. He met his Portuguese wife, Margarida Costa, when they were both studying for their PhDs at the University of Rhode Island. In 1990, they were both invited to join the faculty of the University of the Algarve in Faro. His wife is also an associate professor and her specialties are crustacean fisheries and applied statistics. They have two teenage children and are completely absorbed by their professional and family life. Rzini has dual Portuguese-Moroccan nationality and regularly visits his Moroccan relatives in Tangier—"just a four-hour drive and thirty-five-minute ferry ride from Faro." He doesn't know any other North Africans in Faro, except for a Tunisian researcher at the Center for Ocean Sciences. He is aware that there is a mosque or a prayer hall in the city but does not attend. He too is perplexed as to why Moroccan would-be immigrants haven't tried to land on the broad sandy beaches of the Algarve. His explanation is a combination of factors: distance, language and the lingering image of Portugal as a poor country. "I think the distance would be a deterrent for small vessels. As long as the sea is calm, a five to six meter *patera* could make it here from the northwest coast of Morocco, but it would have to carry a large amount of fuel on board for the roughly 400 km voyage. Then, Moroccans from the north are often fluent in Spanish, so it would be easier to settle in Spain. Also salaries are lower in Portugal, making it less attractive. There is a perception that Portugal is a poor country. Older Moroccans remember immigration in the other direction: Portuguese arriving in small boats looking for a better life in Morocco, during the colonial period!"

Although the Moroccan community in Portugal is tiny compared to Spain, many still feel the need for their own cultural association to help one another adjust to their new society and preserve their identity. Hamou Amgoun is president of the Essalam, an association for North African immigrants and Luso-Arab friendship. Originally from the Moroccan desert city of Ouarzarzate, Amgoun has gone through the typical immigrant experience. He arrived in 2001, when Portugal needed immigrants to build numerous big public works projects, and made the grade as a construction worker building the metro of Oporto. Now, after living in Portugal more than six years and learning the language, he has obtained Portuguese nationality and was able to send for his wife. He divides his time between working at a cyber café and running Essalam.

In 2005, Amgoun and a friend, Rachid, founded Essalam in Oporto, Portugal's northern capital. "Today we have some 250 members—most of them are Moroccan and live in the Oporto area but we have associates in Spain, France and even Holland," the group's leader told me by email.[16] Amgoun said that Essalam helps immigrants deal with Portuguese bureaucracy, provides information on new laws and fights against immigrant traffickers. At the same time, the association promotes integration through all kinds of sports and social activities, classes in Portuguese and Arabic and its blog: www.assoporto.blogspot.com.

"The North African presence in Portugal has always been linked to regularization," Amgoun explained. "Currently Magrebins are leaving Portugal for France and Spain because even though life is difficult in those countries, they think it's better than staying in Portugal where wages are low and it's increasingly complicated to obtain residence permits."

Asked about Islamophobia and racism, the Portuguese-Moroccan said categorically: "There's less intolerance here than in France or Spain, maybe because of our common history but also because Portugal is still a country of emigrants who continue to seek better lives in other countries of Europe and the United States, like the rest of us."

7

PORTUGAL'S CENTRAL MOSQUE AND ASSOCIATES

Sheikh David Munir is Portugal's most popular Muslim cleric, and his Friday prayers at Lisbon's Central Mosque are usually overflowing with hundreds of the faithful. Outside of prayer times, the forty-three-year-old sheikh from Mozambique often serves as tour guide for Portuguese school children and other visitors to the Central Mosque, which includes a *madrasa* (Islamic school), a bookstore and meeting rooms for women, youth, converts to Islam and other groups. Invariably, the soft-spoken sheikh is invited to represent Islam at ecumenical meetings and in radio and television debates. Whenever Muslims anywhere in the world are implicated in terrorist activity, and whenever Islam and its Prophet are insulted, the sheikh is called on by Portuguese and foreign journalists to give an Islamic response. Late in 2009, the Portuguese learned that the imam of Lisbon's Central Mosque had won international recognition for his work on behalf of interfaith dialogue. Jordan's Royal Centre of Strategic Islamic Studies named Sheikh Munir to its honor roll of the 500 most influential Muslims in the world.[1]

Other mosques and prayer halls have sprung up around the Portuguese capital and outlying areas, but none wield the same clout as Lisbon's Central Mosque and its diligent sheikh. Wherever Muslims live and work, they have banded together to rent space in garages, cellars, offices and vacant buildings for daily prayers but, if at all possible, they attend prayer services at the Central Mosque on Fridays and on religious holidays. Although the Central Mosque does not exercise control over other Islamic centers, it keeps ties with most of them and often sponsors their registration process with the Portuguese authorities. Not all the imams speak with the calm and moderation of Sheikh Munir, but if they persist in using intemperate language, they are given a warning by the leadership of Lisbon's Islamic Community (CIL). The Central Mosque, which is Sunni, also maintains good relations with the small Ismaili community, who are Shiites, and occasionally the two traditional rivals worship together.

Not at all the stereotypical Muslim leader, Sheikh Munir answers his own telephone, puts his family before official obligations and prefers jeans and a sport shirt on weekends to imposing white prayer robes. I have talked to the sheikh on numerous occasions—generally brief conversations because of his busy schedule—and he is always friendly and unflappable. What comes across more than anything is his openness; he is the kind of person who will try to respond to almost any question.

Was he concerned about a radicalization of the Muslim community in Portugal after the arrest of youths of Pakistani origin implicated in terrorist acts in Britain the summer of 2006? I asked, during one interview. Sheikh Munir replied without hesitation: "In general Muslims in Portugal are not radical. The situation is completely different from that of other European countries. Most of us came from non-Islamic countries and identify ourselves as Portuguese. There are no religious ghettos here, no places for only Muslims. We try to be good citizens and participate in the social life of the country. And after all it is such a small community—barely more than 40,000—and most people know one another."[2]

Sheikh Munir acknowledged that he had been worried about a possible backlash against the Islamic community after the terrorist attacks of 11 September, in the United States, and in Spain three years later. But there was no sign of anti-Muslim feelings, he stressed, adding: "The Portuguese know the Muslim community here."

Weren't Muslims in Portugal angry about the situation in the Middle East, like Muslims elsewhere, I persisted? Sheikh Munir's response was unambiguous, "Like other Portuguese, the Muslim community is against the war in Iraq and the Israeli aggressions against the Lebanese and Palestinians, and we participate in demonstrations alongside Portuguese political parties. We pray for peace but we tell worshippers: 'Don't bring politics into the mosque.'"

Like many of Portugal's Muslims, Sheikh Munir was born in Mozambique. His father is of Yemeni descent and his mother's family is from India. At an early age, David Munir, though he rarely uses his first name, wanted to pursue Islamic studies. But Mozambique in 1975 had just won independence from Portugal and the volatile atmosphere was hardly conducive to religious discipline. The young scholar went to Pakistan, then India and finally the University of Karachi, where he obtained his BA in education and MA in Islamic studies in 1985. At the same time he began teaching in the Karachi Theological Center and private schools, with a good salary and promising future. In 1986, Munir visited his parents in Lisbon, where they had moved because of the insecurity in Mozambique. The Central Mosque had just been inaugurated and needed an imam. Sheikh Munir signed a contract for six months, and then was asked to stay on. He married a Portuguese Muslim and they have two teenage girls and a young son. The sheikh confided that even he had difficulties with Portuguese bureaucracy when it came to naming his son for the Muslim Prophet Mohammed. An old Portuguese law stipulates that parents wishing to give their child a foreign name, i.e. non-Roman Catholic, must apply to their embassy or church for a certificate. The Central Mosque generally provides Muslims with this service, and Sheikh Munir had to go through the formalities like anyone else.

The Central Mosque towers over Lisbon's busy Praça de Espanha, like a Mesopotamian ziggurat. The sand-colored brick building is dominated by a large dome and tapered minaret with an external ramp. At the entrance, an arcaded patio is flanked by the ablutions room and the Koranic school. Beyond, is the immense red-carpeted prayer hall with its vast chandelier, *mimbar* or preacher's chair, and *mihrab* or central apse, facing southeast in the direction of Mecca. One of two balconies is reserved for women and a basement under the prayer hall is used for the overflow of worshippers. On most Fridays between noon and 2:30 pm, the Rua da Mesquita (Street of the Mosque) is transformed into an African parade ground cum market. Women with rainbow-hued *boubous* and saris, and men in colorful African shirts or long white robes greet one another warmly in front of the mosque. Vendors (mostly gypsies) line the walkway with their trinkets, and beggars mingle with the crowd, praying for Allah's generosity.

Sheikh Munir told me that usually more than a thousand faithful show up for Friday prayers: construction workers from Guinea, Guinea-Bissau and Senegal, shopkeepers and their wives from Mozambique and Bangladesh. He said that during the week, many people go to a prayer hall near their place of work. There are more than thirty prayer halls in Portugal, mostly in the Lisbon area. Questioned about the financing of the Central Mosque, Sheikh Munir said the land was a gift from the Lisbon Municipal Council. A number of Muslim countries and Lisbon's Islamic Community paid for the construction. Saudi Arabia funded the final phase of works on the basement and the exterior and Iran and Turkey offered decorative gifts. The funding of day-to-day operations comes from members' donations and essentially three or four well-to-do families from Mozambique.

Beyond the regular prayer services, the Central Mosque is involved in various activities, Sheikh Munir said. A charity committee helps some 100 needy with food, medical and electricity bills and visits 120 aged and sick persons in the area each month. A Muslim lawyer helps immigrants with legalization problems. The sheikh supervises daily Koranic classes for children and teaches a weekly class on the meaning of the Koran to adults. As part of its public program, the mosque receives daily visits from Portuguese schools, sometimes as many as three busloads a day. There is also a committee to help converts adjust to their new religion, a social group that organizes festivities for religious holidays, and an information team charged with the mosque's publications, including two websites: www.comunidadeislamica.pt and www.myciw.org.

While the Central Mosque's outreach to the growing Muslim community around Portugal has been facilitated enormously by the internet, it still relies on traditional sources like Tablighi Jamaat, an international organization of Muslim missionaries. In his youth, Esmael Loonat was a popular soccer star in Mozambique, vice president of the Sporting Club of Lourenço Marques and a committed member of Tablighi Jamaat. Although he was happy in independent Mozambique, and still hopes to return one day, Loonat came to Lisbon in 1984 for the education of his four children. The following year, he became a coordinator of the newly opened Central Mosque and resumed his missionary work. Now a grandfather, Loonat is a successful textile industrialist but has kept up his religious activities. Wearing the Tabligh's uniform, the long white tunic of the Prophet Mohammed's time, Loonat met me in an office at the Central Mosque in the fall of 2006. Among his concerns were misperceptions in the Portuguese media regarding the Islamic Community and specifically Tablighi Jamaat and its international connections.

"We condemn all acts of violence," Loonat stressed, responding to Spanish allegations of links with Al Qaeda. "We believe that humanity is going through a crisis of identity, and even the values of faith are threatened by materialism. The work of the missionary is to help restore the purity of the soul."[3] Commenting on the situation in Portugal, Loonat noted, "There were no convulsions in Portugal in the wake of 11 September. Everything was peaceful. Thank god most Muslims in this country came from Portugal's former colonies, which meant some 500 years coexistence. Even after the Portuguese revolution, we didn't feel like foreigners. Our community is united. The Portuguese authorities know our organization and know we aren't radical. They understand our need for mobility and we keep them informed of our visits."

But in 2003–04, there were attacks in the Portuguese press accusing the Muslim community, and specifically Tablighi Jamaat, of Islamic extremism, Loonat recalled. For this reason, he decided to give an interview to the daily *Público* in March 2004, which he said was still valid and explained the organization and objectives of the little-known missionary movement. The name Tabilghi Jamaat simply means: Preaching Group, Loonat pointed out in the Portuguese newspaper.[4] Tabligh's mission derives from the 104th verse of Chapter III of the Koran, which states: "Allah said: among you, there should be a group that seeks out or commands Good and prevents Evil.' Portugese Tablighs regularly visit more than thirty mosques and prayer halls around the country, as well as Islamic places of worship in southern Spain, Portugal's former African colonies and Brazil. Carefully evading specifics, Loonat said that "a reasonable number of brothers and sisters" devote three days a month, or forty days yearly, to mission work. When they travel abroad, they go in small groups of five or six persons. The missionaries are chosen for their moral probity, conduct and knowledge of religion. Debunking the public stereotypes, Loonat stressed that the Tabligh's mission was not political but "exclusively religious," that is, getting Muslims to renew their commitment to the five pillars of Islam (faith in one God, five prayers daily, tithes, fasting during the month of Ramadan and the pilgrimage to Mecca). He also insisted that Tabligh preachers did not seek the conversion of non-Muslims nor did they reject values of western society, but simply aimed to preserve the Islamic "faith, identity and culture."

From Loonat's words, I gathered that Tablighi Jamaat has a significant role to play not so much in reviving the flame of Islam in Portugal, which hardly seems necessary, but in monitoring for the Central

Mosque on what is happening in the outlying prayer spaces. Little did I suspect that the missionary group itself would soon fall under suspicion as a cover for the movements of some radical Islamists.

An important offshoot of CIL, the Islamic Youth Association was set up in 1992 to give Muslim students a social structure through activities such as excursions and the celebration of Islamic holidays.

"I am 100% Portuguese, not a Portuguese-Muslim," twenty-six-year-old Zakir Karim asserted confidently, when we met in a reception room at the Lisbon Central Mosque.[5] Slender, with a trim beard and dressed in jeans and a dark jacket, Karim is a leader of the Youth Association. He was born and raised in Lisbon; his parents came from Mozambique and his grandparents from India. A graduate of Portugal's prestigious Institute for Sciences, Labor and Business, Karim is marketing director for Unilever Portugal, the multinational corporation. "Being a Muslim is not a handicap in Portugal, although being black can be," he admitted. Basically, Portuguese society is open to immigrants and known for its "gentle customs" he said, noting the contrast with the Spaniards, "who are very litigious even among their own regions." From the beginning, the Islamic community set out to integrate fully into Portuguese life and has succeeded fairly well, according to Karim. He pointed out that many Muslims, including women, can be found in good jobs in banking, finance, consultancy, business and law. He acknowledged that Muslims have not gone into politics, but that takes time. Karim stressed that Lisbon's Islamic Community has strongly condemned the terrorist attacks carried out by Muslim extremists like the assault on the London transport system. In fact, he noted that since 11 September, many Portuguese wanted to learn about "the true Islam" and some have converted to Islam. "More and more, Portuguese Catholics and Muslims find we have the same values, and we are beginning to see mixed marriages."

Karim said the Youth Association is focused on three main areas: social works such as collecting food for the poor and organizing visits to local hospitals; recreational activities like cultural trips, dinners out and sports tournaments; and intercultural dialogue with other faiths including Jews, Hindus, Ismailis and Buddhists. "We are minorities and understand we must work together," Karim stressed. He added that the subject of the group's next debate would be domestic violence; "something Muslims don't talk about enough."

Nina Clara Tiesler, a German academic engaged in post-doctoral research at Lisbon University's Institute of Social Sciences, is co-author of the first comparative survey of Muslim and non-Muslim young people in Portugal. The study involved 200 Portuguese university students and the 160-member Youth Association of Lisbon's Islamic Center, and was published as part of a broader study on Islam in the Portuguese-speaking world.[6]

The astonishing conclusion of this survey was that the cultural attitudes of the young Portuguese Sunni Muslims revealed "little difference" from those of their non-Muslim peers. What emerged was that generally these young people are "content with their lives," despite what are perceived to be difficult economic circumstances in Portugal, particularly in relation to the labor market. The report shows that a large majority of the respondents (89% of the Muslims and 88% of the non-Muslims) "feel at home" in Portugal. Both groups (76% Muslims and 80% non-Muslims) are critical, however, of the education system and low salaries in Portugal and want to find work elsewhere in Europe. One notable difference is that 44% of the young Muslims attend religious services on a weekly basis (65% males, 19% females) in comparison to only 9% of non-Muslims.

Another group under the wing of the Central Mosque is the Committee to help the New Muslims. Yiossuf Adamgy is a member of this welcome committee and put me in contact with several Portuguese converts. Like Spain, an increasing number of Portuguese have turned to Islam in the wake of 11 September. Unlike the Spanish converts, the new Portuguese Muslims have not assumed roles of leadership in the Islamic Community, which remains the fief of the Asians Muslims. Nevertheless, I have encountered several Portuguese converts who are potential leaders and bridges to non-Muslims.

One of the most active converts is Raúl Braga Pires, a graduate student at the University of Oporto and a co-founder of the Forum of Islamic Studies and the first academic website aimed at Muslims of the Portuguese speaking world, www.islamicos.eu. Pires was raised by his Roman Catholic mother and discovered Islam only at age thirty (he is now thirty-nine). During our first meeting at Lisbon's Central Mosque, he told me he had wanted to become a diplomat and studied international relations at Lisbon's University of the Lusíada. By 1998, his interests turned to the Middle East, and he took a course in religion and Arabic lessons with Sheikh Munir. Insisting that the cleric exerted no pressure, Pires recalls that he had "a click moment" after the events of 11 September, and joined a class at the mosque to become a Muslim. It was this double interest in Islam and foreign relations that led him to the University of Oporto's Center of African Studies and his thesis for a master's degree on "Islam in Mozambique"—the home of Portuguese Islam. His field has broadened to include the Muslims in former Portuguese Guinea as well as in other African states, Nigeria, Mali and Morocco. From his base at Oporto University, Pires has participated in a number of conferences on Islam in Africa. From there it was a logical step to the creation in February 2009 of the Forum of Islamic Studies on the worldwide web, whose aim is to "fill a void in Portuguese scholarly research." The forum publishes news events of special interest to Muslims in the Portuguese speaking world, including Brazil. Still in its infancy, the forum has plans for online debate and the publication of academic works in Portuguese.

Asked about reports on the rise in Islamophobia in Europe, Pires assured me he hadn't seen the phenomenon in Portugal. He acknowledged that since the time of the Inquisition, the Portuguese have been hostile to "the other" and this attitude continues toward gypsies, but not Muslims. "With the new immigration, we are more tolerant," he stressed, adding his favorite expression, "Portugal is becoming another Noah's Ark."[7]

But some Portuguese converts remain in the closet for different reasons. There is, for example, a young high school teacher who lives in a remote farm town of southern Portugal and does not dare tell her family she has become a Muslim. I had expected a shy, demurely dressed woman, fleeing the ills of urban life, but stereotypes can be misleading. We first met in a popular village teahouse, where everyone knew the gregarious, fashionably attired *professora*, but no one was aware that she is a Muslim. Nevertheless, she opened herself readily to a foreigner. Raised by devout Roman Catholic parents, she became interested in world religions as a young woman. Then 9/11 happened and everybody was talking about Islam. While she condemned the terrorist acts, she was horrified at the surge of anti-Arab prejudice. There was no mosque in the region, and she began to read books about Islam and Islamic history. In 2004, she discovered the website of Lisbon's Central Mosque, which addresses current problems facing Muslims and answers their questions. At the same time, she met an Arab businessman on the internet. He helped her see the difference between Islam and Christianity, but did not pressure her to become a Muslim. She learned to pray through the Central Mosque's website and, a year later, she and her Muslim friend were married at the Palmela Mosque south of Lisbon. The new convert said she has been well received by the Muslim community in Lisbon, but there are no Muslims where she lives. Her husband spends most of the time abroad for his import-export business, and so she must live her Muslim life on the internet. As a teacher, she encourages her students to respect Catholicism and other religions and has taken them to visit the Islamic school at Palmela. She is worried about young people in Portuguese society, and points to an urgent need for more investments in education and specifically courses in citizenship and integration. "If youths can't find work and don't have motivation, they turn to drink and, even worse, to extremism," she emphasized.

The Central Mosque's junior partner—and to a certain extent the future of the Islamic Community—lies on a wooded plain about twenty-five miles south of Lisbon, in the shadow of the Palmela Castle, whose fortifications are said to date back to the early years of the Muslim conquest; the eighth or ninth century. The Islamic School and mosque of Palmela started out in 1998 as a primary school for the children of Lisbon's Muslim elite. Every year the school has grown and, by 2008, it went through secondary school also, with 195 students including thirty non-Muslims.

"The Muslim community had been having trouble with its children in the mid-1990s, some were dropping out of Portuguese schools, some were taking up modern vices," Sheikh Rachid Daud Ismael, with a full grizzled beard and an imam's long robe, told me, as we toured the premises. Better known as Sheikh Rizwan, the thirty-eight-year-old headmaster was especially proud of the strict discipline in the school and listed the hard and fast rules: no politics, no smoking, no drugs, no bad language. "Our students are here to study; that's why some non-Muslim families also send their children to us," the sheikh said. He emphasized proudly that they have had only one dropout, a student whose family had moved back to Mozambique. All their graduates have continued their studies.[8]

Like many Portuguese Muslims, Sheikh Rizwan's parents fled from Mozambique with their five children in 1979, to escape the civil war. They opened a grocery shop in Laranjeiro, part of the dormitory town of Almada across the Tagus River from Lisbon. After completing high school, he went to the Islamic Institute in Manchester, England, where he studied Arabic, Urdu and English. There he married an Anglo-

Indian woman, but they decided to return to Portugal "because of the climate and the quality of life." At first, he served as imam of the Laranjeiro Mosque and then worked with members of the Lisbon community to set up the school at Palmela.

A private community school, Palmela follows the Portuguese state curriculum but offers optional courses in Arabic and Islamic sciences. The classes are co-educational. Palmela also provides extra-curricular activities such as music and sports, the latter segregated, according to Muslim custom. The school has a staff of twenty-five professors, mostly non-Muslim Portuguese and all with masters' degrees. Among the visiting professors, Sheikh Munir gives a course in Islamic studies once a week. Sheikh Rizwan said 60% of the school's financing comes from tuition and contributions, and the rest from the Islamic Community in Lisbon. The community has raised the question of subsidies with the Ministry of Education, which gives grants to private Catholic schools, but was turned down.

As I started to leave, Sheikh Rizwan acknowledged that he was worried about Muslim young people, even in Portugal. He pointed out that the Islamic Community had changed since the early 1990s, when most of the Muslims had come from the former Portuguese colonies of Mozambique and Guinea and "were easier to integrate." He noted that the second wave of Muslim immigrants came from Pakistan, India and Bangladesh directly, and many of them didn't know Portuguese. "That makes a big difference and it is going to take time for them to integrate," he stressed. He also admitted that with the increased diversity of the community, it is easier for extremists to come from abroad to try to recruit young people.

Many community leaders told me that the Central Mosque has no control over what is being said in the neighborhood mosques and prayer rooms. And clearly, not all the imams speak in the same gentle language of peace and harmony as Sheikh Munir. For example, there is the popular prayer hall near the immigrants' Martim Moniz Shopping Mall, known as the Bengali Mosque because it is frequented mostly by Bangladeshis and other Asian Muslims. Some of the imams there are said to have engaged in fiery discourse against the enemies of Islam. This mosque was so popular that it nearly collapsed in 2006 and the community had to move into a larger building across the street.

My friend Sérgio Tréfaut managed to film a passionate exhortation by an imam in the Bengali Mosque, although the preacher's name was not disclosed. Here is my translation of the sermon—given in Bengali, Urdu and Portuguese—which rings with nostalgia for Al Andalus ....

"My brothers...
Thanks to Allah All Powerful who gave us the opportunity
to be today in this mosque in Lisbon, Rua do Benformoso,
Martim Moniz, Socorro...
After 500 years, we are going to mark once more the holy day of Friday.
Five hundred years ago, they prayed in this same neighborhood,
and did so 750 years before that.
In those days there were grand mosques here.
They know that Lisbon had many ancient houses.
In the oldest building next to a restaurant, an Arabic inscription says:
"There is No God but Allah and Mohammed is his Messenger."
It is still written there.
Those who devoted their time and money to build this mosque
are today beloved by Allah.
Don't think these things are easy to accomplish.
Their names will remain inscribed in letters of gold
because they tried to recover a tradition
interrupted for more than 500 years.
Thanks to them Muslims can again
commemorate here the day of Friday
and hail their god, Allah."[9]

Every neighborhood mosque is different and some have very different agendas—a reflection of their congregations. In Lisbon's bedroom community of Laranjeiro, across Tagus River, there are two rival mosques; one belonging to a Sufi mystical order, which is open to the world, and the other orthodox and very closed. Worshippers from the Sufi mosque say there is a certain hostility between the two congregations and occasional acts of violence, although the leadership of the Islamic Community doesn't usually acknowledge it. Laranjeiro's orthodox sanctuary was the first mosque built in Portugal in 1982 and aimed at the working class Muslims south of the Tagus. The Sufi shrine, which is known for its lively chants and prayers, isn't listed as a mosque but called the Madrasa Ahle Sunny Jamat and was founded by the Spiritual Foundation of India in 1996. The Indian leader, Syed Muhammad Jilani Ashraf Kichhauchhavi, generally called Baba Jilani, has visited Portugal several times to meet with his followers. Another branch of this Sufi order was opened in Lisbon's burgeoning neighborhood of Odivelas in 1997 and is called the Darul 'Ulum Kadria Ashrafia. In her notable work, "Muslims in Portugal," Alexandra Prado Coelho says that these Sufis are informally known as "salami" (the Muslim greeting) because they chant their benedictions and praises of the Prophet Mohammed for hours at a time.[10]

The Aicha Siddika Mosque, a stately building with arches and a small dome, was founded in 1983 in the heavily immigrant municipality of Odivelas, north of Lisbon, and has gained in influence as the Muslim population has grown in recent years. In recognition of the increasing diversity of Odivelas, mayor Susana Amador organized a Forum for Peace and Prayer in May 2008, with the presence of Catholic, Protestant and Muslim dignitaries. The mayor outlined her plans to develop housing and combat poverty in the neighborhood, and the religious leaders reviewed the social activities of their respective institutions. Asfak Tayob, president of the Islamic Community of Odivelas spoke at length of the history of Islam and the local mosque's charitable activities. Then in an unusual occurrence, the entire assembly of about 100 people of different faiths gathered under a large tent to pray together "for a better world, peace and love for others."

Some imams prefer to be independent, rather than linked to a specific mosque. Moulana Zabir, a large imposing man of thirty-three, with a long bushy black beard, is a former imam of the mosque at Odivelas. He has now chosen the vocation of freelance preacher and is working especially with converts. We met at a café near the subway station of Odivelas. He was accompanied by his wife Zeida, enveloped in a *djellaba* and headscarf, who remained silent throughout our conversation. Like most of the community leaders, Zabir's family came from Mozambique right after independence in 1976 to escape the war. His father owned one of the main furniture companies in Lourenço Marques and had no problem opening a furniture business in Lisbon's central Dona Estefánia neighborhood. After high school, the young Zabir went to Manchester, England, to study Islamic law and Arabic and intended to take his master's degree in Cairo. However, he was horrified by the poverty and bureaucracy in Egypt and returned to Portugal in 1998. His first job was that of a teacher at the Islamic School of Palmela. He was soon offered the post of imam at Odivelas, where he remained for five years.

"In 2004, I felt there were no more challenges in my work at the mosque and I decided to pursue my own projects which involved teaching Arabic and Islam to people who need structure like children, young adults, women and new Muslims," Zabir told me.[11] His first project was a cyber café for young people, which turned out to be too successful. One day he found somebody had stolen all his computers and other equipment, and he didn't have the heart or the funds to start over again. Now he has rented a shop in the neighborhood of Cacém, near Sintra, where he teaches Arabic and Islam weekends to newcomers, mostly Guineans and Senegalese. There are some 9,000 of these Muslim immigrants in the region who don't have access to Islamic studies, he said. Fridays, Zabir delivers the sermon at the Martim Moniz Mosque, which is usually jammed with 600 to 700 worshippers. He also teaches an occasional class in classical Arabic at the school in Palmela. And he is often called on by non-Muslim schools like the Catholic University at Evora to talk about Islam … "That's one of my projects—improve the image of Muslims in Portugal."

One day a week, Moulana Zabir holds tutoring sessions with converts, who are beginning to pose problems. He said that there are currently more than seventy of these new Muslims in the Lisbon area alone—doctors, nurses, engineers, policemen—and they need help. "They are treated like outsiders by local Muslims and by the Portuguese," the educator stressed. He noted that the Central Mosque hasn't got the personnel to deal with converts. They need help religiously, and they need a space, an association, he emphasized, adding that most converts have private identity problems in their social life, job or with family, and some prefer to remain in the closet.

"Then too, we must recognize there are bound to be spies among the converts who try to get information for financial advantage," the preacher added frankly. "We don't have the power to see their intent. If anyone appears suspicious, we call on the president of the Islamic Community in Lisbon, who contacts the Portuguese authorities." It's the same thing for outsiders who come from abroad. "It's a very delicate situation," Zabir emphasized. "The mosque is public and anyone can join it. But we don't want people who make problems. We have close relations with the small mosques. Most of the imams come out of the Palmela school. We can control Friday prayers. There are no politics on Friday only spiritual subjects. We don't want religious people discussing politics. They can pray for peace; we're against violence. We advise the community to keep a low profile and not respond to provocations." The educator remarked that nowadays, whenever he speaks at a public gathering, he sees agents of Portuguese intelligence services. "That's a good thing because that way the Portuguese will know we're not radical."

The only Islamic Center that could vie with Lisbon's Central Mosque in influence is not a rival at all. The worshippers don't even call it a mosque but the *Jamatkhana* or House of the Community, a specific reference to the small community of Ismailis, who belong to the Shia branch of Islam. In fact there is no evidence of the traditional Sunni-Shiite hostility in Portugal but rather positive cooperation between the two communities. The Central Mosque, which is Sunni, reserves a place of honor for the Ismaili leadership on Muslim holy days. Sunni and Ismaili leaders participate side by side, along with Christian and Jewish representatives in the Portuguese Commission for Religious Freedom and at frequent ecumenical meetings. Portuguese Ismailis, who are now said to number about 8,000, shared the same trajectory with most of the Sunni majority, originally coming from India and settling in Mozambique and other Portuguese colonies in Africa. They first appeared in Portugal proper as students in the mid-1960s. Some Ismailis, fleeing the troubles in East and Central Africa, came to Portugal in the early 1970s, but most arrived after Lisbon proclaimed the independence of its African colonies in 1975.

Ismailis differ from other Muslims essentially over the belief in the Aga Khan as their spiritual leader and the 49th imam, a direct descendant of the Prophet Mohammed through his daughter Fatima. In 2007, Karim Aga Khan, who was born in Geneva seventy years ago, celebrated his 50th anniversary as the head of the community of an estimated fifteen million Ismailis across the world, from India and Pakistan to Europe and the United States. Marking the event, the French weekly magazine *L'Express* dubbed the Harvard-educated multi-millionaire, who lives in southern France, as "Prince of the Poor" because of his efforts to improve living conditions in poverty-stricken areas, including Portugal and former Portuguese Africa.

Amidst the gray urban maze of highways and non-descript high-rise buildings in northwestern Lisbon, the Ismaili Center appears like a mirage, a modern-day Oriental palace, with multiple domes, tiled patios, fountains, *mushrabiye*-like latticework walls, and surrounded by a shady flowering park. The Indian architect of the sprawling rose-colored limestone building, Raj Dewal, is said to have been inspired by various Islamic monuments, such as the Fatehpur Sikri in India and the Alhambra of Spain. In the entrance hall, panels of Kufic calligraphy list the ninety-nine names of Allah. At the heart of the complex is the *Jamatkhana*, a large carpeted space with filtered light for worship and meditation. The center also includes classrooms, a library, meeting rooms, a large social hall and offices of the Aga Khan Foundation and the Aga Khan Development Network, described in an earlier chapter.

It was no accident that the Council of Europe chose the Ismaili Center as the site of its colloquium on Inter-cultural Dialogue, Issues and Perspectives in June 2007. Nor was it by chance that the former president of Portugal, Jorge Sampaio, chose this occasion to make his first public appearance as the United Nations High Representative for the Alliance of Civilizations. The Ismailis, like the Central Mosque and its associates, have effectively projected themselves as good citizens and strong proponents of interfaith understanding.

The conciliatory stance of the leadership of Portugal's Islamic Community seemed to be working. No Al Qaeda sleeper cells have been detected in Portugal, as they have in neighboring Spain. Few Islamophobic incidents have been reported, although the number of racial clashes has grown. Portuguese Muslims generally felt they were somehow immune to the growing tension between Muslims and non-Muslims elsewhere in Europe. Then early in 2008, Spain uncovered what has been called the Barcelona terrorist plot, with ramifications in Portugal and France and implicating the Pakistani-based organization Tabligh Jamaat. Although there were no Portuguese suspects, members of this Islamic missionary society play a prominent and active role in Portugal. That spring, the Tablighs held their annual congress at Lisbon's Central Mosque. Later, Sheikh Munir confided to me that a delegation from Spain had been turned back "because we didn't know them."

The idyllic complacency of Lisbon's Islamic Community had been shattered.

8

SPAIN'S MULTIPLE MUSLIM VOICES

It was in 1992, during the commemorations of the Fifth Centenary of the Expulsion of Muslims and Jews, that the Spanish government announced agreements with the three main religious minorities, establishing their rights and obligations. While there was no problem about the representation of the Protestant and Jewish federations, it was more difficult to identify a Muslim partner. The Spanish authorities had hoped to find a single address for their Muslims, but there is no Central Mosque, no uncontested voice like Portugal's Sheikh Munir.

In the end, Muslim communities were encouraged to join one of two officially recognized Islamic federations, the Spanish Federation of Islamic Religious Entities, (known by its Spanish initials FEERI), or the Union of Islamic Communities of Spain, (UCIDE). These two groups, in turn, formed an organization known as the Islamic Commission of Spain (CIE), the body empowered to negotiate agreements with the state. But it was not a satisfactory situation: an artificial Islamic commission, comprised of two rival federations which were not representative of the Muslim majority: the Moroccan immigrants.

"The Muslims must find a place in Spanish society—after all, there are more than a million of them—we have tried to get them to form a representative organization but it hasn't worked," Mercedes Rico Carabias, general director of religious affairs, told me candidly in the spring of 2007.[1] She said that since there was no agreement concerning an Islamic authority on the national level, perhaps a regional solution could be found—a mirror of Spain itself.

In my personal contacts with Spain's Muslim communities, I found the three mainstream groups generally shared the same basic principles but diverged on tactics and leadership. The old Muslims, made up mostly of Middle Easterners from Syria, Egypt and Palestine—a small, educated elite with Spanish nationality—headed UCIDE. The second group, FEERI, was until recently led by Spanish converts and included a number of independent organizations. Finally, a large majority of other Muslims, mostly immigrants from Morocco, did not have their own federation; many of these joined UCIDE and some set up their own associations.

The Abu Baker Mosque, sometimes called the Estrecho Mosque for the subway station nearby, is located in a plain office building in a busy commercial neighborhood of northern Madrid. On my first visit, the mosque was in the throes of a family fiesta. The meeting rooms were crowded with head-scarved women and children chatting noisily, while young boys whooped it up in the corridors. "It's graduation day for children in the Koranic Studies program," Helal-Jamal Abboshi, the rumpled, hands-on administrator of the mosque explained, adding somewhat apologetically; "We really need more space, another mosque."[2] Palestinian-born Abboshi, seventy-one, is also secretary general of UCIDE and chief aide to Syrian-born Riay Tatary Bakry, the federation's leader, who was traveling at the time of my visit. Abboshi first came to Spain in 1968 to complete pharmaceutical studies. After Spain became a democracy with Franco's death in 1975, the Palestinian became involved with the small Muslim community and the mosque ... "which has been my life ever since."

UCIDE is the most important Islamic organization in Spain, grouping 255 communities and growing, with branches in Cataluña, Aragón, Valencia and Andalucía, besides the headquarters in Madrid, according to Abboshi. He stressed that UCIDE's main task was to help with the integration of Muslim immigrants into Spanish life. This is done primarily through contracts with the Ministry of Labor and Social Affairs. The union also receives financial support from the government's Foundation for Pluralism and Coexistence, to support cultural programs, such as Spanish and Arabic language courses, Spanish and Islamic culture courses, and socio-cultural courses for women.

"We have denounced terrorism and our community strongly condemned the terrorist actions against the Madrid commuter trains on 11 March," Abboshi declared, adding: "Those acts were essentially against the existence of the Muslim community in Spain and our coexistence in Spanish society." He praised the Spanish public's "mature reaction" to the train bombings—adding that they've had long experience differentiating between ETA terrorists and ordinary Basques. "11 March was a lesson and won't happen again," the UCIDE representative said firmly. "Although the mosque is open to all, radicals know they don't have the right to preach hatred here. In Friday prayers, the imam emphasizes that Spain let us come in, we have to respect Spanish laws; the Spanish visa is sacred."

The Islamic Center of Madrid boasts a very grand mosque, but has identity problems. *Madrileños* almost universally call it unceremoniously the M-30 mosque because it towers over the usually clogged M-30 ring road on the capital's upper-east side. The mosque's sleek concrete arch facings and tiled insets are Middle East modern without a hint of Al Andalus, which is perhaps another reason why the public is cool to this foreign presence. But the main reason is that the mosque was built with Saudi Arabian funds, runs the only Islamic school in the country and some say it preaches a strict Wahhabi line of Islam, the fundamentalist school which originated in Saudi Arabia two centuries ago. The M-30 mosque was reputed to be a member of FEERI, founded by Spanish converts and the main rival to UCIDE.

I had been told to contact Mohamed Kharchich, from Morocco and the spokesman for the Islamic Center, but he was away. Nevertheless, I was able to meet with the center's secretary, Mohammed Saleh from Jordan, and the imam, Sheikh Moneir Mahmoud from Egypt, who for the most part sounded very much like their UCIDE rival. Both leaders informed me that the Islamic Center had decided to pull out of FEERI and planned to join the ranks of the independents. Although no one explained the reason for the defection, it was apparently connected with FEERI's recent leadership problems. Manuel Escudero, a Spanish convert and the outspoken founder and former president of FEERI, had been ousted by his colleagues in 2005 for issuing a fiery *fatwa* against Osama bin Laden. He was replaced by another Spanish convert, mild-mannered and scholarly Félix Ángel Herrero Durán—head of the Union Mosque in Málaga—but the controversy had hurt FEERI.

Saleh said an average of 2,000 faithful come to Friday prayers at the Islamic Center, mostly Moroccans and Algerians. Among its services to the local Muslim community, the center provides food for the poor, runs a Koranic school for children and a library, and offers classes in

Arabic and Islamic studies, he said. Other activities aim to improve the image of Arabs in Spain through meetings with representative of the other two main monotheistic religions, Judaism and Christianity, as well as exhibits on Islamic architecture, art and sacred books. "The 11 March attacks were a big shock initially, but Spaniards recognized the difference between Islamist extremists and the majority of Muslims," Saleh said in response to my question. He emphasized that the Islamic Center had taken a firm position against the 2004 Madrid terrorist acts, organized three campaigns to collect blood for the wounded, and took part in an anti-terrorism ceremony organized by a Roman Catholic group at the Atocha railroad station.[3]

"The Islamic Center of Madrid is open to all, Muslims, Spaniards and converts," said Sheikh Moneir, the Cairo-born, forty-six year-old imam with close cropped hair, who has lived in Spain for the past eleven years. Emphasizing the "good *convivencia*" between the center and Spanish society, the imam declared that he respected the Spanish people's "mature reaction" to the 11 March attacks and noted there had been few incidents. He was more critical of the Spanish media, accusing some journalists of "fabricating facts" to give a bad image to Islam. "They must respect our identity," he said.[4] Sheikh Moneir emphasized that the problem of Muslim extremists was rooted not in religion but in the political situation, namely what he called "the injustice towards Palestinians and the occupation of Iraq." He insisted that mainstream Muslims must talk to the radicals: "We must sit down with them and show them the right way. We must change their bad thoughts for good ones. I believe we can save many young people. My argument is that jihad is a defensive position and should not be used to attack. I also tell them that in Spain we must respect Spanish law."

In Valencia, I met the leadership of an active Muslim group that belonged to neither of the main federations, UCIDE or FEERI. The independent Islamic Center of Valencia had organized an international congress on the theme of "The Alliance of Civilizations: Another World is Possible." It was the first open Spanish Muslim support for Zapatero's favorite project. In official circles in Madrid, I learned that the vice president of the Islamic Center and congress organizer was a woman, Amparo Sánchez Rosell, married to a Moroccan restaurateur. Sánchez is an example of the new breed of Spain's Muslim converts, who are growing in numbers and often assume roles of leadership in the Islamic Community. Because of their Spanish culture, these *conver-*

sos know how to defend citizens' rights and how to communicate with the local authorities and the press.

"When the prime minister, Zapatero, launched the proposal of an Alliance of Civilizations at the United Nations in 2004 as an alternative to military action, we were enchanted," Sánchez told me after a press conference held in her husband's restaurant. "We sent a letter to the government saying we had connections and were willing to help, but then there was nothing. We decided to do something ourselves and so we have brought together Spanish and Muslim educators, private associations, official representatives and the media to engage in the East-West dialogue for four days."[5] This unassuming woman of almost fifty, in a tight headscarf and loose djellaba, was no Islamic *passionaria*. Born and bred in Valencia, she was a practicing Catholic until age thirteen, when she began to question church practices. She studied business administration at the Valencia School of Commerce and worked as an accountant for an electrical appliances firm. A youthful marriage ended in divorce and she was left with two children to raise.

In a lengthy conversation, Sánchez spoke openly of her initial doubts about Islam and present concerns over Muslim radicals. "I read a good deal and tried to find a philosophical home. I was attracted to left-wing political parties and their emphasis on social justice, but they lacked the spiritual qualities I sought. In my studies of religions, Islam made me afraid at first, although I admired our Arab past. Then I began to meet Muslims and found they were completely different from our image of them. In 1992, I got to know Rachid Ben Hamza from Tangier when he was working in a restaurant in Valencia. His family were good people; when they saw how happy we were together, they welcomed our marriage. My husband did not force me to convert, but I became a Muslim in 1997. What I liked was the spirituality combined with social conscience and the absence of religious hierarchy. At first I thought Muslim women didn't have rights, but then I learned that wasn't so. Everything depends on the different countries' laws. In democratic Spain, Muslims must obey Spanish law. Some Islamic societies are ruled by machismo traditions and for that reason women have problems."

Responding to my question, she acknowledged she was afraid of extremists. "All Spaniards are afraid after the 11 March attacks in Madrid. Those terrorists were drug traffickers, delinquents, mercenaries, working for the ringleaders. Terrorists are crazy and evil; they don't care who the victims are. Remember the attacks in Casablanca on 16 May,

2003; most of the dead and wounded were Muslims. The terrorists had little education, were poor and frustrated and had been brainwashed. Terrorists can travel everywhere. We have to take precautions."

Sánchez stressed that this meant that Islamic organizations must work harder than ever to counter the negative image of Muslims projected by the extremists. After the 11 March bombings, Valencia's Islamic Cultural Center organized a blood drive for the victims. The center is registered with the Spanish government as a non-profit association aimed to promote the full integration of Muslims in Spanish society. As a member of the Immigration Forum of Valencia, the center provides Muslim immigrants with classes in Spanish language and culture and also gives courses to young people on Islamic religion and culture. "We must be bridges to the broader Spanish community and barriers to Islamic radicals," Sánchez concluded.

Pablo Barrios Almanzor, the diplomat charged with "The Alliance of Civilizations" portfolio in the Spanish Foreign Ministry, declared that the Valencia meeting could make an "important input" to the report being prepared for the United Nations. Among the topics discussed were: the political, legislative and juridical mechanisms to achieve the alliance of civilizations, social means to promote understanding, the role of education and the media, and questions of immigration and cultural dialogue.

As I could not remain until the end of the four-day congress, Sánchez emailed me the eight-page report with the conclusions of the meeting. I was particularly interested in the experts' list of recommendations to improve the integration of Muslims into Spanish society. Many of the points could serve as a roadmap for Europe and other western countries:

– Elimination of the "bi-polar" situation between Muslims and non-Muslims by stressing points in common.
– Acceptance by Spaniards of the history of Muslim Spain as their own history.
– Separation between culture and religion.
– Action by Muslims to contain Islamic extremists.
– Efforts by immigrants to learn the language of the country.
– Acceptance and obedience by Muslims of the laws of the country.
– Active participation of women in society.
– Equal working conditions for immigrants.

– Enhancement of the role of imams as mediators between Muslims and the rest of society.

– Elimination of internal Muslim conflicts to enable a renewal of the dialogue with the State begun in 1992.

– Spread of the Alliance of Civilizations beyond diplomatic circles to the local level of cities and towns.[6]

In Granada, I learned about Spain's *converso* problem. There are, to be sure, highly respected converts like Félix Herrero, leader of FEERI, and Amparo Sánchez in Valencia, who serve as bridges between the Muslim minority and the broader Spanish community. There are others, however, like the founder of the Albaicín mosque in Granada, Sheikh Abdalqadir, revered by his followers as a Sufi leader but virulently denounced by his critics as the head of an anti-Semitic cult.

After visiting the wonders of the Alhambra and the Generalife gardens, I crossed the Darro River valley to the Albaicín, the old Muslim quarter with its churches built on the foundations of mosques and bustling once again with Moroccan handicraft shops, Moorish cafés and tea houses, and Arab baths. I was looking for the Grand Mosque, which did not appear in any of my guidebooks. The cornerstone had been ceremoniously laid in 1996 with the presence of the mayor and other personalities, but then there had been long delays because of protests from the neighborhood. Now it stood behind a locked iron gate, an attractive, whitewashed Mediterranean-style sanctuary, surrounded by a garden with a splendid view of the Alhambra. Neighbors suggested I return later, which I did, several times. Finally, I found the caretaker, Mohammed Ziane, a student from Spain's Moroccan enclave of Ceuta, who was unwilling to chat but gave me some basic information: "The leader of the mosque is Sheikh Abdalqadir, a Sufi, author of many books on Islam, and presently living in Cape Town, South Africa," Ziane said, as if reciting a prepared speech. "The mosque was inaugurated on 10 July 2003, in the presence of the leader of the Emirate of Sharjah, Sheikh Sultan bin Muhammad al Qasimi, who had provided funds for the building. The Moroccan imam, who has gone home for the summer holiday, is Sheikh Mohammed Kasbi, a former student of Sheikh Abdalqadir. About 4,000 Moroccans live in Granada and 400 of them usually come to the mosque for Friday prayers."[7]

That would have been the end of the story, except that I met a Turkish calligrapher who insisted I talk to a leader of the Muslim community to learn "the truth" about the Grand Mosque. He took me to meet

Mustafa Akalay, owner of an elegant restaurant at the foot of the Alhambra and a former assistant of the late David Hart, the American anthropologist known for his work in northern Morocco. The restaurateur welcomed me affably, but when I mentioned the Grand Mosque and Sheikh Abdalqadir, he changed visibly. He spoke disparagingly of the "sheikh," a movie actor by the name of Ian Dallas, who had played a minor part in Fellini's classic 8 ½ and then converted to Islam and came to Granada. Why were American journalists so interested in *conversos*? Akalay asked suspiciously. It was a very dangerous subject, and I should beware of the Albaicín mosque, he warned. No serious person in Granada would talk to me about the so-called sheikh.[8] The Moroccan's hostility abated when I said I was traveling to Córdoba where I had an appointment with Mansur Escudero, the former head of FEERI. Akalay said Escudero was a highly respected convert and that he knew Sheikh Abdalqadir well and could tell me about his cult.

Wikipedia, the online encyclopedia, presents the sheikh's unusual CV without comment. Born Ian Dallas in 1930 in Ayr, Scotland, he studied for a career in the theater at the Royal Academy of Dramatic Arts and the University of London. He wrote numerous plays and television scripts, and did some acting before embarking on his new life as an activist for Islam. The convert took the name Abdalqadir as Sufi al Murabit and, in the early 1980s, established the Murabitun World Movement, which called for the restoration of the Caliphate—a unified Islamic rule. He founded the Grand Mosque of Granada, the Jumu'a Mosque in Cape Town and the Dallas College for Muslim leaders in Cape Town, where he currently resides.

Sheikh Abdalqadir's own website claims to be the "world's foremost Islamic site" for analyses of current affairs and guidance to action. Illustrated by a portrait of the leader with black brows and white moustache and beard, wearing a white hooded robe, the website provides the sheikh's views on such subjects as "the Lebanon Crisis," European leaders' position on "the so-called Islamic veil" and Afghanistan, which he forecasts will prove to be "America's third and final Vietnam."[9]

On the other hand, numerous articles on the web present an altogether different picture of the Sufi from Scotland. One of the most critical accounts of the life and times of Ian Dallas/Sheikh Abdalqadir appeared in a series of articles by Denis Campbell in the *Scotland on Sunday* weekly newspaper in the fall of 1995. At that time, according to Campbell, the Muslim leader had set up the Muribatun's headquarters near Inverness and was actively recruiting well-to-do westerners, mainly British, for Islam.[10] More alarming were Campbell's quotations of Sheikh Abdalqadir's own words, such as his praise for Hitler's "great genius and great vision" and his denial of the Holocaust: "no scientific mind accepts the fantastic figure of six million gassed."[11]

I hoped to learn more about the mysterious sheikh from Mansur Escudero. Several Spanish officials in Madrid had urged me to meet the outspoken head of the Islamic Junta when I visited Córdoba. No longer leader of FEERI, Escudero remained an influential voice in the Muslim community in Spain. He agreed to see me at his home on the outskirts of Almodóvar del Rio, a whitewashed town with orange tile roofs, fifteen miles west of Córdoba in the fertile Guadalquivir Valley, dominated by an imposing Arab castle.

I found Escudero and his American-born wife, Kamila Toby, hard at work on their computers in a rambling farmhouse, secluded by olive trees. From their home, the husband and wife team ran the Islamic Junta, which published books on Islam, organized Islamic conferences and contributed to Webislam, the first Islamic website in Spain, which provides a comprehensive news report from the Islamic world. Appearing more like a country doctor than a Muslim militant, Escudero, fifty-nine, with grizzled hair and short beard, wore slacks and sport shirt and spoke in an engaging manner. Born in a village near Málaga of "very Catholic parents," he studied with Jesuits for eight years "and became a Marxist." Completing medical studies at Madrid's Complutense University, he specialized in neuro-psychiatry at Córdoba's Mental Health Center and pioneered Spain's first Center for Group Therapy in Córdoba. In 1974, he did a tour with the Mental Health Communities Services in Tucson, Arizona. There he met Kamila, who had been raised in Islam by her American Muslim mother. "Kamila was a young girl and I don't think I even spoke to her," Escudero recalled somewhat shamefacedly. Only when he had established his practice did he find the courage to ask her to come to Spain and marry him.[12]

Escudero "accepted" Islam in 1979, when he was in Norwich, England. The following year, he founded the first group of Spanish Muslims, called the Society for the Return to Islam in Spain. "I found that Islam gives a balanced way to understand life and behavior," he explained, but admitted he had "difficulties" at first with the ideas of discrimination against women. "I soon learned the difference between the general understanding and practice of Islam and the original precepts," he continued. "One of our main tasks is to recover the genuine interpretation and practice of Islam from the Prophet's time. The Prophet taught the middle way to avoid extremism. Real Islam is democracy. Extremism is a deviation, an aberration."

At this point I asked him about Sheikh Abdalqadir. Was he the extremist of some media accounts or the peace-loving Sufi portrayed on other websites? Escudero said he met the sheikh at the mosque in Norwich and had joined the Murabitun, which started out as a Sufi movement. Escudero remained three years in the movement and then quit. "When you leave, you don't talk," he stressed. My host did say that the Murabitun had become "like a sect, based on the authority of the teacher." The members, he said, were "an elite of the elite." When the teacher left for South Africa, some disciples followed him.

Then, changing the subject, Escudero talked to me about the Islamic Community's relations with the Spanish government. "Prior to the 1992 commemorations of the discovery of America and the expulsions of Muslims and Jews, the State opened negotiations to compensate those religions that had been victims of genocide after the fall of Granada," he said. As head of FEERI, from 1990 to 2003 and secretary general of the Islamic Commission of Spain, Escudero had signed the Accord of Cooperation with the Spanish State in 1992 and the Convention on Teaching Islamic Religious Education in 1996.

"From the outset, we informed the government that since Spain is now a secular state, we wanted the same level of cooperation as it has with the Roman Catholic Church," Escudero said. "The official negotiators refused and unfortunately some other Muslim leaders are reluctant to pressure the government. But we continue to demand equal rights with Catholics." He highlighted the "big discrepancy" in the millions of euros Spain gives to finance Catholic schools, teachers and other institutions, and the few thousand euros for Muslims. The government, he added, was considering more funding for Islamic institutes to counter aid coming from Saudi Arabia. The three main mosques in Andalucía—Marbella, Fuengirola and a new mosque in Málaga—have been funded by Saudi Arabia and belong to the conservative Wahhabi School of Islam, whereas the mosque in Granada was funded by the Emir of Sharja with contributions from the King of Morocco. "I was invited to visit Saudi Arabia in 1995 and they offered to give us financing for a new mosque in Córdoba, on condition that I refrain from criticizing the situation of women in that country," Escudero said with a smile. "Needless to say there was no deal."

The leader of the Islamic Junta gave me a complete file on the "*fatwa* affair*,*" which had got him into trouble with his own organizations. There was the text of the incendiary statement issued by Escudero as secretary general of the Islamic Commission of Spain on the first anniversary of the bloody attacks on the Spanish commuter trains in 2004. It was the first time the leader of a major Muslim organization proclaimed Osama bin Laden and his organization to be "apostates" for his defense of terrorism in the name of the Koran and responsibility for "horrendous crimes" against innocent people on 11 March in Madrid. There were also widespread comments on the *fatwa* against Bin Laden. Sheikh Moneir, imam of the M-30 mosque in Madrid and Socialist deputy Muhammad Chaib of Barcelona had approved of the *fatwa*, while the Mufti of Egypt, Ali Jum'ah, ruled that condemning Bin Laden as a terrorist was "a legal not a religious matter." Escudero himself showed no remorse for his intemperate declaration but rather disappointment that some colleagues had refused to support the *fatwa*. He adamantly clung to his position that "anyone who justifies the killing of innocent people in the name of Islam is outside of Islam."

At this point, Kamila reminded her husband of an appointment in Córdoba. On our way into town, Escudero confided that there was another domain in which Spanish Muslims suffered from discrimination; the recognition of their rights as forced exiles. He hoped to obtain equal treatment for *Moríscos*, Muslims converted to Christianity, as for Sephardic Jews, who are able to acquire Spanish nationality in two years (contrary to ten years for most foreigners). The *Moríscos*, like the Jews, were ousted from Al Andalus and should be given the same special status "in the name of historical justice," he stressed

Escudero actually brought this issue up the following month during a lecture at Córdoba University's summer school, saying: "The King of Spain made a political and state declaration recognizing the expulsion of the Jews but nobody has done this for the Muslims." He also urged holding an international congress on "The Recovery of Andalusia's Historic Memory." The centerpiece of this meeting would be equal treatment for the descendants of *Moríscos* and Sephardim under Spain's nationality law.

Some of Escudero's critics accuse him of being a showman and playing to the media, and it's clear he knows how to push buttons and shake things up. His latest *cause célèbre* was the Grand Mosque of Córdoba. The Spanish convert believed Muslims—and Christians too—should have the right to pray in the vast eighth century Islamic masterpiece with the ornate sixteenth century cathedral planted in its heart. In 2004, Escudero conveyed his dream to the Vatican. "What we want is not to take over that holy place, but create, together with you and other faiths, an ecumenical space unique in the world which would be of great significance in bringing peace to humanity," Escudero wrote in a letter to Pope Benedict XVI. The Vatican reportedly responded that it was up to the Bishop of Córdoba to take a decision. Bishop Don Juan José Asenjo, however, categorically rejected the petition to allow Muslims to pray in the Córdoba Mosque, saying it would only generate confusion among the faithful. Abandoning the diplomatic route, Escudero took action. On Friday 29 December 2006, he took off his shoes and went to the southern wall of the mosque opposite the *mihrab* to say the ritual midday prayer facing Mecca. The entire operation took about five minutes, but it sent shock waves around the world. A Muslim had returned to pray at the Grand Mosque of Córdoba, against the express will of the Holy Roman Catholic Church. On several occasions since, church authorities have reiterated their firm refusal to share the premises of the mosque-cathedral with Muslims.

At his inaugural ceremony in the mosque-cathedral in early 2010, the new Bishop of Córdoba, Demetrio Fernández González, reaffirmed support for interfaith dialogue but emphasized that "sharing the cathedral is not possible."[13] Later in an op-ed piece in the conservative daily, *ABC*, the bishop went on to question the appropriateness of the terminology, mosque-cathedral, noting that it had not served as a mosque since it was consecrated as a cathedral in the thirteenth century. Reporting on "the name debate," *The New York Times* stressed that the mosque-cathedral has been enshrined on UNESCO's list of World Heritage sites. Isabel Romero, a Spanish convert to Islam and spokesperson for the Islamic Junta, is quoted as saying, "The Córdoba monument is a lesson in universalism, in how cultures and religions can meet and coexist."[14]

There isn't even one proper mosque in Barcelona, although the region of Cataluña is the main center of Muslim immigration. Some years back, a group from Saudi Arabia presented plans for a magnificent mosque, worthy of the Cataluña capital with promised financing, but the *Generalitat*, the local government, rejected the offer because they were afraid of Saudi influence. Since then, informal mosques and *oratorios* (prayer rooms) have sprung up all over the region, causing alarm in official circles and angry NIMBY reactions among Cataláns, particularly in rural areas. Finally at the end of 2010, Barcelona's city hall informed a congress of Moroccan Islamic scholars of Europe that the northern capital would have its Grand Mosque, like the M-30 in Madrid.[15] The Union of Islamic Cultural Centers of Cataluña welcomed the news, but observers were skeptical because of the strong right-wing opposition to the increased visibility of Muslims.

On Fridays in downtown Barcelona, steady streams of Muslims can be seen converging on a grim three-story, one-time warehouse, which serves as the city's main mosque. I entered through the back door into a dark corridor packed with young men, mostly Pakistanis and Moroccans, who paid no attention to the stranger in their midst. I was accompanied by Jordi Moreras, Catalán anthropologist and author of several books on Muslims in Cataluña. We pushed our way back out and went around the block to the front entrance, but that was even more crowded, and so we repaired to café nearby where Moreras gave me a briefing on the struggle of the Islamic Community to put down roots in the region.

"The first Muslims showed up in Cataluña in 1970; they were Moroccan migrants, heading north to find jobs in France and Germany," Moreras began. "Then the oil crisis exploded in 1973, and Europe closed its doors. A good many Moroccans were trapped in Cataluña and some stayed as the economy picked up. *Oratorios* appeared in 1978, generally in storefronts rented by Pakistanis, the first Muslims to enjoy economic success. Then some Saudis wrote a letter to the mayor and the *Generalitat* proposing the construction of a beautiful mosque. But the Socialist mayor rejected the offer saying that 'foreign intervention' could not be accepted. I think it was a historic error not to build the mosque. Instead, we have all the *oratorios*, 150 in Cataluña and twelve in Barcelona alone, without any form of control. Some of these have been the object of a growing Islamophobia, particularly in the villages. Others are the source of an increasingly radical discourse. Before 11 September, integration of the Islamic Community was difficult, but after 11 March, the general public sees Muslims as a threat and integration next to impossible."[16]

Moreras said the top priority of the Catalán authorities now was to find an acceptable representative of the Islamic Community. The main Muslim organization, the Islamic Council of Cataluña, led by Moroccan-born deputy Mohamed Chaib, was not recognized by the Pakistanis and other Muslim groups, he said.

When I contacted Chaib, he emphasized that the majority of Muslims in Spain are Moroccan immigrants, or more than 600,000 of them are, of which about 200,000 are in Cataluña. Around 95% of the imams in Cataluña are also Moroccan. He admitted that only eighty of the some 150 Islamic communities in the region belonged to the Islamic Council. There were efforts underway to create a new federation which could speak for all of the region's Muslims, he said. The Socialist parliamentarian acknowledged his concern over the absence of controls over the *oratorios* and stressed that the two main Islamist groups from Morocco had already established a presence in Cataluña. "What worries us is that members of radical religious movements can infiltrate the community, and seek to influence our young people," Chaib said, adding that he had heard reports that some visitors "were speaking out against Spain."

The following spring (2007), I returned to the Islamic Centre of Madrid with an appointment to see Mohamed Kharchich, who had since been named secretary general of FEERI, in addition to his post of communications director at the M-30 mosque. (The Islamic Center had not returned to FEERI, but that didn't seem to matter.) A large man with trim beard, moustache and rimless glasses, wearing a yellow sport shirt and dark suit, Kharchich received me in his small office on the second floor of the Islamic Center. An optician by profession, he came from Tetuan at age twenty and is now in his early forties, and has been waiting five years to obtain Spanish nationality. Besides his post as spokesperson for the Islamic Center, he serves as a Muslim chaplain in Madrid's three prisons and in the Spanish armed forces.

The voluble Moroccan gave the Spanish authorities credit for trying to organize the role of the religious minorities in Spanish society through accords establishing rights and obligations. But he stressed there were difficulties in the implementation of the accords, as far as the Islamic communities were concerned. "The system isn't functioning very well," he said bluntly. "The main problem is about representation. We need one federation, like they have in France. FEERI was the first federation, then the Estrecho Community pulled out and formed UCIDE. And now there's talk of regional federations. It's mainly a question of personalities. Also the structure of the Islamic communities is abnormal, with the proliferation of garage-mosques, which are very difficult to control. Now the Ministry of Justice is considering a big mosque in the capital of every region. Another problem is the imams.

They need training; and they should learn Spanish and the laws of the country. What is necessary is a school for imams in Spain."[17]

The Moroccan leader did not hide his concern for the current situation in Spain and Morocco, both countries threatened by radicals. "Terrorism affects everybody. Fear exists. Spaniards are increasingly preoccupied by the terrorist threat. Terrorism is a new phenomenon in Morocco. We must look for motives: poverty, social injustice, ignorance. We want to give Spaniards another image of Muslims. We are proud of the civilization of Al Andalus. But Spain is a sovereign country and Muslims must respect the country they live in."

As time passed, dissension over the representation of Spain's Muslims only increased. All of the original leaders of the federations were contested, with activists calling for new leadership. In the fall of 2009, Félix Herrero was replaced as head of FEERI by Mohamed Hamed Ali, a Muslim from Spain's Moroccan territory of Ceuta. This pleased some advocates for more Moroccan representation, but some official Spanish circles were concerned since Ali reportedly had close ties with the Moroccan administration.

One of the newest groups, the Muslim Federation of Spain (FEME), is led by a Spanish convert and outspoken journalist, Yusuf Fernández, forty-four, editor of the Muslim website, Webislam. A former spokesman for FEERI, Fernández quit the troubled federation in 2006, and organized FEME with some breakaway groups and regional organizations around a common platform for the resolution of the community's problems. By 2007, FEME was the second most influential Muslim organization in Spain, with 130 associations made up mostly of Moroccans, but also Spaniards, Africans and Asians. Late in 2009, the heavy-set, bearded Fernández publicly declared that that the seventeen-year-old Islamic Commission of Spain "does not represent the majority of Muslims" in Spain. He urged the authorities to open the Commission to other members, including FEME.

The leadership crisis among Spain's Muslims was particularly acute in Cataluña, where the community numbered some 250,000, including Moroccans, Pakistanis, Senegalese and *conversos* by early 2010. "Never in history have there been so many Muslims and never so many organizations claiming to be their spokespersons," wrote Josep Playa Maset in Barcelona's daily *La Vanguardia*, adding that it was difficult to know "how much weight and how representative" were the 180 Muslim organizations in the territory.[18]

The birth of Spain's first Islamic-inspired political party early in 2009 caught most people by surprise, although it was to be expected, considering the number of groups competing to represent the country's 1,300,000 Muslims. There are other Muslim-backed parties in Spain's Moroccan enclaves, but they do not have a national outreach. Mohammed Bakkach el Aamrani, forty-five, a Spanish-Moroccan professor of Arabic, journalist and poet who has lived in Spain for the past eight years, announced that his new Rebirth and Union Party of Spain (familiarly known by its Spanish initials PRUNE) would defend the interests of Moroccans and other immigrants.[19] From the outset the new Islamic-based party was received coolly by traditional Muslim leaders, who said they had not been consulted on the initiative. It was clear they felt that an Islamic party might be seen as a Muslim refusal to integrate into Spanish society, or at least an act of provocation. "This party is suicide for Spanish Muslims," declared Ibrahim López, founder of Granada's Peace Mosque, who suggested it could attract "discontented radicals."[20]

Nevertheless, Bakkach declared that the Granada-based party planned to set up branches in key municipalities around the country and would take part in local elections. He acknowledged facing a major hurdle: the fact that Moroccans cannot vote in Spanish elections until the two countries sign an accord of reciprocity. Bakkach went out of his way to assure the Spanish public that PRUNE "respects the Spanish constitution and condemns terrorism," according to *ABC*. The conservative Spanish daily reported that the authorities had several underlying concerns regarding the new Muslim-led party. It might militate against integration in urban areas and try to impose its customs in municipalities with a Muslim majority. Also it might be influenced by Morocco, "whose interests are in opposition to those of Spain."[21]

Answering critics, Bakkach presented the authorization of the Ministry of Interior on 23 July 2009, as a kind of official endorsement. In an interview with *Europa Press*, he stressed that PRUNE was not Muslim or Islamic but "open to all" and declared: "Its main objective is to give a voice to marginalized people like immigrants, who are not represented by other political institutions." He also claimed the party was independent "with no links to any foreign country or religious movement."[22]

Most Muslims I contacted indicated little likelihood that an Islamic-inspired party could unite Spain's diverse immigrant communities. Rather, it seemed destined to become yet another faction on the nation's fragmented Islamic scene.

Unfortunately it took the death of Mansur Escudero to win national recognition for what he stood for, the integration of Spain's Muslims of all origins on an equal footing in a truly intercultural society. I had planned to go back to see Escudero in mid September of 2010, but had to postpone my appointment a few weeks, and by then it was too late. The president of the Islamic Junta died unexpectedly of respiratory failure during his early morning prayers in his home at Almodóvar del Rio on 3 October 2010. Condolences poured in from Muslim leaders around Spain as well as from the palace, the government and intellectual circles. King Juan Carlos extended his "deepest sympathy" to Escudero's family and all the Islamic community of Spain, through the chief of the Royal Cabinet.[23] José María Contreras, director of religious affairs in the Ministry of Justice, hailed Escudero as a proponent of "modern Islam, a man who fought for the rights of the Muslim community in Spain and a man of dialogue with other faiths."[24] Juan José Tamayo, director of the chair of theology and religious sciences at Madrid's Carlos III, called Escudero "a central figure behind the growth and reform of Islam in Spain and Europe."[25] Declaring that Escudero's loss leaves a "vacuum" in Spain's Islamic community, Amparo Sánchez Rosell, head of Valencia's Islamic Cultural Center, described him as "a great defender of Islam and the rights of Muslims."[26]

But the debate over representation in the Islamic Commission of Spain continued unabated. "Let us do our work; we don't want outside interventions,' declared Mohamed Hamed Ali, president of FEERI, who called a meeting in Madrid in February 2011, to resolve the problem. He accused the head of Spain's religious affairs, but also Morocco and Saudi Arabia, of interfering in the Muslim communities' affairs.[27] But agreement remained elusive. Ana Planet, a specialist in Islam at Madrid's Autonomous University, who attended the conference, told me the new element coming out of the conference was the latest statistics on Muslim groups in Spain. Juan Ferrero, former deputy director of religious affairs, announced that 878 Muslim associations are registered with the Ministry of Justice. Only 576 of these associations (500 from UCIDE and seventy-six from FEERI) are represented in the CIE, which is supposed to encompass all Muslims of Spain. Therefore, he said, 302 Muslim associations plus hundreds of cultural groups are not represented in the umbrella Islamic organization.[28]

My informal survey of Spain's Islamic leadership leaves me with ambivalent feelings. On the surface, the discordant Muslim voices have not well served the interests of the growing Islamic community. The rivalries and absence of a cohesive policy have eased pressure on the authorities to carry out reforms linked to the 1992 accords, such as Islamic education in public schools with numerous Muslim students. At the same time, it is clear that a strong united Muslim front could appear threatening at a time of increased Islamophobia in Spain, the spread of Islamic extremism in Europe and continued threats by Islamic zealots to reconquer Al Andalus. There is perhaps strength in disunity.

9

THE RADICAL FRINGE

In my travels through present-day Spain and Portugal, I found little evidence that the largely Roman Catholic countries are engaged in a global conflict of civilizations with militant Islam. Despite renewed threats from Al Qaeda to recover Al Andalus, the savage terrorist attacks killing nearly 200 Madrid commuters in 2004, and the resurgence of jihadist activity in neighboring North Africa, Iberians by and large contend they do not feel especially threatened by Islamic extremists.

Exception must be made for those Spanish journalists, academics and angry bloggers, who argue that Spain has been at war with Islamic radicals since the jihadist movement appeared in the 1970s. Some even go back to the Reconquista. For example, Gustavo de Arístegui, author of *La Yihad en Espana*, claims that the recovery of Al Andalus has been "an obsession" of Islamic radicals since the Middle Ages.[1]

But Spanish politicians, the media and general public, for the most part appear warier of the challenge from Basque separatists and their armed wing ETA, which has carried out terrorist actions since the 1960s. As for the Portuguese, most claim that Al Qaeda, or even terrorists from ETA, are of no direct concern to them, and are much more worried about the recent rise of violent crime in their tranquil country.

It is generally agreed, however, that Spanish authorities, fixated on their war with ETA and persuaded of their special relationship with the Arab world, were ill prepared for the bloodbath of 11 March 2004, caused by Muslim extremists. Spanish officials go so far as to admit that prior to the attack, the police had discarded some wiretapping records in Arabic because there weren't enough Arabic translators to decipher them.

That has changed. A number of senior officials, specialists, military officers and academics in the two countries acknowledge that the peninsula could be a prime target of Muslim radicals. Governing circles in Madrid and Lisbon are now clearly focused on the dangers posed by radical Islamists. They do not see jihadists in every mosque or prayer hall, and have made deliberate efforts to avoid stereotyping. But there is no doubt that security concerns have negatively affected the integration of Iberia's new Muslim communities.

Portugal's minister of interior told me that all of Europe "is at risk" in the wake of the attacks by Muslim extremists in Madrid in March 2004, and in London the following year. "These attacks could happen here in Portugal; we are all threatened," the minister, António da Costa said, when I asked him about the threat of terrorism. He stressed that the common danger had led to a significant increase in inter-European cooperation in counterterrorist training, detection and prevention.[2]

Spanish leader José Luis Zapatero, whose Socialist party won national elections in the wake of the Madrid attacks, has given new direction and resources to the struggle against terrorism. Within scarcely a year, the Ministry of Interior had put 450 officials to work full time on the terrorist threat in Muslim circles, or three times the force before the 11 March attacks, according to a report by the US Congressional Research Service. Zapatero's government also set up a National Anti-Terrorist Center, tightened controls on the sale of explosives and improved surveillance of radical Islamists in Spanish prisons, which were described as "recruitment centers for Islamic extremists."[3]

Nevertheless, in the months following the arrest and trial of a group of radical Muslims for the Madrid bombings, the Iberian public seemed to relax its guard. Although the media has covered Al Qaeda's sinister warnings against Al Andalus and its violent deeds elsewhere, people give the impression that a dark period is over, probably because there have been no subsequent attacks on the peninsula. Spaniards continue to speak of the Muslims they know—their baby-sitters, shopkeepers, laborers or students—as "moderates" and "hard-working," while Portuguese say they have "no problems" with their Muslim neighbors.

The experts on radical Islam have sought to counter Iberian complacency. Among the recognized authorities, Javier Jordan is senior lecturer at the Department of Political Science and Administration of the University of Granada and a member of the European Network of Experts on Violent Radicalisation, who has written extensively on terrorism in Spain and Europe. Fernando Reinares is co-author of *El Nuevo Terrorismo Islamista: Del 11-M al 11-S*, whose comments appear often in the Spanish press and whom I encountered at a conference on counterterrorism in Lisbon. A leading Spanish journalist covering terrorism is Antonio Baquero, whom I first met in Morocco a decade ago, and who regularly covers traditional Islamist groups as well as the radical fringe. He also keeps watch on the young people—mostly Spanish and Latin American converts to Islam—who frequent the chat rooms on the internet. "They describe themselves as Salafists and call for a return of the caliphate," Baquero wrote in a feature for the Barcelona daily, *El Periódico*. He emphasized that these radicals are anti-system, don't go to the mosque and don't speak Arabic, but condemn terrorism and do not support Al Qaeda.[4]

Other specialists present a wholly negative view of Muslims. José Luis Sánchez Nogales, author of *El Islam Entre Nosotros*, depicts the Muslims of Al Andalus as cruel barbarians, and links them directly to modern Islamists, namely the *Morabitun* of Sheikh Abdelkader (mentioned earlier), although they profess to be non-violent Sufis. José María Irujo's book of 2005, *El Agujero*, deals with "the invasion" of Spain by jihad and portrays Moroccan immigrants as unassimilated loners, susceptible to recruitment by radicals. While former diplomat Arístegui argues that the Muslims' petition to hold Friday prayers in Córdoba's Grand Mosque could lead to Muslim claims on all mosques and other buildings around the peninsula and constitutes the first step toward a total reconquest.

As for Iberia's Muslims, they have generally tried to keep a low profile. When they speak out, it is usually to preach moderation and reconciliation. If questioned, Muslims will invariably denounce terrorist attacks in the name of Islam and attribute them to "politics." Most Muslims know their fellow worshippers and contend that if there is a danger of radicalism it would have to come "from outside." They hold there are few imams known for their fiery discourse or bookstores with incendiary literature. Even Madrid's large Saudi-built mosque is said to be "neutral" and refrains from promoting the Saudis' rigid doctrine of Wahhabism. On the surface, one might conclude that there were no radical Muslims in Iberia, except those in Spanish jails.

For an overall assessment of the presence of Islamic extremists in Spain, the chances of renewed attacks and the measures taken to prevent them, I asked the Ministry of Interior for a high level briefing. A meeting was arranged with one of the country's leading counterterrorist experts and a prime investigator into the Madrid train bombings, on condition that he remain unnamed. That was fine by me since senior officials are often more open on delicate issues such as terrorism when they are reassured they will not be quoted.

We met at the vast police complex of Canillas, a veritable fortress on a hill on the outskirts of Madrid, which was so heavily guarded that a passport, rather than the usual photo ID, was necessary to gain entrance. The official, whom I can identify only as a member of the Central Unit of Foreign Intelligence, appeared well informed and readily responded to all my questions. Therefore, I have transcribed most of his comments from my notes. I began by asking what were Spain's main security concerns regarding the Muslim community: unregulated immigration or uncontrolled prayer halls; unassimilated young people or returning jihadists from Afghanistan and Iraq? The official's answer took me by surprise.

"What concerns us above all is the process of radicalization—not how many Muslims are coming here or where they come from. What matters is the formation of clandestine associations and committees ... and above all, the links on the net.

"North Africans are the main target of Spanish counterterrorism services because the community is so large. We're not talking about those who come by *pateras*. This is not an immigration problem. The danger comes from Salafists—radical members of the pan-Islamic reform movement—who share Al Qaeda's ideology but have no direct links with the international organization. In fact, it is believed there are only a few members of Al Qaeda in Spain but rather like-minded groups that act like franchises.

"Before, it was easy to contain radical Islam, just by confiscating books and videos. Today Salafists recruit operatives among Muslims with minimal education. Not at the mosques and prayer halls, but through Islamic sites on the internet. The irony is that Al Qaeda discovered the internet thanks to the United States, which had destroyed its logistics in Afghanistan. The worldwide web is much more difficult to control than prayer halls. Radical Islamists change sites frequently. We can close one location but they will open a new one.

"There is also brain-washing going on over the net, directed mainly at educated Muslims, encouraging them through misinformation to believe that the United States was behind the 11 September attacks and even 11 March. The recruiter's pitch is invariably defensive. A besieged Islam is said to be under attack by the West. True believers must stand up and defend their religion. Once the recruiter is convinced of the sincerity of his prey, a personal contact is arranged.

"One of the root causes of Islamic radicalization in Spain, but not the only one, is the war in Iraq. After the Zapatero government withdrew Spanish troops from Iraq, Islamic extremists have raised the problem of Spanish forces in Afghanistan and Lebanon, and it doesn't matter that they are under United Nations auspices. Another element in the case against Spain put forth by radical Islamists is the continued Spanish occupation of the Moroccan enclaves of Ceuta and Melilla. The demand for the restoration of Al Andalus is an old Salafist claim, which Al Qaeda adopted in September 2006, when the North African terrorist groups joined the global movement to become Al Qaeda in Islamic Maghreb.

"The Indian-Pakistani community does not present the same level of danger as the North Africans, although some members have been found to engage in money laundering and the traffic of false documents," he added.

In conclusion, he noted that the government has bolstered its counterterrorism unit and now has sufficient Arabic speakers to face the challenge. However, he faulted the present laws, which allow only five days' preventive detention. Emphasizing the importance of Europol (European Police Office) in combating terrorism, the official highlighted "the close cooperation" between Spain and other intelligence services, despite occasional political tensions. He cited the examples of Morocco, which had almost gone to war over Spanish claims to Parsley Island in 2002, and the United States, which had not hidden its anger when Zapatero pulled Spain's troops out of Iraq in 2004. Asked whether there could be a repeat of the 11 March disaster, the counterterrorism expert said: "Probably not, at least not on that huge scale, but of course it can happen."[5]

Barely a month after this interview, the Spanish press reported the dismantling of a terrorist cell at Burgos, 150 miles north of Madrid, which appeared to come straight from the counterterrorism official's textbook. Spain's Guardia Civil, with help from security services in

Denmark, Sweden and the United States, arrested a group of six North African Salafists, accused of recruiting young people for jihad in Iraq and distributing Al Qaeda propaganda. The lead suspect was an Algerian imam of Burgos, who also ran a prosperous Islamic butcher's shop and had been radicalized during a stint in prison. Police sources said that most of the cell's activity took place over the internet and noted they were especially skilled at using chat rooms and creating firewalls.

But the counterterrorist official had not predicted the next major terrorist threat in Barcelona, involving the arrest of fourteen suspected terrorists, twelve Pakistanis and two Indians, in a plot with international ramifications. The Guardia Civil carried out midnight raids the evening of 18-19 January 2008, on Barcelona's principal mosque, a prayer hall and five residences in Raval, the city's main immigrant neighborhood. Bomb-making material, including timers, computers, false documents and mobile phones were seized, but only a small quantity of explosives. Spain's minister of interior Alfredo Pérez Rubalcaba personally announced the anti-terrorist strike, emphasizing that it differed from past actions directed against cells implicated in raising funds or recruits for the jihad. This time, the minister said, the police had uncovered a highly organized Islamist group, "which had gone beyond the stage of ideological radicalization" and was preparing violent action. In an attempt to justify the preventive action by the security forces, Rubalcaba declared: "Spain is mentioned in all statements by Al Qaeda, and so we are on very high alert." He emphasized that the police had acted in cooperation with other European intelligence services.

I was in the United States at the time and followed the dramatic revelations in the Spanish press. It was reported that ten of the suspects had been jailed and the others released, but all had rejected the terrorism charges leveled against them. The group, which allegedly included six potential suicide bombers, was said to be planning attacks on the Barcelona subway system as well as actions in Germany, France, Portugal and the United Kingdom. The operation reportedly had been triggered by the arrival at Barcelona of a Pakistani citizen, known to European intelligence as an Islamist extremist. Several other suspects had also recently spent time in Pakistan, and at least four of the local residents were described by official sources to be "extremists" and linked to Tablighi Jamaat, the Muslim missionary organization.

Leaders of Barcelona's Muslim community confirmed that some of the suspects were members of Tablighi Jamaat, but they stressed that it was an Islamic movement of itinerant preachers, not jihadists. The president of the Association of Pakistan Workers of Cataluña, Javed Ilyas, was quoted by *El País* as saying that the suspects were known to be "very religious men" and that the raids "had damaged the entire community."

However Spain's most prominent counterterrorist academic, Fernando Reinares, professor at Madrid's Rey Juan Carlos University, showed no surprise over the discovery of a cell of radical Pakistanis in Barcelona. In an interview with Antonio Baquero of *El Periódico*, Reinares said Al Qaeda was known to have penetrated Pakistani communities in Europe. He was careful not to brand the Tabligh movement as a terrorist organization but stressed that "many jihadists use the activities of Tablighi Jamaat as a cover for travel and recruiting." Reinares stressed that Spanish security forces have the highest rate of "police efficiency" in Europe, meaning the percentage of detainees who go to trial, but pointed to what he sees as a significant flaw in Spain's anti-terrorist arsenal. "We are the only country that has suffered a major attack that hasn't adapted its legal framework," he declared, noting that other countries accept proof obtained by surveillance methods "that are not acceptable here."[6]

When I returned to my base in Portugal several weeks later, most people had forgotten about the Barcelona plot. The case had been prominently displayed by the Portuguese media for a couple of days and then fizzled out. The informal word in Portuguese press circles was that the affair had been dreamed up by a mole in France who had been under pressure to produce intelligence on terrorist plotting. A senior Portuguese official told me privately that Madrid had reassured him the affair had been overblown by the Spanish press; there had been no concrete plot ready to be implemented, only "vague references to intentions."

Portuguese Muslim leaders, however, were concerned because the Barcelona suspects were linked to Tablighi Jamaat, which boasts prominent members in Lisbon and holds an annual congress in the Portuguese capital. It was the first time that Portugal's Muslim community had come under a negative spotlight and it made them uneasy. Several of these Muslims told me privately that such a plot was not inconceivable. Radicals could easily enter the country from elsewhere in Europe and attempt to exert their influence on alienated young people.

To learn more about Portugal's anti-terrorist operations and whether Tablighi Jamaat was considered a serious threat, I asked to meet Lisbon's director general of Strategic Defense Intelligence, Jorge Silva Carvalho, who agreed to speak to me on the record. We met in his spectacular office in the Alto da Duque Fort, high on a hill at the entrance to Lisbon, surrounded by a moat. The intelligence chief prefaced his remarks by recalling the mood in Portugal after the fall of the dictatorship.

"The Portuguese simply didn't trust secret services and didn't establish an intelligence system until 1984—ten years after the revolution. The law specifically barred any infringement of civil rights and gave the intelligence services no powers except for analysis. Things began to change in 2001 and accelerated after the Madrid bombings in 2004. We now have a Department of National Intelligence—like the United States—under a secretary of state who coordinates the services, except for the military.[7]

"Actually, Portuguese intelligence had begun looking into Tablighi Jamaat in 1997, before 11 September, simply because they were here. The Tablighs come from the Indo-Pakistani *Deobandi* school, a radical Asian current of Islam, generally based in well-to-do circles. We have been tracking the movements of the Tabligh and found them to be very mobile and very well organized. Their international Islamic meetings, known as *Itjmah*, are designed to improve the training of preachers and generally revitalize the faith of Muslims, but they appear to be likely breeding grounds for radicalization and recruiting sites for jihadists. These meetings are used by radical Islam's 'talent scouts' looking for committed men of faith who want to do something important for the *Umma*, the Islamic nation. We know they are looking for recruits who will pass in the West; the whiter, the quieter, the more western the better. Then Al Qaeda takes them to the next level in its struggle for power at home, in Saudi Arabia and elsewhere in the Islamic world.

"We were informed of the Pakistani plot at Barcelona three days before the official announcement. Our Spanish colleagues had been focused on North Africans and hadn't expected terrorists to come from the Asian community. Spanish investigators found the suspects were from Pakistan, the UK and the Netherlands. Four of them were Tablighs, who had visited Portugal. I do not believe Portugal is targeted by Al Qaeda, but we must be concerned because there are more than one million Muslims at our door in Spain."

Returning to Madrid, I requested a new meeting with the Interior Ministry official, who had been so informative. He confirmed that the

Barcelona conspiracy was indeed "a serious matter." He emphasized that it was an operation waged by the CNI (national intelligence service) and the Guardia Civil, with cooperation from foreign services. Police investigations have implicated Tablighs from Pakistan and a local jihadist group, he stated, emphasizing: "Tablighi Jamaat is not a terrorist organization" but has been infiltrated by radical Islamists and is now "a major concern."[8]

The Spanish intelligence official declared that Al Qaeda has lost much of its operational capacity in Europe because of the new counterterrorist vigilance, but it would undoubtedly try to restructure its presence. For the time being, he added, Al Qaeda presents "a big danger" to the countries of Maghreb, and Al Qaeda leaders continue to threaten Al Andalus and Spain's territories in Morocco. He noted that many countries have overhauled their intelligence systems since 11 September. Even Spain, "which has been accustomed to terrorism for a long time," has made important changes, creating the National Center for the Coordination of Anti-Terrorism, under the Ministry of Interior, he said. Madrid has also substantially increased counterterrorist personnel and obliged telephone companies to keep data on all users, and there's enhanced cooperation with foreign intelligence services, including the United States.

Spain's main focus remains on the large North African immigrant community and the attempts to radicalize Muslims through the internet, according to the counterterrorist expert. He stressed that there have been some positive experiences in reaching out to Muslims through "institutions of proximity," adding: "Above all, we count on our Muslim communities to keep the radicals in check."

In the spring of 2008, I was fortunate to hear some of the leading figures in Iberian counterterrorism in a three day conference on "Terrorism: Challenges and Responses" at the New University of Lisbon. It was Iberia's first trans-Atlantic conference on counterterrorism, grouping American, British, Spanish and Portuguese specialists. Speakers from both sides of the Atlantic highlighted progress made in the fight against global terrorism, but did not hide contradictions on the western front.

Portugal's secretary of state for the interior, José de Magalhães, opened the meeting with the assertion that his government has "awakened to the terrorist threats that don't respect borders" and the need for a common European strategy and trans-Atlantic cooperation. In the panel on "Terrorism and the Armed Forces," Lt. Col. António Beja Eugenio, a teacher of strategy at the Portuguese Joint War College, described Portugal's "firm commitment" to the struggle against terrorism since 2003, particularly through participation in NATO's air and naval patrols. However, General José Loureiro dos Santos, former army chief of staff and author of various works on defense and security, raised the constitutionality of Portugal's troops in Afghanistan "without a declaration of war."

"A NATO Approach to Terrorism" was presented by Lt. Colonel Ben Richards, from the Terrorism Threat Intelligence Unit in NATO. He noted that before 2001, terrorism was not prominent on NATO's agenda, although Spain and the UK had experience with counterterrorism. At the Prague Summit in 2002, he said, agreement was reached on strategic policy and guidance, whereby the Alliance "must be ready to deter, disrupt, prevent and defend against terrorist attacks—outside the geographic area." Colonel Richards emphasized the importance of NATO's cooperation with non-members, such as the Istanbul Cooperation Initiative with four Gulf states and the Mediterranean Dialogue with Egypt, Israel and North Africa. "Before these nations weren't interested in multilateral action but now we can survey all Mediterranean traffic, with non-NATO cooperation," Richards said.

American authority Ian Lesser spoke of the changing patterns of international terrorism. Lesser, a senior fellow with the German Marshall Fund of the United States, pointed out that some jihadists had left Iraq and were going back to North Africa and Europe, which could be "potentially a large problem." Lesser was critical of some aspects of US counterterrorism policy. Pakistan and its nuclear arsenal, he said, could pose a much bigger problem than Iran. More resources should be devoted to the nuclear threat. It was a mistake to make counterterrorism drive foreign policy, and risk alienating people. In conclusion, he suggested we should see terrorism "in terms of containment rather than victory."

Another American speaker, Michael E. O'Hanlon, senior fellow at the Brookings Institution declared that since the attacks of 11 September 2001, "a good deal has been done to improve the safety of Americans and other westerners, not only in the offensive war on terror abroad but in protecting the homeland as well." He pointed out that air travel is much safer, many countries have agreed to better regulate sales of surface-to-air missiles, intelligence sharing has improved and the share of FBI resources devoted to counterterrorism has doubled. Suspicious ships entering US waters are screened more frequently. Hundreds of millions of doses of antibiotics and smallpox vaccine have been stockpiled and oversight rules have been tightened on labs working with biological materials. Important bridges and tunnels are protected by police and National Guard forces under terrorism alerts and nuclear reactors have better security.

Spain's most prominent counterterrorist specialists shook up the assembly with accusations that the United States has failed to share terrorism intelligence with its Spanish ally. In his address on "Spain's Strategy for Facing Terror," Fernando Reinares, director of the program on Global Terrorism at the Elcano Royal Institute in Madrid, declared that Spanish police complain of "a lack of reciprocity … that they give more than they get" from American intelligence counterparts. Reinares pointed out that Al Qaeda had Spain in its sights long before the war in Iraq. He recalled that Mohammed Al Suri (also known as Setmariam) had set up an Al Qaeda cell in Spain the fall of 1991 and members of the Hamburg cell had met in Spain prior to 11 September. "11 March (the Madrid train bombings of 2004) was not the work of a local terrorist cell," Reinares stressed, "but part of a dismantled Al Qaeda group and the GICM (an affiliate, the Moroccan Islamic Combatant Group)."

The Spanish counterterrorism specialist stressed that Spain had "a good anti-terrorist system" prior to the 2004 Madrid attacks, but it was really "an anti-ETA system." There was an urgent need to improve the scope of intelligence and correct errors, Reinares noted. Today there are more than 1000 police speaking foreign languages, including Urdu, and more are being trained. Another problem was rivalry among intelligence agencies, which has only now been addressed with the creation of a Center of Intelligence. He reiterated one of his favorite themes, that Spain is the only country that has been badly hit by terrorism that hasn't changed its laws. "But in post-Franco Spain," he stressed, "it's difficult to introduce laws that infringe on human rights."

The star of Spanish justice, judge Baltasar Garzón, addressed the same theme: "Cooperation with the United States was better before 2001, when it involved Communist challenges." The outspoken judge recalled that when he had asked for certain information in January 2004, he received no response from the State Department or the Justice Department. People spoke of "the confidentiality of intelligence," he said. In 2005, the magistrate was looking for the Al Qaeda militant, Al Suri (Setmariam), who had Spanish nationality and was believed to be held on an American base in the South Pacific, but he was refused access. In another case, he had heard of computer messages in Kabul that referred to two leaders of Al Qaeda in Spain. The Americans said they could not give him information on the messages, but the British sent him the computer with the messages. "It's easier to work with Europeans," he commented

American counterterrorism expert O'Hanlon acknowledged that the United States had made "two mistakes" in dealing with Spain: it needed a review process with the power to free prisoners from indefinite detention, and it should have given Garzón an answer when Al Suri was captured.

Professor José Manuel Anes, who heads the Portuguese Observatory for Security, Organized Crime and Terrorism, which sponsored the conference, gave an overall account of "Terrorist Groups that make up the Global Jihad." The Portuguese academic focused on jihadist organizations, in addition to Al Qaeda, which are located in Europe and North Africa. Those groups with a known presence in Spain, he said, included: Al Qaeda in Islamic Maghreb, the Moroccan Islamic Combatant Group, Salafiya Jihadya, Laschar e Tayyba and Jaish e Mohammed.

In the months that followed the terrorism conference, I saw Professor Anes on several occasions. As director of the quarterly magazine *Defense and Security*, Anes is one of the best informed Portuguese on international terrorism. "Most Portuguese are not aware of the danger of global jihad; they feel a world apart from Europe and even Spain," Anes told me over coffee at the Gulbenkian Foundation's cafeteria. He stressed that in Portugal, there was no trace of the radical movements found in Spain. A Moroccan barber had been arrested some time ago for collecting funds for jihad but was said to be acting alone. "We've been very lucky so far," Anes said, expressing the conviction that the terrorist threat could spread to Portugal at any time, though he agreed with the general view that Portugal's Muslim community is well integrated. "Our problem is with recent arrivals, the outsiders, particularly radicalized Asians," he conceded.

The Portuguese security expert noted that, despite considerable opposition, the government set up a Department of Homeland Security under the prime minister's office in the fall of 2008. A secretary of state for security, called by the media "a super policeman," has been put in charge of the police forces and intelligence dealing with counter-terrorism and natural catastrophes. This new agency does not include the armed forces, because the civilians basically don't want the military involved in counterterrorism, Anes stressed. Cooperation among European intelligence services is generally good, Anes said, although relations with Spain could be improved. "We need to get rid of our historical complex," he said.

"The Iberian peninsula has been called Europe's soft under-belly; and they're right; we're soft on border controls, yes, but also soft on vigilance," he acknowledged. For this reason, the Observatory organized the conference on terrorism. "It's clear we need better trans-Atlantic cooperation," he said. "It's absolutely necessary that US-EU relations be improved."

If the Iberian public appears generally disconnected from the threats of Islamic extremism, there is an invisible wall of disbelief around the Muslim community as a whole. Almost all the Muslims I have encountered are thoroughly convinced that a small group of Arabs based in a remote corner of Afghanistan would be incapable of organizing a lethal attack on the world's premier superpower like 11 September. They are equally persuaded that the West, led by the United States, is engaged in an all-out war against the Muslim world for one basic reason: to gain control of its energy resources. These are not anti-American Muslims but people who hoped that President Obama would change American policy on issues of concern to Muslims.

At the Autonomous University of Madrid in the fall of 2007, several Moroccan graduate students still questioned Osama bin Laden's "anti western" credentials, pointing out that he had received American support in the war against the Soviets in Afghanistan. "Muslims don't kill innocent people," Said Kirhlani, president of the Moroccan Students Association stressed. He also expressed the widespread doubt that the Madrid bombings were planned by a group of radical North Africans. Adil Barrada, thirty, who has obtained a doctorate in Spanish literature and plans to return to Morocco to teach, said he had read a number of articles and books raising questions about the authors of the attacks on the Twin Towers in New York as well as those on Madrid's commuter trains. "These skeptics say the United States fabricated a pretext to invade Afghanistan and Iraq," Barrada said, apparently giving them credence. "In fact, after 2001, the world changed and the Americans had found the way to control the world," he stressed.[9]

It was, however, Mansur Escudero, head of the Islamic Junta and married to an American convert, who best articulated the profound skepticism of Muslims in Spain regarding the War on Terrorism. I met him for the second time the summer of 2008 at his farmhouse at Almodóvar del Rio. He reminded me that he had originally issued a *fatwa* against Bin Laden for claiming the 11 September attacks, but added: "There have been too many lies."

"I never believed that Bin Laden was capable of coordinating that operation; he simply didn't have the capacity," Escudero said, asserting that "Bin Laden is a product of the Saudis, the CIA and Pakistan." Admitting that he didn't know who was behind the terrorist attacks, he said: "Whoever it is, they are using Islamic terrorism against Islam."[10]

The Spanish Muslim leader pointed out that numerous texts and videos on the net contend that certain global organizations have developed a strategy that "Islam is the enemy" and have tried to provoke a conflict, even before the fall of communism. According to these sources, "big economic powers" have used the War on Terrorism as a justification to gain control of oil in Iraq, Kuwait and Saudi Arabia. Other videos attribute statements to the US Association of Scientists alleging that the fall of the World Trade Center was an act of "controlled demolition," he noted. "I believe there was a conspiracy behind 11 September, even though anyone who questions the events is discredited," Escudero said. As for the Madrid attacks, Escudero was adamant: "11 March was not Islamic terrorism. The bombers were petty criminals, police informants, traffickers, not even practicing Muslims, who were used by others. I have said before, this deed had nothing to do with Islam; it was of no benefit to Muslims and only served to stir new Morophobia." He insisted there were no extreme Islamist groups active in Spain, no zealot imams, no radical literature. "The internet is easy to use and there's no control but the videos are about Chechnya and Bosnia not attacks in Iberia," he stressed.

Portuguese Muslims are less prone to indulge in conspiracy theories but equally persuaded that a small group of Arabs in Afghanistan could not conceive and carry out such a complex attack as 11 September. Muslim convert Raúl Braga Pires said too many questions had been raised about 11 September online. "From my perspective, both Osama and Saddam were controlled by the CIA and I do not know how they became American enemies," the graduate student from Oporto University remarked. "The Americans had their own agenda; maybe they knew about Osama's plans and let it happen."[11]

After the reports of the Barcelona plot and the detention of suspects from Portugal, I called on Sheikh Munir at the Central Mosque. "We don't have radical groups in our community," the sheikh repeated several times during our conversation. "All our imams are moderate," he said, adding that he meets every month with the preachers. He acknowledged, however, that some smaller prayer halls were not controlled.[12]

The Portuguese Muslim cleric admitted that there could be problems with "outsiders." He disclosed that a few years back a radical Islamist leader had come from England and attempted to establish a cell in Lisbon, but the local Muslim community had rejected him. More recently, in the wake of the Spanish allegations of a terrorist threat from members of Tablighi Jamaat, a delegation of Tabligh scholars from Spain was barred from the annual congress in Lisbon. "We didn't know them and we are trying to avoid trouble," he said candidly.

Only late in 2010 with the release of the controversial WikiLeaks documents, was there evidence of how serious the American embassy in Madrid considered the threat of Islamic radicals in Spain. The Madrid daily *El País*, considered close to the Socialist government, was the only newspaper in Spain given direct access to the WikiLeaks releases and published the most relevant ones in English. American diplomatic dispatches of 2005 portrayed Spain as an "active front in the War on Terror." A cable from September 2005 emphasized that "Spain is both a significant target of Islamic terrorist groups and a major logistical hub."[13] Included is a lengthy history of so-called Islamic terrorism in the country, starting with the 1985 bombing near Torrejón Airbase outside Madrid attributed to Islamic Jihad that killed eighteen people and wounded eighty-two. The embassy noted that the first Islamic terrorist organization was founded in the late 1980s by Syrian Muslim Brothers, among them Setmariam, who reportedly raised funds for terrorism through Moroccan criminals engaged in fraud, robbery and theft of mobile phones. The movement was later reinforced by radical Algerians, Salafi Moroccans and South Asian extremists. The cable emphasizes that since 11 September and the dismantling of the Muslim Brotherhood network, Moroccans have been "in the forefront of the jihadist community in Spain … providing an ample supply of poor alienated young men and access to funds from drug trafficking and other illegal activities."

Reporting on active terrorist groups in Spain, the US embassy names some organizations which have been dismantled, and fails to include South Asian groups. Here is the sketchy American list:

– Syrians linked to Al Qaida and other organizations inspired by Al Qaida, but not led by it.
– the Moroccan Islamic Combat Group, with connections to the Madrid train bombing.
– the Algerian Salafist Group for Call and Combat supporting global jihadi causes.
– Ansar al Islam, which recruited suicide bombers for Iraq but was dismantled in June 2005.
– Salafiya Jihadya, Moroccan veterans of the anti Soviet Union war in Afghanistan.
– Hizbullah, a small presence, not considered a terrorist organization by the European Union.

The same cable quotes the Spanish police as saying there are "at least 300 active Islamist radicals" and counterterrorism expert Fernando Reinares's estimate of "as many as 1000 extremists." Spain faces a "long struggle against Islamic militants" the US embassy predicted.

A classified cable, dated 2 October 2007, stressed that Spanish and US authorities have identified Cataluña as a "major Mediterranean center of radical Islamist activity." It said the US has proposed the creation of a "counterterrorism and law enforcement hub in Barcelona." The proposal suggests that the US consulate general in Barcelona could become a platform for a multi-agency, jointly coordinated counterterrorism, anticrime and intelligence center to work with Spain in combating what was described as "the target-rich environment of terrorist and criminal activities centered in the region."[14]

Neither Spain nor the United States has commented on the information in the cables. However, *El País* counterterrorism expert José María Irujo remarked in a videotape, "The US is obsessed by the effervescence of jihadism in Cataluña."[15] He goes on to write that, according to the secret documents, the decision to set up the agency against terrorism and organized crime was taken in October 2007 and the center was operative two years later. Irujo notes that another classified cable of 10 March 2009, again focuses on Cataluña, emphasizing the effort to increase the activity of the multi-agency spy center "which has been set up in the Consulate in Barcelona'."[16]

Official Spanish sources made no mention to me of a "US-Spanish spy center" in Barcelona, although they confirmed that anti-terrorism collaboration between the two countries has improved in recent years. They indicated that the reports were misleading. On the other hand, these sources pointed out that anti-terrorism cooperation with France had begun in the 1980s over Basque problems, and later over Islamic extremists, and was now "total."

At the end of 2010, Spain's vice president and minister of interior, Alfredo Pérez Rubalcaba, made it clear that Spain was fully engaged in the fight against Islamic extremists. In a closed-door session with parliamentary leaders, Rubalcaba reportedly said that terrorism by radical Muslims had replaced ETA as Spain's "number one security threat."[17] This was not, however, a signal to launch a witch hunt against radical Muslims in Spain. Instead, the minister noted the escalation of jihadist activity in the Sahel south of the Sahara, which he said has become a sanctuary for Al Qaida's North African operations and a source of possible attacks on Spain. He took pains not to magnify the threat and stressed that the security alert for Spanish forces was four on a scale of one to eight; lower that of other European countries.

Madrid's *ABC* warned of the growing presence in northern Spain of *salafis*, whom it described as followers of "the most extreme current of Islam." *ABC* noted that in 2010, ten *salafi* congresses had been held in Spain, compared to only one in 2008. The newspaper added that seventy to eighty imams from Morocco and Algeria who preach in prayer halls in Cataluña and the Basque country were known by security services for their "radical discourse."[18]

While there is no doubt that the number of radical Muslims has grown in Spain as elsewhere, all of my contacts insisted that this is not a clash of civilizations but rather the threat from an extremist fringe. These *marginaux* are fed by external events, misunderstandings, faulty information and prejudices which have led to a state of growing tension between Muslims and non-Muslims. In fact, it is rather remarkable that the Iberian public has reacted with such restraint to threats and other provocations from Islamic extremists.

10

JEWISH ROOTS

Long before Muslims returned to present-day Iberia, Jews had begun to trickle back. Despite painful memories of the Inquisition, burnings at the stake and forced conversions and exile, some Jews seized the earliest opportunity to return to their roots in Sefarad, as they called the peninsula. So much has been written about Jewish history in Spain and Portugal that I will provide just a brief background to the current situation.

The Jewish presence in Iberia is said to date back to about 800 BC, when Greeks and small numbers of Jews set up trading posts along the Mediterranean coast and some inland rivers. The first significant influx of Jews came after Rome conquered Jerusalem in 70 AD, leading many Jews to settle in the far reaches of the empire. Under Roman rule, the Jews of Hispania (as Iberia was known) had prospered. Then in the fourth century AD, Vandals and other Germanic tribes invaded the peninsula. By the fifth century, the Visigoths had taken over the remains of the Roman Empire, opening a strife-ridden period in which Jews and other peoples of Iberia fared poorly. Historian Stanley Payne states: "To most of the population, the conquest was represented as a liberation."[1] The new Muslim conquerors often named leaders of the non-threatening Jewish community to positions of responsibility over the Christian majority. A prime example from the eleventh century is Samuel Ibn Nagrila, better known as the Nagid or head of Granada's Jewish community, and a gifted poet in both Hebrew and Arabic, who was appointed prime minister of the Muslim kingdom and commander of its army. In fact, Jews exercised many influential roles in the Muslim courts and society, as physicians, astronomers, cartographers, financiers, tax experts and artisans. By most accounts, the Jewish minority enjoyed relative security and prosperity in the Muslim kingdoms for a long period, free of the discriminatory legislation that prevailed in much of Europe during the Middle Ages. But by the thirteenth century, the era of tolerance had declined with conflicts between the advancing Christian forces and the Moroccan tribesmen, who had come to aid the embattled Muslim kingdoms of Al Andalus. The fourteenth century was a time of drought, hunger, plagues and hardship, particularly for the Jewish minority. While some Muslim monarchs continued to protect their Jewish subjects, the Christian masses became increasingly intolerant of well-to-do Jews, favored by the Muslim courts. Violent incidents occurred between Jews and Christians, at times instigated by members of the clergy, who portrayed the Jewish community as the root of the peninsula's evils. As is generally known, the fall of the last Muslim kingdom at Granada in 1492 also meant an end to the brilliant Jewish community of Al Andalus. With the victorious Christian Reconquista, Spain's Catholic monarchs, King Ferdinand and Queen Isabella, ordered the expulsion of all Jews, granting them four months in which to leave. Thus, thousands of Jews fled to Portugal with their skills and their wealth, and were initially well received. British authority on the Inquisition, Henry Kamen, says as many as 120,000 Spanish Jews sought refuge in the neighboring kingdom "to become about one-fifth of the total population."[2] Later, however, when Portuguese King Manuel I sought to marry the oldest daughter of the Spanish monarchs, his bid was accepted only on condition that Portugal expel all heretics, Muslims and Jews. Thus in December 1496, the Portuguese king issued his expulsion decree, giving Jews and Muslims ten months in which to convert to Christianity or go into exile. Reluctant to lose the valuable Jewish community, King Manuel tried to convert Jews by force, closing the ports and sending hundreds of Jewish children to Portugal's island colony of São Tomé off the coast of Africa. Those Jews who accepted nominal conversion were given another twenty years to adapt to their new faith.

No one knows how many Sephardim were expelled from Spain and Portugal, how many were converted by force, how many continued to practice their religion in secret and how many perished during the Inquisition, which lasted some 300 years. Estimates of the number of Jews to quit Spain after the 1492 expulsion range between 165,000 and 400,000, according to Kamen.[3] Statistics for the victims of the

Spanish Inquisition are generally piecemeal by region. Reliable estimates suggest that some 4,000 people were burned at the stake by
1520 (including Muslims and Protestants).[4] Of 150,000 *conversos* who
went on trial from 1550 to 1800, some 3,000 were put to death by the
Inquisition.[5] Historians estimate 80,000 Jews left Portugal during the
expulsions, but the majority remained, accepting conversion to Catholicism. The death toll of New Christians by *auto da fé* in Portugal was
put at 1,387 in the period from 1543 to 1684.[6] A recent study, *The
Persecution of the Jews and Muslims of Portugal*, offers an intriguing
comparison: "In Portugal, it was the Jews who were forced to convert
and the Muslims who were expelled whereas in the rest of the Iberian
Peninsula, it was the Jews who were expelled and the Muslims who
were forced to convert."[7]

What is certain is that Iberian Jews suffered persecution at the hands
of Christian rulers and many, forced to leave their place of birth, were
dispersed around the world, to the benefit of their new homelands.
Those with money went to Europe—England, Italy and, particularly,
Holland—and were among the early settlers of New York. Others with
lesser means went to Morocco, the Ottoman Empire, and Spanish and
Portuguese territories in Latin America.

I began my tour of Portugal's Jewish community at Lisbon's synagogue, named Shaaré Tikfa ... the Gates of Hope. Inaugurated in
1904, it was the first Jewish temple built in the country since the forced
conversions of 1497, the expulsions and the long struggle to regain recognition of their rights. It is a handsome oyster-colored building with
stone trim, set back discreetly behind a high wall in Lisbon's modern
business district. At the beginning of the twentieth century, only Catholic churches were allowed to have direct access to the street. On the
inside wall, commemorative plaques honor prominent members of the
Jewish community and a few notable Portuguese supporters. Among
the latter are Aristide Sousa Mendes, former consul in Bordeaux, who
disobeyed Salazar's order to refuse visas to Jews and "other undesira-
bles" in 1940, and thereby saved the lives of more than 30,000 people.
The wall also bears the names of the former president, Mário Soares,
who in 1989 publicly demanded pardon for the Inquisition and other
atrocities against Jews, and his successor, Jorge Sampaio, who in 2004
attended the inauguration of a synagogue for the Crypto-Jewish community of Belmonte, which had worshipped in secret for 500 years.

"Jews wanted to return to Portugal because it was their land, where
their ancestors were buried," says Samuel Levy, former president of

Lisbon's Jewish Community. In his late 70s, Levy is a retired economist from a major Portuguese holding company, who traces his family back to the Inquisition and even before. His family's story encapsulates the long odyssey of Portugal's Jewish Diaspora.[8]

"My grandfather fourteen times removed, Mair Halevi, was a merchant born in Lisbon in 1465. When Spain pressured King Manuel to expel all unconverted Jews, Halevi left Lisbon in 1510 for the Portuguese trading post of Safi in Morocco. Bearing contracts from King Manuel to deal in textiles, Halevi got along well with the Portuguese Governor of Safi and served him as an interpreter. Sometime later, Halevi was detained and hanged by the Moroccan king, presumably for his close cooperation with the Portuguese authorities. His son and grandson, however, were allowed to continue operating their concession. After Portugal abandoned Safi in 1541, the Halevis moved to Tetuan in northern Morocco, where many Jewish and Muslim exiles from Spain were concentrated, and some Halevis became judges in the Jewish court. When the British fleet captured Gibraltar in 1704, Jews were welcome to settle in the territory. My family went there to be closer to Portugal. Finally, my great great great grandfather, Moses Levy, a shipowner and grain merchant in Gibraltar, was authorized by Prince-Regent Don João VI (in voluntary exile in Brazil) to return to Lisbon in 1807. Levy received this special permission thanks to a brother-in-law, Isaac Aboab. It is through the Aboabs that we are related to the former president, Jorge Sampaio, whose grandmother converted to Catholicism. Although the Inquisition was extinguished in Portugal in 1821, some Levys remained abroad. Moses Levy's son, Isaac, returned to Tetuan to study the Torah and established a Yeshiva there. My grandfather, Joshua Levy, was born in Gibraltar, served as honorary consul of the Bey of Tunis and wrote three books on the Kabbalah. My grandmother, Donna Benoliel de Levy, founded the Portuguese Welfare Association in Lisbon in 1865 and later opened a Jewish hospital, which would help refugees in Portugal during World War II. Their son, Solomon, my father, was born in Lisbon but kept his British nationality. My mother is a Sequerra, whose family goes back even before the Inquisition and moved from Portugal to London to Gibraltar to Portugal. But it would take too long to tell the story of that side of the family…" Levy did tell me about two cousins on his mother's side, Samuel and Joel Sequerra, who signed transit documents for some 70,000 Jews escaping from the Nazis during World War II. The Sequerras were sent to northern Spain by the American Joint Distribution Committee to help refugees crossing the Pyrenees reach safety. They acted as representatives of the Portuguese Red Cross since the American Joint "was not accepted" by the Spanish authorities.

Jews were not allowed to stay in Portugal but were sent on to Palestine, Australia, Mexico, Cuba, the United States and Canada. That way the lives of 100,000 Jews were saved."

Emphasizing the importance of Soares' denunciation of past injustices towards Jews, Levy says the Jewish community today is well integrated and has excellent relations with the government and local Christians and Muslims. "Our problem is there are only 500 to 1000 Jews left in all Portugal," he said with sad resignation. "All my family is outside and I am the last of the line in Portugal."

In fact, Portugal's Jewish community has a greater projection today than its numbers would imply because of leaders like Esther Mucznik. When we met at the synagogue, Mucznik was giving an impassioned speech to a group of Jewish visitors from France. She spoke in French but would have been just as effective in English or Portuguese. A vibrant woman with long auburn hair and hazel eyes, Mucznik was born in Lisbon of a mother from Warsaw and a father from Ukraine via Galicia. She studied sociology at the Sorbonne, married a Portuguese journalist (non-Jewish) and raised two daughters in the Jewish faith. She is currently vice president of Lisbon's Jewish Community, writes a column for Portugal's newspaper *Público* and several magazines, teaches a course at Lisbon's Catholic University, was co-founder of the Association of Jewish Studies and the Abrahamic Forum of Portugal, and is the Jewish representative on the National Committee for Religious Freedoms.[9]

One of Mucznik's most important projects is the Portuguese translation of *Tell it to Your Children: A Book on the Holocaust in Europe 1933–1945*, with funding from the Portuguese government, which assured its distribution to all public schools. Surveys have shown that Portuguese students know very little about the persecution of Jews on their doorstep. The Portuguese edition of the book includes a brutally frank quotation from a spokesperson for Salazar's national socialist trade union movement: "There is no Jewish problem in Portugal. To defend the race, this problem was resolved like the solution of Hitler's Germany today. Since the time of Dom Manuel I, there has been no need to fight against the sons of Israel."

For a long time, Mucznik tried to get the Lisbon city hall to put up a memorial to mark the 500th anniversary of the Lisbon Massacre, of which most Portuguese have little or no knowledge, but the time was never right. The ugly incident of 1506 is engraved on the memory of Portuguese Jews and demonstrates how precarious was the position of the New Christians, at the mercy of Roman Catholic zealots and a superstitious public. Troubled by severe drought and an outbreak of the plague, Lisboners, praying for help in the Church of São Domingos, claimed to witness a bright light on the Crucifix and tears in the eyes of the Virgin. A New Christian who contested the miracle was murdered by the worshippers. Later, members of the clergy were said to have instigated the crowd to commit more violence with shouts of "Death to the Jews" and "Death to the New Christians." Portugal's first pogrom ended in the murder of some 2,000 Jews, held responsible for all of the country's vicissitudes, according to Portuguese historians. King Manuel punished the leading perpetrators and renewed his pledge that the New Christians would not be molested for sixteen years. But many New Christians were skeptical, and thus began the first exodus of Portuguese Jews.

In view of the massacre and all the other incidents, I again asked: why would Jews return to Portugal after so much suffering? "Jews had been happy here in the past," Mucznik responded. "They were very respected, enjoyed complete liberty of worship, were relatively well-off, and served in key positions, and they certainly lived better here than elsewhere in Europe." More optimistic than her colleague Samuel Levy, Mucznik estimates there are about 1,500 Jews in Portugal, including some fifty Brazilians who came in the late 1990s and early 2000s. She is convinced there would be more Jews if conversion were not so difficult. "The process of conversion before the Rabbinical Tribunal is so long that many people give up. We need people. This is our drama. We can't continue to have a ghetto mentality. Judaism needs to open up. Many people feel Jewish. Let them come." Mucznik noted that in the 1991 Portuguese census, some 6,000 people said they were Jewish.

Mery Ruah is wife of Joshua Ruah, prominent urologist and former president of Lisbon's Jewish Community, a busy mother and grandmother, and a leader in her own right. Co-founder with Muzcnik of the Portuguese Association of Jewish Studies, Mery Ruah has done much to restore Portuguese Judaism to its place as a historical center of the Jewish Diaspora. Her activism dates back to the eve of 1992, when

Spain organized elaborate ceremonies to commemorate the Fifth Centenary of the Expulsion of the Jews and "totally ignored Portugal."[10]
Israel's ambassador to Lisbon, Colette Avital, suggested that something
should be done to present the role of Portuguese Jews in the Diaspora
and turned the mission over to Mery Ruah. Despite some local "resistance," she organized a two-month-long blockbuster exposition on
"Portugal's Jews and the Diaspora" at the Gulbenkian Museum, with
1000 people at the opening. Since then Ruah, who is treasurer of the
Jewish Studies Association, has organized numerous conferences,
debates and study tours around Portugal, Spain, Israel, Morocco and
as far as India and Poland—wherever the Sephardim struck roots.

Born in Lisbon of a mother from former Spanish Morocco and
father from Istanbul of Russian origin, Mery married Joshua Ruah, a
childhood friend whose family also came from Morocco. At first she
worked as secretary for her husband and later for the Urology Institute. "We are Portuguese," she said, "we feel Portuguese." Emphasizing that the Portuguese were "different" from other Europeans, she
suggested there was a much greater *convivência* (sense of companion-
ship) perhaps because of Portugal's inter-racial policies in the former
colonies. She acknowledged however that there is "a political problem" nowadays, not so much with the extreme right, which has no
influence, but the left. (I was to hear similar complaints from Jews in
Spain.) "The Portuguese left doesn't make a difference between Jews
and Israelis. They confuse the two and tell us: 'You did such and such
a thing to the Palestinians...' We don't agree with all Israeli politics,
and certainly not the fence, but we defend Israel."

Like other Jewish leaders, Ruah is worried about the future of the
tiny Portuguese community and has pinned her hopes on immigration.
"There are people of the Portuguese overseas nation who are languish-
ing for their country. We believe more Jews would like to emigrate to
Portugal from Brazil. There are still Jews in Amsterdam who say their
prayers in Portuguese and Jews in Istanbul who speak *Hakitie*, which
is a mix of Portuguese, Hebrew and Turkish. Many Jewish Moroccans
wanted to come to Portugal in the 1960s during the unsettled times
after independence. Ruah's dream is the creation of a Jewish museum
in the Portuguese capital. "Lisbon's Jewish community has rich collec-
tions of memorabilia, which should be put on public display ... like
they did in Belmonte," she stressed.

The saga of the Marranos, or Crypto-Jews, of Belmonte in north-
eastern Portugal, who practiced their faith in hiding for centuries, has

captured imaginations of Jews and non-Jews around the world. In recent years, Belmonte's Marranos—forced converts, in Hebrew—have cautiously emerged and publicly embraced their Jewish faith, but some are said to be reluctant to give up their own traditions. Also, it is believed there are other pockets of Crypto-Jews in rural Portugal, but no one knows how many. Historians generally believed that after Dom Manuel's Expulsion Order of 1496, many Jews left the country, and those who remained as New Christians tried to fade into the overwhelmingly Catholic society. Marranos say that they never left their villages but maintained their Jewish traditions and rituals in secret, while living the life of the Catholic community around them. Recent research substantiates the Marranos' testimony. Maria Antonieta Garcia, who heads the Center of Judaic Studies in the northern city of Covilhã, has uncovered documents from the Inquisition which record the presence of inquisitors in Belmonte investigating cases of alleged heretics throughout the period, from the sixteenth to the eighteenth century. The absence of religious leaders, the lack of holy texts and the network of inter-community cultural exchanges could have led to the assimilation of the Jews of Belmonte, according to Garcia. The miracle, she says, is that they resisted, perpetuated their rituals and created a specific religion which they lived clandestinely.

It is generally agreed that Samuel Schwarz, a Jewish mining engineer from Poland "discovered" the Crypto-Jews of Belmonte, when he was working in the tin mines of nearby Gaia. Schwarz recounts how he met the Marranos, won their confidence and joined their religious celebrations in his book, *New Christians in Portugal in the XXth Century*, published in 1925. This was a major revelation for Jews around the world, who generally believed that the Crypto-Jews had all died with the Inquisition or been absorbed by the Catholic society. A leading Portuguese figure who embraced the cause of the Marranos in the wake of Schwarz' revelations was a highly decorated army captain, Artur Carlos Barros Basto. Born in a New Christian family, Barros Basto converted to Judaism and took the name of Ben Rosh. Assuming the mission to wean the Crypto-Jews back to orthodoxy, in 1927 Barros Basto founded the Rosh Pinah Yeshiva in Oporto, attended by many New Christians in the region. He also opened synagogues in Bragança, Covilhã and Oporto. But the times were not propitious for winning the hearts of the Marranos. Salazar had come to power and established his authoritarian state and national socialism concepts. With the advance of Nazism and anti-Semitism throughout Europe, Portugal's Crypto-Jews sought cover once more.

Mery Ruah and her husband were among the first members of Lisbon's Jewish community to establish relations with the Crypto-Jews of Belmonte in the late 1960s. This was a time when Catholics rejected the Marranos because they claimed to be Jewish, and some Orthodox Jews were concerned because they had been baptized and married in the Catholic Church, she explained. "I remember a small group came from Belmonte in 1964 to see how the Lisbon community observed Yom Kippur, and they were very suspicious of everyone," Ruah recalls. She said she met with members of the community again in 1968 in Madrid for the inauguration of the synagogue, "and that was when our friendship started."

My first glimpse into the secretive world of Iberia's Crypto-Jews was through Laura Cesana's absorbing book, *Jewish Vestiges in Portugal*.[11] Born in Rome, Cesana grew up in the United States and has a master's degree in economics from the University of Rome and in visual arts from Boston. She has lived in Portugal since the mid-1970s and is a professor of visual arts at Lisbon's Teachers' Training College. With a grant from the Gulbenkian Foundation, she spent two years researching the Jews of Portugal. Through words and artwork, Cesana describes the customs and practices of Jewish origin, which are still prevalent among Crypto-Jews. Among these traditions is the eating of unleavened bread during the Christian Holy Week, making sausage with poultry instead of pork, and putting a broom behind the door to encourage unwelcome guests to leave.

For some time, I had been reluctant to join the rush to "discover" Belmonte. I felt that the Marranos, who had struggled so long to preserve their faith in secret, deserved the right to privacy. Now, however, since the community has its synagogue and museum, I felt they must be ready to receive visitors. A visiting friend from New York, interested in the story of Crypto-Jews, provided the pretext for a visit to Belmonte in the summer of 2007. The 300 kilometer journey from Lisbon to Belmonte and the castle towns of the Estrela Mountains, which used to be a major expedition, turned out to be a delightful excursion on Portugal's recently built super-highways.

And unlike the past, the townspeople of Belmonte greeted foreign visitors warmly, confidently. Did we want to see the synagogue, they asked? It would be best to park on the square near the castle and walk down the narrow cobble-stoned street to the temple, easily recognized by the large red door. We found the synagogue without any trouble, a whitewashed building with orange tile roof and a large sign in Hebrew and Portuguese that said: Sinagoga Bet Eliahu. But it was closed. A passerby, who introduced himself as the deputy mayor of Belmonte, offered to drive us to the Jewish Museum, where Miguel Vaz, the young man in charge of the museum, volunteered to call the leader of the local Jewish community and a meeting was arranged at the synagogue. Meanwhile we visited the first Jewish museum in Portugal, built and run by the Belmonte municipality. Opened in 2005, the museum received some 11,000 visitors the following year. It was a tribute from the town of Belmonte "to Jewish history and culture in Portugal" and dedicated "to the victims of Inquisition," according to a pamphlet published by the town council. The main collection came from Portuguese historian Adriano Vasco Rodrigues, and includes a particularly fine Torah, several menorahs, Shabbat lamps, a Mezuzah or religious scroll, and other items from Crypto-Judaism practices.

"The rabbi is in Israel on holiday but will be back in two weeks' time," the community leader, Abílio Henriques, said, explaining why the synagogue was closed. Senhor Abílio is a burly businessman of sixty-eight, co-owner with his brother of a factory which produces jeans and men's trousers. We sat at the entrance to the temple, where Senhor Abílio could watch out for visitors, while he told us about Belmonte's Jewish life. The synagogue was built in 1996 by the Azoulay family in honor of the late Rabbi Eliahou Azoulay Zal from Morocco, but now the community has problems raising the money to pay for salaries, maintenance and other expenses. "It's very difficult for me as president of the community. We get visitors from all over—the United States, Holland, France and Spain—and some of the Americans and other foreigners give us contributions. But the community in Lisbon doesn't give us anything. That's why we have to ask a three-euro admission fee."

Senhor Abílio acknowledged there were only 130 people in Belmonte's Jewish community, but added that the population was "stable." Responding to my question about the future, he said firmly, "The community will continue; there are forty children and they will stay and find jobs in tourism." Then he added with special pride: "Seven or eight of our youths have already learned Hebrew."[12]

But I wondered how long Belmonte would be able to keep its Jewish sons, now that they had been recognized and integrated into the society. One of the young men I met during my visit confided to me that he was in contact with an American friend, who had told him how to get a visa for the United States. "I want to leave and get a good job and a wife; there are so few Jewish girls here," he said, admitting he hadn't told his parents of his plans. I concluded that it would be difficult for even the most entrenched traditions to resist the inevitable changes from the completion of the E-80 highway from Lisbon to Salamanca and points north, Burgos and France.

In the spring of 2008, Lisbon's fragile Jewish community saw the realization of a dream: the memorial to the 2000 victims of the 1506 massacre. On São Domingos Square in the heart of the capital, where the slaughter occurred, the Jewish Community has placed an austere semi-sphere decorated with the Star of David and an inscription in Portuguese that states: "In memory of thousands of Jewish victims of intolerance and religious fanaticism assassinated in the massacre begun 19 April 1506 in this square. 5266–5766," followed by a verse from the Book of Job in Portuguese: "O earth, cover not my blood, and let my cry find no resting place."[13] And on the northern edge of the square, a mural commissioned by Lisbon's city hall bears the words: "Lisbon City of Tolerance" in thirty-four different languages.

Finally, the winter of 2010, Portugal demonstrated that it was prepared to embrace its Jewish heritage as part of the national identity. This was the main message to come out of the First International Festival of the Sephardic Memory, held in the rugged frontier region of the Serra da Estrela, or Mountains of the Star. The seven-day festival was organized by a group of towns, villages, Jewish communities and the Serra da Estrela tourism office, under the patronage of the president of Portugal with the presence of the secretary of culture and the ambassador of Israel.

The welcome reception was held at the Jewish Museum of Belmonte, and gave me the opportunity to see how the community had fared since my visit three years earlier. To all appearances, Belmonte and its Jewish citizens were flourishing. The once secretive village has been transformed into a thriving town of 4,000 inhabitants that exudes energy. The Jewish Museum has received 79,000 visitors since its opening in 1996. There are now five restaurants, plus a superb new *pousada*, or inn, in the thirteenth century convent of Our Lady of Hope. The medieval Jewish quarter and thirteenth century castle and church of Santiago have been spruced up. And a spectacular Museum to the Discovery of the New World was opened in 2009 to honor native son Pedro Álvares Cabral, who is said to have discovered Brazil. The Jewish community numbers 150, or a slight increase since my last visit. There's a permanent rabbi and a new community leader, António Mendes, who told me that a majority of his constituents now welcomes visitors and thinks that the festival will have a positive impact. "Today we have good relations with our Christian neighbors," he stressed, adding that there have even been mixed marriages "unfortunately."[14]

The main event of the festival was a three-day congress of Portuguese and foreign scholars in the medieval fortress city of Guarda, which had boasted a dynamic Jewish community until the expulsion order in 1496. The theme of the congress, attended by some 150 people, was a belated homage to two towering figures of Portugal's Jewish history: Aristide Sousa Mendes, the Portuguese consul in Bordeaux who saved so many Jews during World War II, and Dona Grácia Nasi, a Jewish woman who helped many Jews escape Portugal and became a leader in international banking and trade in the sixteenth century. Jorge Patrão, the head of the Serra da Estrela Turismo, announced that Guarda would be the center of a new Network of Portuguese Jewish Sites, similar to Spain's Routes of Sepharad, launched in 1995.

* * *

Traveling around Spain in the summer of 2007, I was impressed by how many *juderías* and other vestiges of the Jewish past I encountered—yet how few Spanish Jews. The ancient Jewish quarters are located mostly in towns and cities of southern Spain where Jews prospered under the long Muslim rule, but also in Barcelona, Girona, Zaragoza and even in villages of Galicia in the north. The best known *juderías* are those of Seville, Córdoba and Toledo, which have been scrupulously renovated and maintained to form an integral part of the cities' historical center. Now there is a general rush by municipalities to uncover a Jewish heritage and revive the old *juderías* which, like Arab mosques and castles, have proved to be popular tourist attractions.

The Network of Spanish Jewish Quarters actively promotes cultural, tourist and scholarly programs through its website (www.redjuderias. org). The stated aim of this not-for-profit organization is to defend the urban, architectural, historical, artistic and cultural legacy of the

Sephardim in Spain. The network lists twenty-one towns or cities on its roadmap and provides a calendar of cultural events, such as Sephardim concerts and an exhibit on Jewish memory in Ávila, story telling and workshops in Girona, and a photo exhibit on "The Essence of Sefarad" in Córdoba.

In Toledo, however, there are efforts to create something different, something more than just a magnificent medieval tourist attraction, and rather an embodiment of the coexistence of Judaism, Christianity and Islam that existed in Al Andalus. The city possesses the Sefardi Museum, a rich collection depicting Jewish history in Spain in the superbly-restored fourteenth century Sinagoga del Tránsito. The thirteenth century Sinagoga de Santa María La Blanca is under restoration, as is the tenth century mosque, the Mezquita del Cristo de la Luz, nearby. The fourteenth century Mezquita de las Tornerias is being used as a handicrafts center, and the grandiose Alcázar, tenth century Arab fortress badly damaged during the civil war, is currently undergoing works to house Madrid's army museum. Dominating everything is Toledo's splendid gothic cathedral, built on the site of a Visigoth basilica, which served as the central mosque until Alfonso VI captured Toledo in 1085 and, contrary to his pledge, destroyed the mosque. This remarkably well preserved city is therefore an appropriate backdrop for attempts to revive "the spirit of three cultures."

It was the International Jewish Sefarad Committee of 1992 that decided to reopen Toledo's School of Translators as part of the commemorations of the 500th anniversary of the expulsion decree. The school had been an important center of learning in the Middle Ages, grouping prominent scholars in the Hebrew, Arabic and Latin languages. Another recent initiative was the establishment of the Toledo International Centre for Peace, whose declared purpose is to make a Spanish contribution to the Middle East peace process. I tried to arrange visits to the Translators' School as well as the Peace Center, but was told that no one was available to show me around at the time of my visit—which coincided with the city's important Roman Catholic holiday, Corpus Christi, when most of the city closes down for a week of religious processions and other festivities.

Frustrated, I resorted to the internet and learned that the Translators School of Toledo (www.uclm.es/escueladetraductores) had reopened in 1994 as a research center of the University of Castilla-La Mancha. It is located in the fourteenth century Mudejar-style palace of King Don

Pedro, and includes a library specialized in documentation on Toledo in the Middle Ages. Initially the school aimed to train translators from Arabic and Hebrew into Spanish. Miguel Hernando de Larramendi, professor of Arabic and Islamic studies at the University of Castilla-La Mancha and director of several courses at the Translators School, responded personally to my email query. More than 900 students, the majority from Spain, but also from Morocco, Lebanon, Algeria and Egypt, have completed the course for specialists in Arabic-Spanish translation. He added that the school plans to broaden its activities to include immigration management in schools, intercultural research and teacher training courses in Moroccan language and culture. He acknowledged, however, that no seminars in Hebrew were scheduled for the 2007–08 school year, for lack of applications from a minimum of fifteen students per seminar. I later learned that the 2010–11 semester opened in Toledo with forty-two students in Arabic and seventeen in Hebrew.

Subsequently I visited the website of the Toledo International Centre for Peace (www.toledopax.org), which reveals that the institution was founded in June 2004 under the auspices of FRIDE (the Foundation for International Relations and External Dialogue), a Madrid-based independent research center. The Toledo center's interest in the Middle East peace process is evident, judging from its board members, vice presidents Shlomo Ben Ami, a former Israeli foreign minister, and Nabil Shaath, former negotiator of the Palestine Liberation Organization. The Spanish government is represented by foreign minister Miguel Ángel Moratinos, listed as a trustee. But there was virtually no information on the center's current activities.

I left Toledo with a bittersweet feeling of letdown. José María Contreras, who headed the government's Foundation for Pluralism at the time, acknowledged that there is not even a Jewish community in Toledo. And I certainly saw fewer Arabs there than in other Spanish cities. Toledo—the city's name still carries a mystique—remains a great museum city, but has a way to go to become that vital center of diverse faiths, arts and learning and that it once was.

Where I found a thriving Jewish community was the upscale Costa del Sol resort of Marbella, which only made its debut on Spanish maps in the 1950s. The Beth El Synagogue, an airy modern building flanked by greenery, was consecrated in 1978 and is the first Jewish temple built in Andalucía since 1492. Recently the community opened a social center in an adjacent building with a large garden. Families from around the region frequently gather at the large celebrations hall to observe Jewish festivals or the birth of a baby, a bar mitzvah or a bat mitzvah. During my visit on a Sabbath the summer of 2008, the synagogue was crowded, and there were worshippers from France. The local community had organized a Peace Festival at a nearby restaurant, where it usually celebrates weddings. The Marbella Jewish Community is made up of about 700 families, mostly elderly couples, according to the community's quarterly magazine *Focus*. The population is stable because of a continual inflow of people, mostly Moroccan-born Jews from France, drawn by the amenable climate and the atmosphere of the Costa del Sol.

"The Jewish population in Spain numbers about 40,000 and is located mainly in Madrid, Barcelona, Andalucía and Melilla," said Jacobo Israel Garzón, president of the Madrid Community and the Federation of Jewish Communities. "They are aging communities but continuing to grow, thanks to immigration from Latin America, particularly Argentina." Receiving me in his office in an elegant business quarter of the capital, Israel Garzón, a youthful sixty-five, told me that I had seen so few Jews in my travels because they are well integrated. "Spain's Jews are an immigration success story; they are professors, engineers, communications experts, economists, lawyers, accountants; they look Spanish and speak Spanish."[15]

Born in Tetuan, Morocco, in 1942, Israel Garzón has lived in Madrid since 1959. An agricultural engineer and specialist in communications, he is author of numerous books on Jews in Spain and Morocco and director of the magazine, *Raíces Revista Judía de Cultura*. One of his most important works is *Escrito en Sefarad*, which presents a fascinating gallery of outstanding Jews who have lived and worked in Spain since the end of the Inquisition and their contributions to Spanish society.[16]

Israel Garzón told me he wasn't worried about skinheads in Spain—there aren't that many and there are laws to take care of them—but like the Portuguese Jews, he was concerned about what he called "the new anti-Semitism of the Left." He emphasized: "The Spanish public and the media are increasingly anti-Israel; how can we prevent that from becoming anti-Jewish?"

Spain's Socialist officials have been openly critical of Israel, particularly the 2006 attacks on Lebanon and the assault on Gaza in 2008, but they contend that criticism of Israel is not anti-Semitism. In fact, both Socialist and conservative administrations have gone out of their way to woo Spain's Jewish community in recent years and take a more balanced position on Middle East questions. Spain, which only recognized the State of Israel in 1986 out of fear of a negative reaction from the Arab world, has been trying to play a more active role since the Madrid Conference for Peace in the Middle East on 30 October 1991. Simultaneously Madrid has sought to make amends with Spanish Jews for past injustices since the commemorations of the fifth centenary of the expulsion. On 31 March 1992, the king of Spain formally asked for pardon in a ceremony in the Madrid Synagogue. Later that year, the Spanish parliament approved an accord of cooperation between the State and the Federation of Jewish Communities of Spain. A 1995 reform of the Spanish penal code declared anti-Semitism and discrimination for anti-Semitic motives to be felonies. An accord between Madrid's Jewish Community and the Ministry of Education and Culture in 1998 provided state funding for the Jewish high school in Madrid.

While public demonstrations in favor of Palestinians have become commonplace, the Jewish Community of Madrid organized its first rally for "Peace in the Near East and Solidarity with Israeli Victims of Terrorism" only in 2002. That same year the Jewish Community also sponsored a meeting in "Solidarity with Israel," which was the first of its kind in Spain. To honor Spain's Jewish heritage, the Madrid Book Fair held a Day of the Jewish Book in June 2003 and several months later, the Museum of the City of Madrid held an exhibit on "The Sephardim from northern Morocco, a bridge with Spain." The following year, Madrid was site of various events marking the 800th anniversary of the death of the great Jewish philosopher Maimonides. Barcelona's Jewish Cinema, then in its eighth year, was held as scheduled in July 2006, despite widespread criticism of Israel's military action in Lebanon.

Of special note are the efforts to pay belated homage to the victims of the Holocaust. "The Holocaust was taboo under Franco; people here know very little about it," Mercedes Rico, the former director general of religious affairs in the Justice Ministry, told me, explaining the need for public education on the subject.[17] In January 2005, the Spanish parliament recognized for the first time the Official Day of the Holocaust and Prevention of Crimes against Humanity. The following year, official commemorations marking Holocaust Day were attended by the king and queen of Spain and members of the government. In 2007, two memorial ceremonies honored the Holocaust victims. That April, the mayor of Madrid, Alberto Ruiz-Gallardón, inaugurated the capital's first monument to the victims of the Holocaust in the presence of the Israeli ambassador and Jewish community leaders. Located in an olive grove in the new Juan Carlos I Park near the Palace of Expositions, the monument is a dramatic tribute to the victims of the Nazi rule. A column of steel shafts with clusters of wooden slats are said to represent the railroads that carried Jews on their last journey to the extermination camps. At the base of the statue lay a laurel wreath with the national colors of Spain and Israel.

Under the auspices of the Spanish Ministry of Foreign Affairs, the Casa Sefarad-Israel has nurtured the Spanish public with a constant flow of Jewish culture since its opening in 2007. This institution has become one of the most active organizations on Madrid's cultural scene. Successfully avoiding the pitfalls of propaganda, the Casa Sefarad sponsors a rich and varied program of concerts, exhibits, film showings, book presentations and conferences on a broad range of subjects, including the Middle East question.

During a liturgical ceremony preceding the inauguration of the Casa Sefarad-Israel, Grand Rabbi René-Samuel Sirat, vice president of the European Conference of Rabbis, pronounced a moving speech: "For the Sephardim around the world, the spiritual and affective ties with Spain are ambivalent. On one hand, it is the memory of exile, forced conversions and indescribable suffering endured by the Jewish community. On the other hand there is the incomparable attachment which binds the Sephardis to their second motherland after Jerusalem, second motherland to which they have given all their love and for which they have conserved one predilection: to remain faithful for five centuries to Ladino and Judezmo which cradled their infancy and allowed them to keep intact the remembrance of their spiritual heritage in the lands of Iberia … If it were necessary to prove the tenacious hope in the hearts of Sephardi Jews that a Casa Sefarad would once again open in the capital of the Spanish Kingdom, one must only recall the numerous families named Toledano who have kept as a legacy of their past life the key to their home in Toledo."

It was the answer to my much repeated question: why return?

11

THE IBERIAN MODEL

"We must be more sensitive to immigrants because we are immigrants too," Federico Mayor Zaragoza, former Spanish cabinet minister and longtime head of UNESCO, says of the recent waves of newcomers.[1] Mário Soares, former president of Portugal and a two-term euro-deputy, argues that Europe needs immigrants because of aging demographics: "We can't afford a wall or a fortress, but must reach out to our new communities, including Muslims, through intercultural dialogue."[2]

Although the two national figures no longer hold political positions, Mayor and Soares continue to speak out on the most urgent challenges confronting their countries, the Spaniard as chairman of the Foundation for a Culture of Peace and the Portuguese as head of Lisbon's Commission on Religions and the Mário Soares Foundation. Fervent Europeanists, they have co-authored a book in which they express the conviction that Iberia must play a progressive role on the European scene on major issues such as immigration. Barcelona-born Mayor writes that the Mediterranean has separated peoples too long and must become "a meeting place, a permanent forum, a constant dialogue between the peoples and cultures that surround it." Referring specifically to the Muslim states of Morocco and Mauritania, Mayor said: "We must recall that the Moors remained on the Iberian peninsula for almost eight centuries, and so they are to a large extent part of us and vice versa."[3] For the Portuguese leader, immigration is "one of the most complex problems facing the European Union today." Pointing out that European economies desperately need skilled labor, Soares wrote: "Immigrants must be accorded a status (if possible common to the European Union) that recognizes their dignity, their rights and duties as residents of the European space as well as their languages, different cultures and services to the European Union."[4]

The words of the Iberian statesmen best encapsulate the persistent efforts by Spain and Portugal to fashion what is described as a "humane approach" to two of the most contentious and inter-related issues facing Europe today, soaring immigration and the integration of growing Islamic communities. Iberians do not claim any miraculous solutions but have begun to piece together new strategies based on lessons from other Europeans and their own historical experiences. Initially, their innovative and tolerant policies appeared to gain ground despite pressures from northern neighbors for more restrictive action. But it would be foolhardy to predict the course of events in the volatile Mediterranean region.

Spain and Portugal were long known as lands of emigration, and only joined the ranks of destination-countries in the early 1970s and 1980s. The main reasons for this fundamental change were the rapid development of southern Europe, including Italy and Greece, and the tougher immigration policies of northern Europe. In fact, the Iberian states, suffering from demographic decline, tended to welcome immigrants, regardless of their status. Spain's Law on Foreigners favored Latin American immigrants because of old cultural ties, and Portugal offered preferential treatment to migrants from the Portuguese-speaking world like Brazil and former Portuguese Africa. Only in 1991, upon joining the European Union's Schengen Accord, which provided for free movement among the members, were Madrid and Lisbon obliged to establish more controls. For a time, Spain and Portugal tried to resolve the problem of a growing presence of undocumented immigrants through periodical amnesties. But other Europeans, who had resorted to similar mass legalizations earlier, were of no mind to condone any more laxity and insisted that the southerners comply with EU rules. While the Iberians have desisted from further general regularizations since 2006, they have attempted to craft a generous immigration policy—even toward those with irregular status. Spain is the only European country that allows the *sin papeles* to enroll on municipal registers. Both countries grant even undocumented immigrants the right to health care and education for their children.

"Political leaders understood that a large part of the Spanish population is opposed to a policy involving raids and mass expulsions," writes Carmen González Enriquez in her authoritative report on immigration in Spain. She notes that from 1 January 2002, to 14 June 2004, the administration issued 117,768 expulsion orders but only 32,749 (28%) were carried out. The authorities cite the cost and absence of repatriation accords as reasons for non-execution of expulsion orders, according to González. She emphasized: "Thus irregular immigration is tacitly accepted, like the underground economy. Unlike other developed countries, Spanish citizens rarely report illegal aliens, except cases of forced prostitution or harsh exploitation at work."[5]

Along with their attempts to pursue immigration-friendly policies, Spain and Portugal—relative neophytes in dealing with Muslim immigrants—have tried to develop patterns of integration that would avoid mistakes of other Europeans. Much has been written in the European press about the frustrations of second generation Muslim youths in Britain; the anger of French Muslims in crime-ridden suburbs; the exclusion of Turkish guest workers and their offspring in Germany; the anti-immigrant radicalization of the once tolerant Dutch; and the uprooting of North Africans (and gypsies) by Italy's right-wing authorities. Both Spain and Portugal have deliberately tried to avoid the creation of ethnic ghettos and parallel societies. To their credit, the Iberian governments have reacted prudently to Al Qaeda's threats, the terrorist attacks and alleged plots by Islamic extremists on European soil. While they have introduced new security measures and reinforced intra-European cooperation against global terrorism, Spain and Portugal have gone out of their way to distinguish between the majority of law-abiding Muslim communities and the radical fringe.

The two nominally Roman Catholic countries, with their long history of intolerance, have made great strides to accommodate the increasing religious diversity of their societies. As we have seen, Spain recognized the rights of the main minority religions, Protestantism, Islam and Judaism, in 1992, and has set up a Department of Pluralism and Coexistence to help integrate the religious minorities into Spanish societies. Lisbon approved a new Law of Religious Freedom in 2000, which sets forth the rights of religious minorities, including tax exemptions, the celebration of non-Catholic marriage and respect for their holidays.

It is widely held that Iberia's—and Europe's—awareness of the dual problems of rising immigration and the integration of new Muslim communities came into focus with the events of 11 September 2001. Since then, a number of European states have established tougher controls and urged their Iberian partners to do likewise. But despite the globalization of illegal immigration and renewed threats from Islamic extremists, Spain and Portugal have made a conscious effort to pursue more flexible, conciliatory policies. More and more Iberian voices are calling for greater understanding of "the other," particularly Muslims. Drowning out anti-immigration rumblings, conferences and seminars hosted by universities and non-governmental organizations (often with official support) advocate more inclusive policies towards immigrants. Intercultural dialogue and, specifically, Christian-Muslim encounters in these once insular societies have become commonplace.

Iberia's first comprehensive response to the new immigration challenge was the year-long Gulbenkian Immigration Forum, launched in March 2006 to mark the 50th anniversary of the Calouste Gulbenkian Foundation, established by the eponymous legendary Armenian immigrant and pioneer of the Iraqi oil industry. More than 100 international experts met in workshops to discuss all aspects of immigration and forms of integration. They came up with a lengthy list of recommendations for governments and civil society that covers the management of migratory movements and reception of newcomers, the role of municipalities, trade unions, political parties and immigrant associations, questions of social welfare, the integration of immigrant children and unskilled and overqualified labor, as well as relations with the countries of origin. The culmination of the forum was a two-day conference on "Immigration: Opportunity or Threat?" It was a constructive exchange with representatives of immigrant-importing and exporting countries and international agencies involved in migrations.

The Iberian contingent clearly came down on the side of immigration as an opportunity. Portugal's Socialist prime minister, José Sócrates, set the tone for the meeting when he declared "From my point of view, migrations are desirable and possible to regulate … a factor of development when regulated and controlled." He stressed that Portugal, which assumed the presidency of the European Union in 2007, did not see Europe as a fortress, but considered migrations as a positive phenomenon, particularly in view of Europe's aging population.[6]

Manuel Marín González, a major voice in Spain's ruling Socialist party and chairman of the Spanish Congress of Deputies, set out to dedramatize the debate underway in northern Europe over "the immigration threat," declaring that the mobility of peoples was "a reality of the times and a reflection of the world's problems, namely poverty and the terrible disparity between rich and poor."[7] Marín noted that immigration had increased sixfold in the last ten years and stood at 9% of the population of forty-four million. "We're very happy with this level," the deputy said. "It is a sign of success, and the Spanish miracle, like the German miracle earlier, needs labor." He stressed that Spain was changing because of immigration, with an increase in social security revenues, a fiscal surplus for the first time, more foreign weddings and an increase in births. Spain has adopted a multicultural model of integration "which is working for the time being," he said. Marín acknowledged that after the Madrid train bombings, there was concern how the public would react toward the growing Muslim community in Spain. He stressed, however, that Spaniards knew the difference between Muslim extremists and Muslim workers and "there is no problem of religion."

It was André Azoulay, advisor to the king of Morocco and member of the UN secretary general's High-level Group for the Alliance of Civilizations, who sounded the alarm about "a rupture" in the intercultural dialogue worldwide. He praised the Iberians for their approach of "calm reflection" on the immigration issue, which he said had assumed "a tone of drama and tragedy" at other European meetings. Describing himself as "an Arab-Jew involved in Jewish-Muslim relations for the past thirty years," Azoulay declared: "Since September 11, the world has made a great leap backward. Because we don't pray to the same god, there's been a breach in relationships, a regressive clash of civilizations. Religion is not the cause of the clash. The problems of Islam are political, not religious: they are Palestine, Iraq, Afghanistan." Consensus is more difficult to reach in "this culture of revenge," he emphasized.[8]

Sometime after the Gulbenkian Forum, I encountered António Vitorino, the Portuguese commissioner of the event and principal architect of Portugal's fledgling immigration policy, who told me the assembly had reached a consensus that Europe's immigration policy must be more flexible with more open admissions linked to "the capacity for integration with dignity."[9] A former European commissioner for justice and home affairs, Vitorino pointed out that other European models for the integration of immigrants were in a state of crisis; Britain's multiculturalism has resulted in "alienated communities," while France's assimilation policies haven't eliminated "discrimination at the workplace." The fifty-year-old Portuguese lawyer stressed that there is no unified European policy on immigration, no central authority to decide on admissions and each state is free to develop its own rules. "We are searching for our own way," he said, pointing out that the Spanish and Portuguese approach to immigration was "more open, less discriminatory" than that of their European partners. "In the 1960s, we were the migrants and the northern Europeans were talking about deporting undocumented Portuguese and Spaniards," Vitorino recalled.

António Luis Santos da Costa, Portugal's Minister of Interior, whose security forces are charged with defending the country's borders from illegal intruders, showed the same open attitude towards the influx of immigrants. In fact, the forty-seven-year-old cabinet minister boasted in an interview that he is a product of Portugal's colonization in India and Africa. His father was Orlando Costa, poet and playwright from Mozambique; his mother is Maria António Palla, a Portuguese Journalist.

"We can't be a fortress or an open door," remarked Costa, a leader of the Socialist Party, who later resigned to run for mayor of Lisbon. the minister pointed out that Portugal needs immigrants "mainly to do jobs Europeans don't want to do," but he insisted there must be controls. Costa said that a common European immigration policy would be "desirable" but stressed that circumstances differ radically from one European country to the next. For example, unlike Spain, Portugal isn't overwhelmed by *pateras* washing up on its shores because of North-South Atlantic wind patterns and the inhospitable Atlantic coast. Portugal, however, has a problem with Latin American, African and Asian migrants who arrive by air and East Europeans who come overland and overstay tourist visas.[10]

By the spring of 2007, the Socialist governments of the two Iberian states, which have a long history of mutual suspicion, decided it would be in their interest to coordinate immigration policies in response to increasingly inflexible trends in the rest of Europe. Spain's ambassador to Lisbon, Enrique Panés Calpe, hosted the first Hispano-Portuguese seminar to work out "An Iberian Vision of Immigration in Europe." Leading figures in immigration from the two countries met in the ambassador's residence, the rose-colored seventeenth century Palhava Palace on Lisbon's Praça da Espanha, to exchange views.[11]

Consuelo Rumi Ibáñez, Spain's secretary of state for immigration and emigration who engineered the 2005 mass legalization of irregular immigrants by winning over the labor unions and employers, declared that one of her government's main goals was a comprehensive

European immigration policy. Rumi, fifty-one, with cropped blond hair, stressed that Spain had undergone Europe's highest rate of immigration increase in a short time, with the number of foreign residents soaring to 2,200,000, or 5%, of the population in May 2007, from half a million in 1995. The Spanish official spoke of her government's efforts to manage the flow of undocumented immigrants with the help of the European Union and emphasized what has been done to integrate immigrants under the Strategic Citizenship and Integration Plan 2006–2009.

Spanish director general of integration, Estrella Rodríguez Pardo, forty-nine, who has a master's degree in social services, declared that the Integration Plan was based on the principle of equal rights and duties for all citizens and equal opportunities for immigrants and Spanish citizens. She stressed that it was a comprehensive plan involving education, housing and public health and had been drafted with the participation of civil society—university circles, businesses, local government and immigrant associations. A Fund for Integration has been raised to 200 million euros from seven million euros in 2004, with most of it going to programs of the autonomous communities, the town halls and non-governmental organizations.

For his part, Lisbon's high commissioner for refugees, Rui Marques, noted that Spain and Portugal had gone through parallel migratory cycles. The Iberian neighbors had been countries of emigration for centuries; then at the end of the twentieth century they became immigration destinations. In one decade, Portugal saw the number of immigrants quadruple, reaching 430,000 in 2005, or 4.3% of the population. Like Spain, Portugal's Plan for Integration of Immigrants had been crafted after a lengthy debate among government departments, non-governmental organizations and immigrant associations. The Spanish and Portuguese experiences, Marques suggested, "could be a reference for a global European plan on the question of integration."

Jarmela Palos, head of Portugal's Department of Foreigners and Borders (SEF), who rarely makes public statements, emphasized that cooperation with Spain on border security was "exemplary." He stressed Portugal's participation in most FRONTEX patrol operations in the Mediterranean and the Atlantic, which he called "fundamental" for the control of European borders. He declared that when Portugal assumed the presidency of the European Union, in the second half of 2007, it would seek "more practical and effective" means of dealing with immigration, raising questions of "circular immigration" or short-term labor contracts, more practical development aid for Africa and the participation of North Africa transit countries in security operations.

The shared premise of Iberians at the time, and many other Europeans, was that Europe needed immigration but it should be better regulated. Roberto Carneiro, a former conservative cabinet minister who heads Portugal's Immigration Observatory, brought out a notable study in the fall of 2007 on "Europe: the Challenge of Diversity and Acceptance." Emphasizing that Europe has always been "the cradle of the principal migratory movements since the Age of Discoveries until the present day," Carneiro presents compelling arguments as to why Europe depends on a continued influx of immigrants. "A major and decisive factor in the current destiny of the European Union is its demographic deficit," he writes. "The Europeans exhibit the lowest rate of fertility of any region in the world, condemning Europe to accelerated ageing, a decline in innovation, the progressive unsustainability of its social security model, and the net import of labour to feed its production system."[12] Pointing out that second and third generation immigrants rapidly adopt the sociological and birth rate standards of their host country, Carneiro concludes, "For this reason, the serious demographic deficit shall only be overcome by a combination of birth rate + immigration." But he hastily adds: "The truth is that today there is no longer any doubt that proper management of migration flows has emerged as a major European priority."[13]

From the beginning, a key thrust of Iberian immigration policy has been to win the cooperation of the migrant-exporting countries of Africa to exercise greater surveillance of their borders. This policy can be defined as containment at the source. Both Spain and Portugal have given top priority to improving relations with Africa, not only to develop trade and investments, but also to bring the migratory flow under control. The Spanish Ministry of Foreign Affairs and Cooperation has essentially divided the neighboring continent in two: North Africa and sub-Saharan Africa. Spain has extensive bilateral and multilateral relations with its North African neighbors, through the Barcelona Accord and the more recent Mediterranean Union. But in the past, Madrid had generally paid only "sporadic and superficial attention" to sub-Saharan Africa, according to the Spanish foreign minister, Miguel Ángel Moratinos.[14]

At the Foreign Ministry, located in a Serrano tower on the northern side of Madrid, I met briefly with Manuel Gómez-Acebo, the head of the North African desk. Immigration from North Africa has "stabilized," he stressed, adding that integration was "not an important problem," even after the 11 March attacks.[15] Spain maintains "good strategic relations" with Algiers, the official said, pointing out that Algeria is a major supplier of natural gas to Spain. On the other hand, he noted, ties with Morocco are much more comprehensive, starting with the fact that there are more than 600,000 Moroccan workers in Spain (there are only 40,000 Algerian residents) and some 800 Spanish companies in Morocco. While there have been "differences" with Morocco, the atmosphere has improved, he said.

In another part of the Foreign Ministry, I met ambassador Antonio Sánchez Benedito, director general of the Africa Plan, which is the framework for Madrid's enhanced relations with the countries of sub-Saharan Africa. When Spain launched the Africa Plan for 2006–2008, it was billed as a kind of Marshall Plan for the world's poorest continent, pledging a substantive increase in Spanish development funding, food aid, investments and debt relief. According to conventional wisdom, an important aim of this altruistic plan was to stem the exodus of undocumented African migrants to Europe. "The Africa Plan is not a response to the migration crisis," Ambassador Sánchez declared at the outset of our conversation, insisting that it was "a new global approach" to the region. Although Spain has developed relations over the years with traditional partners like Angola and Mozambique, it has been largely absent from the rest of sub-Saharan Africa.[16] With the Africa Plan, Spain has launched "a big offensive," particularly in West Africa, the official said. He highlighted the fact that Spain's development effort in the region has increased fourfold to 500 million euros from 125 million in the past two years. Madrid was opening new embassies in Mali and Cape Verde, Niger and Guinea, and expanding existing ones. The prime minister traveled to Senegal, his first visit to sub-Saharan Africa, and received the presidents of Mali and Liberia. Spain's deputy prime minister hosted a meeting of Women from Africa, which has now become a regular event. Regarding immigration problems, ambassador Sanchez said: "We are opening avenues to legal immigration and combating illegal networks through bilateral accords with Mali, Guinea-Conakry, Cape Verde and Senegal." He stressed the important shift on immigrant labor from government to contractual arrangements through private business. In closing, the Spanish diplomat gave me a copy of the 159-page Africa Plan. This is my resume of the seven main objectives of the comprehensive plan, which is as good a blueprint as I have seen for even-handed cooperation with this much abused continent.

– Participation in the consolidation of democracy, peace, security and human rights.
– Contribution to the fight against poverty, pandemics, desertification and for effective economic development.
– Encouragement of African cooperation to regulate migration through border controls, combat of illegal trafficking of migrants, repatriation of irregular immigrants with respect for human rights.
– Promotion of trade and investments with special focus on fishing in sub-Saharan waters and cooperation in the exploitation of oil and gas resources.
– Enhancement of cultural and scientific cooperation through UNESCO's program "World Alliance for Cultural Diversity," the spread of Spanish language courses in the region and the development of exhibits, film festivals and other cultural events through the Casa Africa, based at Las Palmas in the Canary Islands.
– Strengthening Spain's political and institutional presence in the region by opening new embassies and technical offices of cooperation and the creation of a Spanish Africa Forum with representatives of civil society.
– Reinforcement of the European Union's Strategy on Africa as set forth by the European council in December 2005 and endorsed two years later by the EU-Africa Summit at Lisbon.

Likewise Portugal has placed high hopes on new partnership arrangements with Africa, to replace the existing neo-colonial connections that are based essentially on the exploitation of manpower and natural resources, which had supplanted old colonial ties. Serving as the rotating president of the European Union in 2007, Lisbon organized a Euro-African summit in December, aimed at defining a new relationship between the neighboring continents to be based on fairness and mutual benefit. It was a comprehensive approach encompassing ideas from Spain's Africa Plan and France's plans for a Mediterranean Union. Muammar el Qaddafi of Libya shook things up on the eve of the summit, by declaring: "The colonial powers must compensate the people they colonized and whose riches they plundered."[17] And heated debate over trade policies revealed that colonial grudges are not easily overcome on both sides of the Mediterranean. Nevertheless, the Spanish prime minister, Zapatero, raised serious questions concerning African migration to Europe. In a dramatic plea, Zapatero called for a pact between the two continents to end the crisis in Africa, "where life expectancy is 46.3 years or half of that in Europe, about 2,800 Africans die of malaria daily, two out of three persons with AIDS are Africans, and 100 million children have no schooling."[18] The eighty nations assembled in the Portuguese capital managed to agree on a strategy for relations between the two continents for the next three-year period. The Lisbon Plan of Action lists eight priority areas for cooperation: peace and security, development, higher education and science, immigration, climate change, energy, trade and regional integration, democracy and human rights.[19]

"What we were able to achieve is a new approach in relations between Europe and Africa, not that of donor and receiver but equals in a legal sense ... a partnership with joint commitment and responsibility," said João Gomes Cravinho, Portugal's vigorous secretary of state for foreign affairs and cooperation, discussing the long-term results of the summit.[20] He stressed that there was a new realization among the participants that a regional approach was needed to face the globalization of problems like migrations, climate change, trade relations, wars and the political instrumentalization of religion.

As long as Spain's economy was flourishing and Portugal was holding its own, the two countries needed immigrants and could withstand pressures from their EU partners, especially France and Italy, to take a firmer stance on immigration. But when jobs started to go, it was much more difficult for the Iberian states to implement a generous immigration policy, not so much because of European demands but pressures at home to restrict foreigners. The global economic meltdown was particularly severe in Spain, which had prospered from prolonged economic development based on the booming construction industry and immigrant labor, including undocumented workers. Portugal had already suffered an economic downturn in recent years and so was in a way inoculated, and unemployed Portuguese were doing what they had done in the past, migrating to Spain, only now there were no jobs to spare. As Spain's economy soured at the end of 2007, anti-immigration attitudes in northern Europe began to resonate in Iberia in conservative and right-wing circles, reaching even the center-left.

Winning a second term in the March 2008 elections, Zapatero pledged to pursue the immigration policies initiated in his first administration. But his actions soon belied his promises. Disregarding senior voices in his own Socialist Party and press, Zapatero came out in support of controversial legislation issued by the European parliament, known as the Directive of Return, which enables a member of the European Union to expel undocumented aliens, even minors, or intern them for up to eighteen months. At the same time, the prime minister named a new tough-minded minister of labor and Immigration, Celestino Corbacho, a fifty-eight-year-old former mayor from Cataluña, who appeared willing to set aside his predecessor's Comprehensive Immigration plan for 2007–2010 whenever expedient. One of Corbacho's first initiatives was to offer incentives to unemployed foreign workers to go home, suggesting that 1.2 million immigrants, or half the total, might sign up. Those eligible for unemployment benefits would receive lump sum payments, on condition they give up their work and residence permits and pledge not to return to Spain for three years. Official sources emphasized that the measure was voluntary and only involved a score of countries with which Spain has social security accords, thus excluding most of Africa and Asia. The initial response was unenthusiastic, and after several months, Corbacho downsized expectations, suggesting that between 10,000 and 20,000 foreign workers might agree to repatriation. In a serious blow to the program, the Moroccan Workers Association (ATIME) announced that, according to its survey, 83% of Moroccan residents were not interested in the offer. Kamal Rahmouni, president of ATIME, told *El País:* "To return isn't in the mind of most Moroccans. They're not going to give up their residence status after everything they've done to get it."[21]

In the summer of 2008, Corbacho stirred new controversy with his approval of a Catalán plan for separate immigrant schools, calling it "an audacious idea." The regional government announced that it would create four Education Welcome Spaces as an alternative to public schools, specifically designed to introduce immigrant children to Catalán language and culture. The measure, which aimed to help the assimilation of children, was received with cries of "racism" and "apartheid" from teachers, immigration groups and human rights organizations. They warned that the Welcome Spaces would be turned into "educational ghettos," placing immigrant children at a disadvantage in relation to their Catalán peers and only harming integration. The Catalán government insisted on the voluntary nature of the program, but the Spanish press widely questioned the legality of immigrant schools, emphasizing that extra language courses should be available to foreign children in regular public schools, as in other European countries. In the end, most Spaniards agreed.

Further protests from immigrants and immigrant associations followed Corbacho's announcement of new restrictions on family reunion, barring parents and in-laws. But the labor minister won criticism from all sides in early September 2008 with his rash plan to reduce the number of workers hired abroad to "roughly zero." Contract labor had been the cornerstone of Zapatero's immigration policy and its main tool to curb the flow of undocumented migrants. Angry reactions came from employers and immigrant associations, as well as foreign governments, with which Spain had labor contracts. The deputy prime minister, María Teresa Fernández de la Vega, hastily contradicted her labor colleague, saying that Spain would continue to hire overseas workers but at a "reduced rate." Corbacho said that his words had been "misunderstood" and that he favored importing foreign workers. He stressed, however: "There are 2.5 million unemployed in Spain ... It seems reasonable we should try to fill jobs with people already here."[22] But the agricultural companies were hardly mollified and demanded a free hand to import seasonal labor. Employers in the southern province of Andalucia, where most of Spain's fruits and vegetables are grown, pointed out that thousands of foreigners were needed to fill farm jobs that unemployed Spaniards refused to take. Even the right-wing People's Party, which has led the opposition to the government's immigration policy as too lenient, wasn't satisfied with the new clampdown. Deputy secretary general Esteban González Pons was quoted as saying that the elimination of foreign labor contracts "will only close the door to those who come legally" and serve as an incentive to the irregulars."[23] On the other hand, the pro-government daily *El País* criticized the new restrictions on immigration. "The Labor Minister is playing with fire by linking unemployment with immigration policy," *El País* warned.[24]

Spain's backsliding on the immigration issue was hardly a surprise since the country was Europe's primary destination for immigrants in 2007 (702,000 immigrants, not counting illegal immigration) and it also boasted Europe's highest rate of unemployment at more than 11% at the end of 2008. But neither secretary Rumi nor other senior officials would admit to a substantive policy change on immigration. "We are developing a flexible policy able to adapt to the new circumstances," was the way Rumi put it to *El País*.[25]

In fact, it was reported that Zapatero had exercised a moderating influence on the "European Pact on Immigration and Asylum," presented by France as head of the European Union in 2008. The French president, Nicolas Sarkozy, had initially sought an outright ban on the mass legalization of immigrants, but the Spanish leader prevailed in the final document, which states that future regularizations should be carried out on "only case by case … for humanitarian or economic reasons."[26] Zapatero was also able to water down the French proposal of an obligatory "integration contract," stipulating that immigrants must learn the language of their new home and adopt its "national identity" and "European values." The pact's final wording on this is vague, suggesting merely that the member states should promote local language classes for immigrants and the latter should "recognize" European values.[27]

The Immigration Pact, which sets forth basic principles of European immigration policy for the first time, was approved by the summit meeting of the twenty-seven members of the European Union on 16 October 2008. Although immigrant-friendly states like Spain helped soften the tough language of Sarkozy's original proposal, the end result is a document more focused on expanding immigration controls than measures of integration. It also includes the widely criticized Directive of Return, allowing the detention of undocumented aliens for up to eighteen months. An innovation that garnered broad support from the EU members was the creation of a Blue Card (shades of the US green card but not so generous), which aims to attract highly skilled immigrants. The EU's new Immigration Pact clearly set a restrictive tone for European policy. While emphasizing greater cooperation with countries of origin and transit to control illegal immigration, the Pact states as a basic principle: "Illegal immigrants in Member States' territory must leave that territory."[28] For immigration advocates, the saving grace of the Pact is that it is non-binding.

As the European economies, particularly Spain's, continued their downward slide through 2008 and 2009, I wondered what could be salvaged of Iberia's liberal immigration model. I tried repeatedly to see immigration secretary of state Rumi during the spring of 2009, but she apparently did not want to discuss Spain's immigration policy with a foreign journalist. David Chico Zamanillo, an advisor to the secretary, was instead delegated to answer my questions. "We have not changed our immigration policy but are adapting it to new circumstances," he said, reiterating Rumi's earlier declaration. "Spain has not shut its doors to foreign labor, but based its forecasts for contract workers on the needs of the market in consultation with business and the unions." A specialist in EU law, Chico Zamanillo pointed out that the Immigration Pact left the number of foreign workers to be imported up to the individual states. "For Spain, as a border country, the main achievement of the Immigration Pact was the declaration that *pateras* are a European Union problem," he stressed.[29]

I did get to see Estrella Rodríguez Pardo, head of the Department of Integration in the Labor Ministry, who acknowledged that the unemployment rate for immigrants was 25%, considerably worse than that of Spanish nationals at 17%. Nevertheless, she informed me that the Strategic Plan for Citizenship and Integration was "still intact," although they had feared budget cuts. The Integration Support Fund, which goes mainly to education and municipal projects, stood at 14,267,000 euros for 2009. "We hope that we won't have to change the action plan, which is based on the equal rights of immigrants and citizens," she stressed.[30]

At Spain's Foundation for Pluralism and Coexistence, the director, José Manuel López Rodrigo, also assured me that the program for religious minorities had not been affected by the economic crisis and the budget for 2009 was five million euros, the same as the previous year. But he noted that the number of Muslim communities had grown substantially to 650 registered with the Justice Ministry, compared to 250 three years earlier. "Many Muslims immigrants are not aware of their rights in Spain," López Rodrigo said, pointing out that the foundation had launched a new course for imams on Spanish democracy at the beginning of 2009.[31] Scholarships were given to forty imams from around the country to take the online course, administered by the National University for Long Distance Education (UNED), which included weekly classes with prominent Spanish academics. He invited me to attend the final session of the course at UNED's Madrid campus.

I seized the opportunity since I knew the principal lecturers, Ana Planet and Bernabé López García, professors at Madrid's Autonomous University, and José María Contreras Mazarío, director general of religious affairs in the Justice Ministry. I had also long wanted to meet the other speaker, Riay Tatary, secretary general of the Islamic Commission of Spain. Above all, I was interested in the reactions of the imams, who were mostly young Moroccan men in informal western dress. They listened attentively as the professors gave an objective account of

Islam in Europe, specifically France, Germany and Holland, and the different patterns of integration. "The Spanish model is still a process in construction," Professor Bernabé emphasized.[32]

The imams took part in a lively exchange with Contreras on the current problems of the Islamic communities. The question of representation stirred an emotional debate, summed up by one imam: "We respect the old leadership, but we want new leaders; and we want all Muslims represented in the Islamic Commission of Spain." The Justice Ministry official agreed: "We know the situation has changed and we too want all registered Islamic communities represented in the Commission." Another controversial issue: the failure of local governments to introduce Islamic education in schools. Contreras stressed that according to the law, a minimum of ten students could request Islamic (instead of Catholic) classes in public school, but the implementation of the law was up to the municipalities. "The State hasn't got the competence to intervene, but we're trying to convince municipalities," he stressed. He gave the same answer to those imams who pointed to difficulties in obtaining permission to build mosques, adding: "This is the most recent Muslim community in Europe ... Before 1992, Muslims didn't even have the right to a place of worship. Now they have many rights ... Muslims in Italy and German don't have the same rights as Muslims in Spain."

The final speaker, Riay Tatary, a grandfatherly figure with trim white beard, recalled "the hard and difficult negotiations" leading to the accord with the Spanish government on 10 November 1992, which he described as "a historic date." He noted that when he first came to Spain as a university student, there were few Muslims, almost no Islamic structure and no place to pray, but the atmosphere was welcoming. Today, he said there are 1,310,000 Muslims and eighty-six different nationalities, mostly workers. He said he favored small mosques, since the Muslim communities are poor and neighborhood mosques play an important sociological role, but after the attacks of 11 March, the garage-mosques became known as "dangerous places." Since 11 September, there have been "some outbreaks" of Islamophobia but they were generally the work of the small ultra-right or part of an election campaign. He declared there was no "inter-Muslim conflict" and that his association, UCIDE, includes "all Islamic tendencies." Emphasizing the importance of Spanish law, Tatary pointed out that when there were public attacks against the hijab, the Ministry of Interior defended a woman's right to wear a headscarf. "We have a cohesive relationship with the State and political parties," the Muslim leader declared. "We are brothers."

* * *

Unlike Spain, Portugal has not been confronted by a mass of jobless immigrants, essentially because many foreign workers, once legalized, have moved on to other European job markets. "They know they can get twice the wage in Spain; we have the luck of poverty," António da Costa, the mayor of Lisbon, remarked, when I met him at a peace conference. The former minister of interior emphasized that Portugal's new immigration law, which went into effect in the fall of 2007, would expand legal immigration through a system of country quotas for workers in all sectors, linked to the country's needs and worked out with employers.[33]

Lisbon's immigration reform, however, was seen by immigrants and their advocacy groups as the closing of yet another door to Europe. Up until then, the conditions for Portuguese residence had been very liberal, requiring little more than evidence of means of support. A Portuguese residence permit enabled an immigrant to move to northern Europe and better-paid jobs. On the eve of the law's promulgation, there was such a stampede of prospective immigrants seeking residence that the Department of Foreigners and Borders had to shut down their Lisbon services for a week.

"EU rules prevail on immigration policy but member states are still free to work out their own policies on integration," Rosário Farmhouse, new head of Portugal's immigration agency, now known as the High Commission for Immigration and Intercultural Dialogue (ACIDI), told me in an interview the spring of 2009.[34] "The European Union has introduced minimum standards and we try to do better than that. Until now we are very open to migrants; our main problem is that there are not enough jobs." For example, the EU's Directive of Return stipulates that undocumented migrants can be held in internment centers for up to eighteen months but Portugal holds them a maximum of two months, she said. Unlike some Europeans, Portugal has not expelled unaccompanied minors but examines each case to determine if the minor would be better off with family at home. Lisbon's new nationality law provides access to citizenship after five years' residence, contrary to ten years in Spain, except for Latinos. Nor does Portugal penalize humanitarian organizations for "crimes of solidarity with undocumented migrants," Farmhouse noted, "only people motivated by money, like human traffickers."

Portugal was one of the first countries to suffer from the economic crisis and some immigrants, mainly Brazilians, have gone home, according to the high commissioner. At the same time, Portuguese emigrants to Spain and to the United Kingdom have started to come home, she stressed. Unlike Spain, Portugal doesn't have a program of incentives for immigrants to return to their countries, but there is an accord with the International Organization for Migrations (IOM) for voluntary departures. The IOM in Lisbon has funds to aid the return of up to 500 migrants a year, such as "people in vulnerable situations, without family or job, who want to go home," according to director Monica Goracci.[35] In 2008, they enabled the voluntary return of 347 migrants, 80% of them from Brazil, and the others mainly from Angola, Cape Verde, Ukraine and Russia.

Despite the general recession, ACIDI is expanding its services for the integration of immigrants with help from the European Union, Farmhouse stressed. She cited the *Escolhas* (Choices) program for children of immigrants and other ethnic minorities, which now runs 120 projects involving 62,000 young people in "difficult neighborhoods" around the country. Muslims and Christians take part in the projects, depending on where they live, she said, underlining that "the problem is poverty, not race or religion." One of *Escolhas's* most effective programs is a campaign against violence, she said. With the help of Portugal's champion kick boxer, popular rock musicians, an actress and other celebrities, *Escolhas* takes the message of social peace to problematical neighborhoods. "We're starting with kindergarten children, because if they learn to respect rules at an early age, it makes a difference," Farmhouse pointed out, suggesting I observe her team's next visit to Cova da Moura.[36]

Cova da Moura is Lisbon's Far West. It can't be found on most maps yet it is reputed to be the most dangerous, the most unruly, the most crime-ridden neighborhood in the area, a place to be avoided at all costs. Residents like to say Cova da Moura was born with the Portuguese revolution in 1974. Before, there was nothing but wheat fields, a quarry, a few dairy cows and workers' huts. With Portugal's hasty decolonization, thousands of Portuguese colonials and native Africans, lumped together under the label of *retornados*, flooded the Lisbon area in hopes of work and put up *baracas*, or makeshift shanties, wherever there was space, like Cova da Moura. Over time, the squatters improved their shacks and the neighborhood association won the attributes of civilization for their *bairro*, like water, sewers, electricity, streets, telephone lines and a primary school. In 1980 a small group of residents created the Cova da Moura Association of Social Solidarity, ostensibly a social club for sports, culture and recreation but essentially to defend the rights of their clandestine settlement. Residents admit the growth of the neighborhood was chaotic and security lax, and their associations weren't able to keep out the negative influences; for example, drug dealers, robbers and youth gangs.

My taxi driver, who had never been to Cova de Moura, a stone's throw from Lisbon's main shopping centers, was visibly terrified when he saw the surly-looking young men, most of them Africans, idling along the nearly deserted streets, the mounds of empty beer bottles, and walls covered with menacing graffiti. After several false leads from reticent bystanders, he deposited me with relief at the gate of the large, freshly painted Basic School #1.

What is violence? The two ACIDI monitors addressed the noisy circle of about sixty primary school children, almost all of them of African origin. At times the monitors answered their own questions other times, the children responded. A: Violence is like when somebody beats you up in school. Q: Why does an older child beat up a younger one? A: Because he's insecure. Q: How many of you have had this happen to you? A: A few timid hands raised. Q: What can you do? A: Talk to your teacher. Q: I'm sure you all have dreams … what do you want to do with your life? A: A school teacher, a soccer star like Cristiano Ronaldo, a doctor, a dancer. Monitor: Whatever you want to do, it's important to continue your studies and learn discipline. A celebrity, a former fashion model, intervened: I used to cry a lot because I didn't want to go to school. But to be a model, you have to learn to read and write. One monitor wraps up the session with a message of encouragement: You're the future. It's important to respect one another. You've got to study to make a better life.[37]

Across the street from the primary school, the Solidarity Association, which has partnership agreements with ACIDI and other public and private organizations, offers the youngsters help with their schoolwork and leisure activities like roller skating and *Capoeira* (Brazilian foot-fighting), gymnastics and art workshops. For young people of all ages, there are sport teams, dance, music and theater workshops, and free access to computers. The Solidarity Association, in partnership with the Portuguese Youth Institute, has taken part in debates on racism, xenophobia and intercultural training. "Our objective is to keep the kids off the street," a leader of the association said, proudly noting they have 580 members out of a total population of 6,000 in Cova da Moura.[38]

But outside, the teenage boys and young men were still there, loitering on every street corner. I thought privately that what Cova da Moura needs, more than leisure activities, is jobs.

* * *

The global economic crisis, particularly severe in Spain and Portugal, achieved what all the border controls and restrictive legislation had been unable to do: slow down the arrival of new immigrants. Some Latinos and East Europeans returned to their countries early on. Moroccans did not go home in significant numbers, but many prolonged annual vacations to wait out the crisis. During my visit to Morocco the summer of 2009, many Moroccans encountered were cool to the idea of going to Spain, contrary to the experience of past years. Word had spread that the job situation on the peninsula was worse than in Morocco.

The scarcity of jobs is the number one problem in Spain and Portugal, according to all immigrant community leaders. They are also worried about a tightening of immigration laws and negative stereotyping of immigrants in the two Iberian nations, which used to be known for having the most liberal immigration policies in Europe. A major concern of immigration advocates is that the European Union may become more repressive on immigration issues and Spain and Portugal will be obliged to fall in line by their own public opinion.

European parliamentary elections of 9 June 2009, clearly affected by the gravest recession since the 1930s, resulted in a rout for the center-left throughout most of the region, and gains for conservatives and the far right. Handicapped by a record low turnout, the ruling Socialists in Spain and Portugal and Labour in Britain suffered severe losses, as did the socialist parties in France, Germany, Italy and the Netherlands, with victory only for the socialist opposition in Greece. The conservative European People's Parties group wound up with 267 seats compared to 159 for the Socialists, reaffirming their domination of the 736-seat assembly. Significant gains for the extreme right, like Italy's Northern League, Holland's Freedom Party and Britain's National Party meant trouble for Europe's immigration policies, already under pressure from the right.

"The EU's Immigration Pact is not really compulsory but rather a political declaration of intentions, and so there's still ample margin for flexibility for EU member states like Portugal and Spain to implement border controls and immigration and asylum policies," Ana Gomes, a Portuguese Socialist Euro-deputy reelected to the European parliament, told me. "The pact, however, does reflect a significant political shift in the direction of 'control first' policies, with too much focus on fighting illegal immigration and less in facilitating legal migration. I'm pretty sure we will see a much uglier, restrictive and security-driven EU with the reinforcement of the right-wing and the extreme xenophobic right in the European parliament."[39]

* * *

As the economic crisis dragged on, the hardening of attitudes towards immigrants in Spain became apparent. The case of Vic was a graphic illustration of public pressure on the government. The mayor of Vic, a Catalán town of 40,000 inhabitants—nearly one-quarter of whom are North African immigrants—announced that as of February 2010, undocumented aliens would not be able to register as residents of the municipality. This meant they would no longer benefit from public education and health services, which has been the cornerstone of Spain's humane immigration policy. In the heated debate that followed, Vic's leaders insisted they could no longer afford social charges for "illegals," and several other municipalities appeared ready to follow suit. Government officials, labor unions and civic organizations condemned Vic's action as illegal and discriminatory. It was highlighted that a 1997 law, passed by the conservative People's Party (PP) government, stipulated that municipalities must register all foreigners, regardless of their legal status. The current PP leader, Mariano Rajoy, suggested the law should be changed, but other political groups backed the government. Finally protesting that Vic was not xenophobic, mayor Josep María Vila d'Abadal agreed to comply with the law but urged the government to provide financial aid to municipalities with a high percentage of immigrants. Progressive forces won this battle but the public mood was uncertain.

When Spain assumed the rotating presidency of the European Union in January 2010, the outspoken minister of labor summarized the Iberian position on the contentious immigration issue to a European parliamentary commission. "Europe must wager on regular, legal and controlled immigration," Corbacho declared. He insisted that Europe would need more immigrants because it needs labor to continue to grow and stressed that it would be "an error" to take into consideration only the present economic crisis.[40]

Despite the worsening of the economic and financial crisis and the increasingly shrill anti-immigrant voices in other European countries, Spain and Portugal appeared doggedly determined to pursue their intercultural model of integration during the troubled summer of 2010.

"The Spanish government's immigration policy remains the same in terms of rights; whoever lives in Spain has access to the basic services like health and education, and this is the standard norm of the country which does not change in spite of the economic crisis," a senior policy maker in the Spanish administration asserted in an interview. Requesting not to be named, the official stressed: "Furthermore, the policy of migratory management, introduced in 2004, links admissions to the labor market. The system functioned during the period of economic bonanza (when Spain needed foreign labor) and is working in times of crisis because the demand for foreign labor has decreased and so has the number of immigrants. We have entered a new phase in which the Spanish labor market has little need for unskilled workers. We are now preparing the new Strategic Plan for Citizenship and Integration for 2011–2014, and undoubtedly the budget will change in line with the new constraints on public spending, but the plan will continue to promote measures to facilitate integration and strengthen *convivencia* in diversity."[41]

Asked whether the government's immigration/integration action was national policy, the source, who is close to the Socialist leadership, responded candidly: "There is no national pact on immigration, and therefore an electoral victory by the PP could mean some changes. There is no margin to change what is regulated by the European Community but there could be less emphasis on efforts made in recent years to regulate the flow of immigration and promote *convivencia*. Of greater concern would be the change in discourse. The People's Party continues to associate immigration with insecurity (now it's the economic crisis as well). Furthermore, the opposition party has shown in the "burqa affair" it is prepared to make immigration an election campaign issue, linking the nebulous fears of "the other" to the current concerns of Spanish society."

As the anti-Muslim fever spread from France and other European countries to Cataluña that summer of 2010, I wondered whether it was a temporary electoral phenomenon, as many people indicated. Or was it rather a revival of deep-seated antagonisms that could jeopardize Cataluña's and Spain's efforts to construct a new society of intercultural harmony? For the answer to my questions, I went to see one of the most knowledgeable and influential Cataláns dealing with these sensitive issues.

Oriol Amorós, secretary of immigration in the Cataluña *Generalitat* or government, received me at his office in central Barcelona with some impressive facts. Some 1,200,000 foreigners have come to live in Cataluña, or 16% of the region's 7,500,000 population, most of them in the past decade. About 30% of the foreigners are Muslim, the great majority from Morocco. He suggested that these facts explained in part the recent rash of anti-Islamic incidents and the rise of the extreme right-wing political party, *Plataforma per Cataluña*.[42]

The immigration chief acknowledged an increase in tension over jobs and economic survival: "For the first time, immigrants have demanded their rights as citizens, members of the society, and the Catalán public is not used to hearing such demands." He noted that the *Plataforma per Cataluña* has profited from the malaise over immigration to launch an Islamophobic campaign. The right-wing extremists, he said, were strong in only eight or nine villages but there was a risk of "contamination" in the current atmosphere of political polarization.

"Fortunately the far right has chosen to wage their fight against the burqa, which isn't important here, and not against social services for immigrants," he stressed, pointing out that 80% of the population still supports health and education for all, even undocumented immigrants. What concerned him more than the occasional anti-Muslim outbreak was the problem of dropouts among immigrant children in Cataluña. There are 11,500 children aged twelve-sixteen in secondary schools and only 634 in high school and 1,456 in vocational schools, he disclosed. "Where are the others? On the streets or working? Doing what?" he said, noting that the unemployment rate was 45% among immigrants, which was more than twice the national figure.

"We have a progressive policy of immigration and will continue in this direction, despite the economic crisis," Amorós assured me. He said this policy was spelled out in a ninety-page document entitled, "An Agreement to Live Together: National Accord on Immigration," signed by the president of the Catalán government and representatives of some thirty political, economic, social and immigrant institutions on 19 December 2008. The accord is based on a set of Action Principles, namely: guaranteed equal rights and respect of duties for the whole society, the right to access to public services like education and national health care, the promotion of equal opportunities and the fight against racism and xenophobia. The Catalán official ended the conversation on a hopeful note. While the central government has been forced to cut funds for integration substantially (65%), the Catalán administration has increased its contribution to make up for much of the loss. "So we can continue to work with hundreds of immigrant groups to improve literacy, language skills, job training and placement."

It was a similar tone in the Spanish Ministry of Justice. "Just because there's less money, doesn't mean a change in policy," emphasized José María Contreras, head of religious affairs, who had seen his own job downgraded in the budget squeeze.[43] The Justice Ministry official said that his department was in contact with the main religious communities to obtain their input for the draft of a new religious law. All the minorities have raised bureaucratic problems, like restrictions on sites for places of worship and complaints about overcrowding and noise from worship services, according to Contreras. He said Muslim groups have reiterated their long-standing demand for representation on the Islamic Commission of Spain and have been assured that under the new legislation all Muslims will be included in the body. Muslim leaders have also expressed concern that Spain might follow the French ban on headscarves in public schools. Pointing out that French secularism is different from the Spanish position, Contreras stressed that Spain permits individuals to wear religious symbols, as long as they are not imposed or threaten public order. "The State must defend women and their right to wear religious or cultural symbols, but we cannot let fundamentalist imams force women to wear head-coverings," he noted. He pointed out that the majority of Muslims were not radical, just as the majority of Spaniards accept diversity. "We have tried to show that religion is an element of social cohesion, not confrontation," he stressed, noting the proliferation of meetings on religion. "The initiative comes from the different religions, who realize they must work together."

The Foundation for Pluralism and *Convivencia*, funded by the regions and municipalities as well as the central government, has not suffered from budget cuts and is still financing new projects by religious minorities. In fact it has expanded its focus and is now working with local administrations on specific problems like permits for new houses of worship or space in cemeteries, according to director José Manuel López Rodrigo. "We're also working with movie producers to get them to eliminate stereotypes on TV," López said, adding that the foundation has researched American television serials to see how they incorporated African Americans and homosexuals into mainstream.[44]

But as jobless figures remained frozen at more than 19%, the country's mood became increasingly anti-immigrant, particularly in Cataluña. Nevertheless, the central government announced a new pilot program to promote integration in some of the most immigrant-populated towns of Cataluña: Salt, Badalona, Hospitalet, Terrassa and El Vendrell. Speaking over Cataluña Radio, the secretary of state for immigration, Anna Terrón, defined the region's main social problem as "unemployment, uprootedness and exclusion."

By the end of 2010, official statistics showed a slight increase in the foreign population to 4,754,502, which did not help the situation. Yet if the critics bothered to study the figures, they would see that the immigration problem was resolving itself with the prolonged economic crisis. The increase in foreign residents applied only to those members of the European Community who counted 2,358,798 in September 2010 or 2.21% up from the previous year, while the number of other immigrants had actually dropped by 1.67% to 2,395,704 because of the loss of jobs.[45] This positive trend was confirmed by the 2010 figures for the heavily immigrant city of Barcelona. *La Vanguardia* announced that the Catalán capital had lost 7,609 inhabitants in one year, mostly foreigners, breaking the recent trend.[46] The main reason given for the decrease in foreign residents was the high unemployment, which meant fewer arrivals and more immigrants going home under the official return program.

Although the Spanish economy remained in the doldrums in 2011, the government stressed that it was not closing the door to immigration in the future. Estrella Rodríguez Pardo, director general of the Labor Ministry's Department of Integration, announced that unemployed immigrants who voluntarily went home would be given "priority" to return to Spain when the situation improved. Speaking on the government's return policy at Madrid's Casa America, Rodríguez said that thus far 23,435 immigrants had enrolled in the return program begun at the end of 2009, which stipulated that volunteers would not return to Spain for three years.[47]

* * *

Like its neighbor, Portugal has been hammered by the global crisis and had to make stringent cuts in administrative expenditures. Nevertheless, in mid August 2010, the government approved a new Plan for the Integration of Immigrants, which actually expanded services. "We're still an island but I don't know how long it will last," commented Rosário Farmhouse, the high commissioner for immigration, when asked if Portugal could afford to pursue its generous immigration policy in the face of increasingly restrictive trends in most of Europe. The 2010–2013 plan provides for continued support to immigrants in areas like health, education, culture, and housing, as well as four new areas: diversity, intercultural relations, elderly immigrants and unemployed immigrants.

Portugal's advantage, (over Spain for example), is that the main opposition, the Social Democrats, see eye-to-eye with the ruling Socialists regarding immigration policy, according to Farmhouse. She said only the small Christian Democratic Party says "Migrants go home if you don't have work!" including in this documented migrants. "We don't see any signs of Islamophobia, and all Portuguese, including the Christian Democrats, respect inter-religious dialogue," she stressed. "More than that, we believe in intercultural dialogue. In sum, what we're trying to do is learn how to live together with respect."[48]

12

WRESTLING WITH PHOBIAS

Iberians tend to argue that intolerance is a phenomenon of the past and point to guarantees of freedom of religion and expression, enshrined in their democratic constitutions. Spanish and Portuguese leaders speak with pride of their nations' new diversity and underline what has been done to integrate religious and ethnic minorities. While there have been occasional outbursts of collective racism against Moroccan immigrants in Spain, against Africans in Portugal and against gypsies in both countries, the peninsula has lived through less racist violence in recent times than other European neighbors. Anti-immigrant movements exist, but have not acquired the same virulence and influence as elsewhere in Europe. Perhaps this is because most immigrants come from Latin America, and Iberians still cling to the notion of a special relationship with their erstwhile colonies. Then, too, the Portuguese are naturally open to other cultures and proud of their mestizo traditions. And while Spaniards admit to racist hangovers from the past, this is outweighed by a strong empathy for immigrants, which may explain the wealth of volunteer organizations devoted to tolerance and multiculturalism and opposed to xenophobia.

Nevertheless, as we have seen in the previous chapter, the prolonged economic crisis and soaring unemployment have begun to take their toll. Public opinion, particularly in Spain, appears increasingly antagonistic towards foreigners, because they are associated with the loss of jobs, strains on social services and a rise in criminality. As the Muslim communities have grown and become more visible, there are new signs of Islamophobia in Spain and even Portugal, but public protests over mosques and minarets, veils and Islamic law have been less heated than in other European countries. The main explanation given for the relative tolerance of Iberians towards Muslim immigration—the issue that torments much of the rest of Europe—is the newness of the phenomenon and the still modest numbers of Muslims. As noted earlier, there are nearly 1.5 million Muslims in Spain and 50,000 in Portugal, compared to four million in Germany, five million in France and 2.8 million in Great Britain.[1] Also highlighted are the efforts of the Spanish and Portuguese leadership to learn from other European experiences in curbing religious intolerance.

Yet, despite multiple efforts to promote understanding with Muslims, Iberians have had to face a very unpleasant fact: anti-Islamic attitudes are on the rise on the peninsula, particularly in Spain, and with them, anti-Semitism, if one is to believe various polls, independent reports and anecdotal evidence. Spain, which has the dubious honor of holding the highest negative opinion of Muslims in Europe, has seen a growing number of Islamophobic attacks. Even Portugal, which prides itself on religious harmony, has begun to witness anti-Muslim attitudes and stereotyping.

Spain's leadership has been concerned about the creeping racism that accompanied the recent influx of North African and sub-Saharan immigrants (and to a lesser extent East Europeans and Latin Americans), which has been exacerbated by the recent economic downturn. The authorities in both Spain and Portugal have been especially worried about the rise of anti-Muslim opinion since the 11 September 2001, terrorist attacks in the US and the 11 March 2004, attacks in Madrid, and periodic reports of radical Muslim activity in Europe.

To deal with this issue, Spain hosted the first conference on "Anti-Semitism and Other Forms of Intolerance," convened by the Organization for Security and Cooperation in Europe (OSCE) at Córdoba in June 2005. The meeting devoted a special session to "Fighting Intolerance and Discrimination against Muslims." In 2007, Madrid, as president of the OSCE, made up of fifty-six European and Central Asian countries, organized a summit on "Discrimination and Anti-Muslim attitudes." Again the venue was Córdoba, internationally recognized as a symbol of the positive coexistence of Islam, Christianity and Judaism. As the conference got underway, Spain's foreign minister Miguel Ángel Moratinos was quoted as saying that intolerance toward Muslims was "an alarming problem." The agenda included a discussion of

the roots of discrimination and hostility towards Islam and the consequences, as well as the role of the media in facilitating Muslim integration and respect for cultural diversity.[2] Arab League secretary general
Amr Moussa, co-president of the conference, seized the opportunity to
voice a long-standing demand of Spain's Islamic community; that Muslims be granted the right to hold religious services in Córdoba's cathe-
dral/mosque. Córdoba's bishop, Juan José Asenjo, reiterated the
church's position in favor of inter-religious dialogue, but stressed that
the "shared use of churches and places of worship would not be help-
ful to dialogue and would only create confusion among the faithful."[3]

While leaders of Spain's Roman Catholic Church have generally
embraced interfaith dialogue, they do not hide misgivings over an
Islamic revival in this still largely Catholic society. In particular, church
officials have expressed concern over Muslim plans for the construction of large mosques in Medina Zahra, Granada, Seville and Córdoba. "Spain's bishops are alarmed by ambitious plans to recreate the
city of Córdoba—once the heart of the Islamic kingdom of Al Andalus—as a pilgrimage site for Muslims throughout Europe," Elizabeth
Nash wrote in London's *The Independent*.[4] An authority on religions,
Nash said that the bishops of those cities were alarmed at the construction of ostentatious mosques, "fearing that the church's waning influence may be further eclipsed by resurgent Islam financed from abroad."

Spain's Islamic communities have regularly faced problems in opening mosques and even unpretentious prayer halls. When all necessary
permits are obtained, projects are often delayed by petitions from hostile neighbors, who protest against more traffic and greater insecurity.
The proposed mosque in Seville caused a particular stir because of its
visibility. The city authorities had actually given the Muslim community the land in the district of Bermejales, and the Arab Emirate of
Sharjah was expected to finance the construction. But the local neighborhood association campaigned against the project, calling it much
too big. A petition against the mosque garnered thousands of signa-
tures, and activists left several butchered pigs' heads (pork is considered impure under Islam) on the site to discourage Muslims from the
endeavor. The Seville municipality reneged on its offer, but local Muslim leaders hoped another site could be agreed upon.

When asked about Islamophobia, however, most Spaniards do not
see themselves as anti-Muslim. In fact, a survey by the authoritative
Elcano Royal Institute claimed in late 2007 "there is no Islamophobia

in Spain."[5] The report did not hide negative opinions of some aspects of Islam, but stressed that they were motivated by "the growing secularism" of the Spanish public. The Elcano poll said that 80% of Spaniards were worried about Islamic fundamentalism, and felt threatened by Islamic terrorism. But emphasizing that only 37% of Spaniards had a negative opinion of the Muslim religion, the analyst stressed that they "differentiate perfectly between Islamic fundamentalism and Islam." The same poll said that 65% of Spaniards think the threat of international terrorism in the world is greater now than before the US-led invasion of Afghanistan.

A leading watchdog on the growth of religious intolerance is the European Network against Racism (ENAR), which has been critical of Spain's record. In a report for 2007, ENAR points out that the rise of bigotry in Spain is linked to immigration problems and faults Madrid for the absence of a clear policy on the integration of immigrants. "There is a total lack of political focus on citizenship and equal access to universal rights," ENAR noted, adding, "There are no public policies in place to support the victims of racism."[6] Worse, the report gives examples of discrimination against immigrants in housing, education and access to health services, as well as wages, despite legal guarantees. ENAR also criticizes the Spanish authorities for failing to keep official statistics on hate crimes, but notes that "numerous signs of fanaticism" are present in the media and on the internet. There were some 4,000 incidents of violence in 2007, the report says, citing the Movement against Intolerance, which is supported by the Ministry of Labor and the European Union. Assaults—namely knifings and beatings—were reported to have been directed against "vulnerable groups," such as immigrants, and particularly Latin American women, the destitute, homosexuals, gypsies and Muslims. Furthermore, over 100 websites and forums were said to be dedicated to racist, xenophobic and neo-Nazi propaganda.[7] ENAR gives the Spanish government credit for several initiatives to curb hate crimes but suggests it should do more. Spain's Ministry of Labor and Immigration has published a Guide to Good Practices on the treatment of immigrants in the media, and a National Observatory against Racism and Xenophobia has done a commendable job with little means.[8]

Overtures to Islam by José Luis Zapatero have increasingly come under attack by the conservative opposition and press, which do not conceal anti-Muslim attitudes. At a reception in Istanbul, marking the

11 September attacks, Zapatero reportedly said that Spain was "proud of the influence of Islam" in its past. He went on to say that Spain wanted "to pay respect to all religions ... to be tolerant of all faiths and ideologies." At home, his remarks stirred the ire of his critics. "Many observers are noting that as Spain's economy descends further and further into chaos, Zapatero's rhetoric on religious and moral issues is becoming increasingly radical," said Soeren Kern, a senior fellow at Madrid's Strategic Studies Group.[9]

From the outset, Spain's Socialist government has shown its resolve to improve relations with the country's new Muslims, and is generally given high marks for its efforts. Nevertheless, the Socialists have made some blunders in their relations with the Muslim community, which have added to the tension. For example, disregarding the furor in France over a ban on veils in public schools, the Spanish minister of equality, Bibiana Aído, angered Muslims by declaring that headscarves "undermined the rights of women." Making matters worse, she added: "Not all cultural practices must be protected and respected." Members of the Islamic Community indignantly responded that "the minister should not talk about what she does not know."[10] Aído dropped the matter, and women remained free to wear headscarves.

It was, however, a widely publicized poll from the Washington-based Pew Research Center that shook Spanish complacency about relations with the Muslim community. In a survey, carried out in March-April of 2008 in twenty-four countries, anti-Semitism and Islamophobia were said to be up in most of Europe. Spain was in the lead, with 52% unfavorable opinion of Muslims, Germany second with 50% unfavorable and Poland third with 46%. Spain also led with 46% unfavorable opinion of Jews, Poland second with 36% and Germany third with 25%. Attitudes in Britain showed little change with only 23% holding a negative opinion of Muslims and 9% of Jews. The United States shared Britain's tolerance, just 23% with unfavorable views of Muslims and only 7% of Jews.

At the same time a Spanish think tank, the Center of Studies on Migrations and Racism, published a report pointing out that Moroccans had replaced gypsies as the main victims of racism in schools. The encouraging fact was that "visceral racism" was down and considerably lower than polling figures for the general population. According to this survey of thirteen to nineteen-year-olds, 48.6% of the students had wanted to expel all Moroccans in 2002 (after the 11 September assaults) and that percentage had dropped to 39.1% in 2008. In response to another question, 23.7% of the students didn't want Moroccans in their class in 2001 and, despite the Madrid terrorist attacks in 2004, the figure was in fact down a little to 23.1% in 2008.[11]

Professor Bernabé López García, the head of North African studies at Madrid's Autonomous University, acknowledged that Spaniards are increasingly anti-immigrant because of the economic crisis, but noted they are anti-Latino immigrants and anti-East Europeans as well as North Africans and Africans. He pointed out that during the olive harvest in December 2008, there were thousands of Africans (Christians and Muslims) in Jaén and Córdoba provinces, who could not find work because unemployed Spaniards were taking seasonal farm jobs. "That caused local tensions, but I don't think you can speak of increasing Islamophobia in Spain," he told me. "There are now about 700,000 Moroccans with legal residence in Spain and the degree of acceptance is quite normal," Professor Bernabé stressed.[12]

It was a Muslim cleric at Madrid's course for imams, organized by the Foundation for Pluralism and Coexistence, who provided an insight on the apparent contradictions in Spaniards' view of Muslims. Mustafa Snabi Himri, vice president of the Federation of Muslim Communities of Castilla La Mancha, who has lived in Albacete for twenty years, had this to say. "No, we cannot say the Spanish are Islamophobic. Their problem is a historical fear, a fear of the return of Islamic rule. But that was the past. They must understand these are new times of multiculturalism. They should recognize that Islam is part of their history."[13]

The imam's words reminded me of the *Cristianos y Moros* festivals, celebrated with such ardor in southern and eastern Spain. I had wondered for some time if these were relics of the Reconquista mentality or, on the contrary, a recognition of an Islamic past? Initially I was prejudiced against the festivals, which seemed to be a promotion of interfaith animosities and no way to ease tensions. In particular, I questioned the wisdom of continuation of such rituals in the Alicante area and Andalucia, where there are so many North African immigrants. In the summer of 2009, I decided to see for myself whether these fiestas perpetuate phobias, or are just another harmless tourist attraction.

Vila Joiosa is a colorful fishing port about twenty miles north of Alicante and the site of one of the most popular Moors and Christians Festival. This is not the usual celebration of the Christian triumph over their former Muslim rulers but rather a reenactment of the city's struggle against Barbary pirates from Algeria. Legend has it that in 1538, a fleet of corsairs prepared to attack Vila Joiosa, when Saint Martha intervened, stirring up a flash flood that destroyed all the ships. The townspeople declared her their patron saint, and for the past 250 years have held an elaborate fiesta of *Moros y Cristianos* in her honor at the end of July.

In the Vila Joiosa *turismo* office, an official was delighted to talk to me about the fiesta. It was too bad that I would miss the main event, the Landing of the Moors, which took place on the fifth day of the festival. At daybreak, some twenty Moorish boats would land their troops at the base of the fortress, where the Christian forces were waiting. A fierce hand-to-hand combat would take place (formerly they had used wooden swords, now considered too dangerous) and the Moors would take the fortress, raising their banner with the Muslim crescent. That evening the Christians would re-conquer the fort and "symbolically" chase the Moors back to sea. The next day, Christians and Moors together would attend a solemn mass in honor of Saint Martha followed by a procession and fireworks. The twenty-nine-year-old *turismo* representative told me that she had taken part in the festivities every year since age seven but regretfully had to work this year. "I've always been a Moor—a Bedouin—but my sister is a Christian," she said, explaining that families could have divided loyalties. She informed me there were twenty-two "companies" evenly divided into so-called Christian and Moorish teams, with names like Cataláns, Hunters, Fishermen, Laborers, Sailors, Smugglers for the Christian or red groups, and Black Guard, Merchants, Bedouins, Berbers, Riffans and Tuaregs for the Moors or blue team. A total of 4,000 participants, all local Spaniards, take part in the events, paying for their own food and costumes—about 550 euros for the week. "It's our history, our festival—not for tourists, although visitors are welcome," the *turismo* representative stressed. As far as she knew, there had never been any protests from Muslims about the festival in Vila Joiosa, although she recalled an incident in another town a couple of years ago, when it was falsely reported that some people were carrying pictures of the Muslim Prophet in the procession.

As I made my way to the headquarters of the Saint Martha Association, I passed by the Camp of the Islamic Artillery, where a joyous group of "Muslim" actors was seated at a long table, feasting on meat stew and fried fish, washed down with beer and sangria. "It's our day off," the revelers explained, inviting me to join them, but I said I'd already had breakfast. At the Saint Martha Association, an off-duty policeman told me he and several members of his family would be marching with the Muslim pirates. The association had been preparing for the festival for a year. This year, the Christian king was leader of the smugglers and the Muslim king was a Tuareg. While the Christians were gathering for the procession, I solicited the opinions of the only authentic Muslims around, several Senegalese from Benidorm, who had come to hawk sunglasses, straw hats, fans and beads along the parade route. Asked what they thought of the Christians and Moors reenactment, their response was enthusiastic: "It's fine for business! A good chance to make money." Finally the King of the Smugglers and his retinue appeared and made their way to the Moorish camp, where they paid a "courtesy visit" to the King of the Tuaregs and his followers. The two monarchs and other dignitaries repaired to the large tent where a copious banquet was laid out for them. Meanwhile, the Tuareg band played a rich repertory of Oriental music, which had Christians and Moors alike close to belly dancing. In turn, the smugglers' band played a selection of Christian tunes with equal *élan*. Several participants urged me to stay over for the Landing of the Moors and the big fight that would follow. "Of course we know that the Christians will win in the end," a pirate told me, "but the Moors don't lose." Shelving my prejudices, I decided that at least Vila Joiosa's festival was no show of Islamophobia but a colorful page from Iberia's past, much like the games of cowboys and indians in the United States.

But clearly the Christian and Moors festivals differ in tone and content. My Algerian friend Mekia Nedjar, who teaches Arabic language and culture at the University of Alcalá de Henares, told me she was appalled by the festival celebrating the reconquest of Granada. "I was especially horrified at the glee with which the Christian soldiers trampled on the Moors," she recalled.[14] It was, therefore, no surprise when a group of Spanish human rights organizations demanded that Granada city hall abolish the *La Tomada*, or "Seizure Day" festival. Calling themselves the Platform for an Open Granada, the group sent a letter to the mayor emphasizing that the fiesta "defends racism and stirs a clash of civilizations."[15] But their appeal was ignored. On 2 January 2011, Granadines celebrated the 519th anniversary of the seizure of Granada with a religious ceremony presided over by the archbishop, Javier Martínez, who extolled the Catholic monarchs for the "extraordinary" and "humane" conquest. Thousands of joyous participants rejoiced over the Christian victory, marred only by minor clashes between small groups of activists from the far left and far right. Rather than join the street protests, the Platform for an Open Granada organized a parallel event with poetry and music at the Euro-Arab Foundation. At this time, Esteban Ibarra, president of the Movement Against Intolerance, called for the creation of a Public Prosecutor for Hate Crimes in Granada, similar to existing offices in Madrid and Barcelona.[16]

Faced with the absence of clear data on Islamophobia in Spain, the OSCE's Office for Democratic Institutions and Human Rights announced the publication of an unusual guidebook on Spain, aimed at raising European awareness of anti-Muslim prejudices and stereotypes. This *Reference Guide on Muslims in Spain* was backed by the Spanish Foreign Ministry with the cooperation of the Casa Árabe. Presenting the new work in Madrid, Janez Lenarčic, director of the human rights body, said it was the first in a series of such guidebooks in response to "the increase of anti-Muslim hate crimes across the OSCE region." Lenarčic praised Spain for its action against anti-Muslim discrimination and efforts to promote greater awareness of Muslim culture through institutions like the Casa Árabe.[17]

The eighty-seven-page guide describes an estimated 1,300,000 Muslims living in Spain and their religious institutions and associations, with special attention to youth, women and Muslims in the media. It also includes the views of a number of Muslim leaders (several of whom I had interviewed) on problems facing the community in Spain. A member of the Muslim Association of Córdoba, Mauritanian Sambo Yero Diop, aged thirty, who works in a telephone center, said Muslims are partly to blame for their negative image in the Spanish media because they failed to respond to acts of aggression. "We simply give up," he lamented.[18]

How serious is the reported surge of Islamophobia, and how would it affect Spain's attempts to integrate its Muslim community? I went to see José María Contreras, director general of religious affairs in the Ministry of Justice. He admitted he had been surprised by the results of the Pew poll, particularly because the Ministry of Interior's annual poll on Muslim immigrants in 2008 showed that 86% of the community had adapted to life in Spain and 76% felt at home here. Those who were unhappy gave as reasons the lack of work or absence of family and friends. They did not speak of Islamophobia. Sixty-seven percent said they were practicing Muslims and 80% said they had encountered no obstacles in practicing their religion. "It's a strange situation; if the Spanish public is so anti-Muslim, why do only 4% of the Muslims feel badly adjusted to life here?" Contreras asked.[19]

"Spain today is very different from 1980 when the new democracy passed its first organic law on religious freedom," Contreras emphasized. Pointing to the rapid growth in religious diversity, he noted that fifteen years ago the overwhelming majority of the population was Catholic and today there are 1.5 Evangelicals, more than a million Muslims and 300,000 Orthodox Christians. "We need a mechanism to deal with these religious minorities and their problems, and for that reason the government is working out changes in the religious law," he said, emphasizing that there would be "more freedom, more equality" under the new legislation. Contreras acknowledged that there had been more racist and xenophobic incidents as a result of the economic crisis and soaring unemployment, "but nothing like the anti-immigrant demonstrations in Italy." There had also been some acts of anti-Semitism, insults and graffiti during Israel's attacks on Gaza, but he stressed that the authorities were working with the religious communities to resolve any problems in this domain.

* * *

Portugal, on the other hand, has been generally commended for its record on religious tolerance. The European Network against Racism or ENAR declared in 2007 that discrimination for religious motives was "almost non-existent" in Portugal. "The Muslim communities in Portugal coexist peacefully with the rest of society," ENAR said, although some anti-Islamic attitudes were noted.[20] The report stressed that Lisbon has a "panoply of very progressive legal instruments" in human rights, but public opinion increasingly links immigration to the struggle against terrorism and organized crime. ENAR points out that there have been reports of racial violence, directed mainly against gypsies and young people of African descent. These incidents were said to involve groups of skinheads but also the police.

The basic problem is the sketchy information on discrimination based on racial or ethnic motives. This is generally attributed to the fact that Portugal was late to join the ranks of immigrant-host countries in the mid-1970s and, therefore, has not been faced with many problems of racial or religious discrimination. The official Commission for Equality and Against Racial Discrimination registered only forty-five cases of ethnic discrimination in the period between 2000 and 2004. These complaints involved mainly labor questions and treatment by the security forces and were made mostly by Africans, Brazilians and East Europeans.

To correct the lack of official data, the European Union's Monitoring Center on Racism and Xenophobia (EUMC) commissioned a group of scholars to make a survey of migrants' experiences of racism and xenophobia in Portugal. Questions related to religion were excluded and would be dealt with in a separate report. The study focuses on the four leading immigrant communities: Brazilians, Cape Verdeans, Guineans and Ukrainians, and the Portuguese Roma (gypsies). The results of the research were made public in the spring of 2009, and confirmed the conventional wisdom that the Portuguese are relatively tolerant of foreigners but have problems with gypsies, as Roma are generally called in Iberia. However there were a number of surprises. More than 90% of the respondents in all the groups reported no occurrence of violence or serious crime committed against them due to their ethnic origin. Yet, about 40% of the foreign groups (60% for the Roma) reported having been denied several times the opportunity to rent or buy a house or apartment, on ethnic grounds. More than half of the Brazilians and Ukrainians said they had been denied the possibility of buying on credit. About half the Roma complained of bad treatment by the police, while between 20% and 30% of all the immigrant groups said they had experienced bad treatment from the Borders and Foreigners Service. Finally, on questions regarding integration, the Roma demonstrated the highest degree of identification with Portugal or 67%, (quite natural, as they are Portuguese citizens), and the newly arrived Ukrainians showed the lowest at 8%. As for the state of xenophobia in Portugal, the Guineans more than any other group said that it has decreased or decreased considerably (36%), while Brazilians were more critical, with 40% responding that xenophobia has increased or increased considerably.[21]

Evidence that the Portuguese authorities were aware of an incipient problem of intolerance came in the form of an amendment to the Penal Code, passed on 15 September 2007, prohibiting racist organizations and racist propaganda. Barely ten days later, the police arrested thirty-six extreme right-wing activists for the vandalizing of Lisbon's Jewish cemetery and the illegal possession of weapons. Denouncing this act of anti-Semitism, several cabinet ministers, along with Christian and Muslim leaders, took part in a public demonstration of solidarity with the Jewish community. On 3 October 2008, a Portuguese court announced its first convictions on charges of racial discrimination in connection with the cemetery incident. Mário Machado, leader of the neo-Nazi National Front, was sentenced to four years and ten months in prison and five others were given prison time, while eighteen received suspended sentences and seven were acquitted.

Several Portuguese Muslims told me they had been the object of anti-Islamic slurs but had not reported the incidents because they did not want to make waves. The mild-mannered Sheikh Munir acknowledged that since 11 September 2001, Muslims living in the West, even in Portugal, have been subject to an increase in Islamophobia. "The public is worried about an Islamic threat," the Muslim cleric explained, noting that if a Muslim forgets a newspaper or a bag in the metro, he or she can have problems.[22] He recounted that two weeks earlier the police had detained two Muslim women who were sitting in the metro merely saying their prayers with a prayer counter, like an abacus.

An unexpected glitch in interfaith harmony came from Lisbon's cardinal patriarch Dom José Policarpo, who has played a prominent role in the current rapprochement between the Catholic Church and minority religions. Speaking on Portuguese state television about the increase in Muslim immigration and mixed marriages, Cardinal Policarpo bluntly warned Portuguese girls against marrying Muslims. "I suggest be cautious with love. Think twice before marrying a Muslim, think about it seriously," he said, adding that such unions "lead to a pile of problems that not even Allah knows where they will end." The cardinal went on to say: "I know if a young European of Christian family marries a Muslim, as soon as they go to his country they'll be subject to the rules for Muslim women. Just imagine that!" The Catholic leader emphasized that dialogue with the Muslim community in Portugal has been "very difficult, but small advances" have been made recently.[23] The Conference of Bishops issued no apology for the cardinal's ill-considered statement. Instead, a spokesman endorsed his advice as "indispensable realism."[24]

Portugal's Muslim leadership reacted with characteristic restraint. In a communiqué, the president of Lisbon's Islamic Community, Abdool Majid Vakil, expressed "surprise" and "pain" over the cardinal's declaration, in view of "the fraternal and cordial relations and the fruitful dialogue" between the two religions in Portugal. Vakil regretted, however, that there still exists "a great ignorance of the Islamic faith in Portugal."[25] But the Portuguese press prominently played up cardinal Policarpo's remarks which seemed to challenge the country's proud policy of miscegenation and interfaith entente. Lisbon's leading daily, *Público*, published several pages of positive testimony from Christian-Muslim marriages under the headline "Senhor Cardinal, 'You don't have to worry about us.'"[26]

Portugal could not remain indefinitely impermeable to the winds of Islamophobia sweeping the rest of Europe. Portuguese friends (not Muslim) were shocked to receive on 8 October 2010, a virulently anti-Muslim email message entitled: "The tremendous Islamic Threat." The text in Portuguese read: "Europe's problem is not really the gypsies but the Muslims, many of whom are already European citizens." The message contained a series of photos said to have been shot at a recent demonstration in London on "The Religion of Peace." Angry young men brandished posters in English, with Portuguese translations provided: "Slay those who insult Islam!" "Europe, you will pay!" "Destruction is on its way!" "Behead those who mock Islam!" "Butcher those who mock Islam!" "Europe take lessons from 9/11!" "Islam will dominate the world!" Scariest of all was a woman enveloped in a black niqab with a sign saying: "Be prepared for the real Holocaust!"

* * *

It is inevitable that Spain and Portugal should be influenced by their partners in the European Union, which are increasingly hostile to immigration and Muslims in particular. As the global recession spreads, the Socialist governments of Iberia have followed the lead of their conservative EU partners in tightening border controls, reducing imported contract labor and restricting immigrants' family reunion. As tension mounts elsewhere in western Europe over the increase in Muslim immigrants and their visibility, Iberian public opinion is showing signs of anti-Islamic, anti-immigrant or, simply, anti-foreign attitudes.

Quite naturally with the rapid expansion of the Muslim communities in Spain, the number of incidents involving Muslims has multiplied. Most cases of Muslim abuse have been denounced by the Islamic community, which is a sign that Muslims are striving to adapt to the norms of Spanish society. A rash of negative reports involving Muslims, especially in Cataluña late 2009-early 2010, provoked a flood of alarmist comments on the web: Islamic Fundamentalism was spreading in the province; Cataluña was in danger of being Islamicized; even talk of Cataluñistan. It began with the news that a group of radical Muslims in the region of Tarragona had formed their own ad hoc Islamic court and ruled that a Muslim woman should be stoned to death for committing adultery. The mainstream media reported that ten Moroccan suspects had been jailed in November 2009; later three were set free and by February 2010, the others were released without bail. The woman who made the charges failed to show up before the judge on several occasions, and reportedly had gone home to Morocco. Some observers questioned the veracity of the story, pointing out that the stoning of women may occur in some ultra-conservative Muslim societies, but it is not a North African tradition. The damage had been done, however. For the public, it appeared that a group of Muslims could set up an Islamic court and rule the stoning of a woman in twenty-first century Spain.

In swift succession, there were reports of the misdeeds of Muslim leaders in different parts of the country. The most flagrant case was that of the imam of the El Algar Mosque in the province of Murcia, who was accused of the sexual abuse of minors in February 2010. The forty-eight-year-old Moroccan man was said to have molested five girls between the ages of eight and eleven attending his Koranic classes. It was the families of the victims who had denounced the imam to the Spanish authorities. The cleric succeeded in taking flight before he could be apprehended. A spokesman for the Muslim community in Murcia condemned such abuse as "immoral," but that did not curb the angry rants on the web against Muslim pedophiles

Another widely publicized story involved the head of the Islamic Association of the Catalán resort of Cunit on Tarragona's Golden Coast, who was accused of threatening a Spaniard of Moroccan origin because she refused to wear a veil. Fatima Ghailan, thirty-one, intercultural mediator for the municipality, brought charges of threats and harassment against the sheikh, and accused him of trying to get her fired. The Police Union wanted to expel the sheikh, but the Socialist mayor sought to placate the community leaders in order to preserve calm. An indignant Ghailan told the press she could not understand why the mayor had not come to her defense.

At the same time, Abdelwahab Houzi, the imam of Lérida, known for his radical discourse, attracted public attention by refusing to shake women's hands and refusing to be interviewed by a woman. Several weeks later, the imam's wife, a Spanish convert, denounced him to the Guardia Civil on charges of polygamy and mistreatment.[27] The imam denied the accusations, but shortly afterwards he left for Saudi Arabia allegedly to resume his religious studies. The Islamic Community of Lérida began a search for a new imam, but there was no doubt that the case served to blacken the reputation of imams in general.

Taking advantage of the growing anti-Muslim mood, Ángel Colom, a leader of the right-wing nationalist party, Convergence and Union of Cataluña, introduced a bill calling for the expulsion of all radical imams. This action brought forth an angry response from the middle-of-the-road Islamic Junta of Cataluña and eleven other Muslim associations denouncing the "witch hunt" against imams.[28] The Catalán government rejected Colom's bill, pointing out that "you can't expel someone because you don't like the way he thinks."[29] But the Spanish online commentary generally supported Colom and his anti-imam rhetoric.

As Catalán-Muslim relations soured, simple press photos of Muslims praying in the streets brought forth a flood of protests on various Spanish websites. In early February 2010, the conservative Spanish daily newspaper, *El Mundo*, reported that the inhabitants of Badalona, a suburb of Barcelona, complained that Muslims held their prayer services in the streets. "It hasn't been easy for Muslims to find a place to pray in Badalona," the reporter, Jordi Ribalaygue, wrote, pointing out that there were only two prayer halls in the city, and Muslims have long asked for a proper mosque.[30] The electronic news organ, *Minuto Digital*, published *El Mundo*'s article, adding photos of street prayers in other Catalán towns. "Never in history have there been so many Muslims, as seen in these photos of Santa Colona and Lérida; they have physically taken over Cataluña's streets," *Minuto Digital* editorialized, pointing out that there were 250,000 Muslim immigrants in Cataluña, in addition to Spanish converts, in 2007.[31] Online reactions verged on panic, with no sympathy for Muslims who could not find a decent place with a roof to worship. "They're drowning our nation!" "Stop the invasion now!" bloggers screamed.

As long as the diatribes remained anonymous and confined to the net, the Spanish authorities and NGOs involved with immigrants did not appear overly concerned. But when Spaniards clashed with immigrants in the streets, people grew alarmed, fearing contagion of the ethnic riots in neighboring France. In fact, Spain had lived through a fortnight of race riots at El Ejido in 2000, and all sides had tried to avoid any recurrence of the violence with relative success. With rising tensions over the series of Muslim incidents in 2010, however, it was inevitable that a minor altercation should degenerate into a racial outburst. It began with a routine police identity check of a group of North Africans on the afternoon of 17 February 2010, in the town of El Vendrell near Tarragona. The Mossos d'Esquadra, or Catalán police, noted the suspicious behavior of a nineteen-year-old Moroccan and, searching him, found what looked like hashish. The Moroccan was arrested, and his companions began throwing stones and other projectiles at the Mossos, injuring one. The police sent in reinforcements and several dozen immigrant youths assembled for what turned into a pitched battle with a number of wounded on both sides. Although spirits calmed down the next day, right-wing political circles magnified the incident, in line with their anti-immigration campaign.

Josep Anglada I Ruis, leader of the extreme right-wing Platform for Cataluña, made a widely publicized declaration announcing that: "The ethnic war has begun." He argued that the North African immigrants "want to live in ghettos in order to set up separate zones, where there is no law and they have complete control." Anglada went on to predict that the El Vendrell clashes "would spread around the country like a drop of oil—the same thing that happened in the suburbs of Paris."[32]

It was the racial explosion at Salt, just ten days after El Vendrell, which troubled the nation and caused Spaniards to question immigration policies, with new urgency. Salt is a bedroom community of Gerona with a population of 31,000, of which 43% are immigrants, one of the highest percentages in the country. In fact, the city is known as the capital of Cataluña's Muslim community, with some 5,000 North Africans and 4,000 sub-Saharan Africans. Like El Vendrell, the confrontation began with a minor incident: an argument between an African immigrant and a Spaniard over a parking space. In no time, there were hundreds of native Spaniards and immigrants exchanging insults of *Moros! Ladrones! Racistas!* and clashing with each other in front of city hall. Police reinforcements were sent in to restore order but only added to the tension. Finally, the Socialist mayor, Iolanda Pineda, announced that "a coexistence pact" had been reached. A Board of *Convivencia*, with representatives of the different groups, would advise the authorities on complaints and demands from the community. "Today we have opened a new page in our common history, although we have a lot of work to do," the mayor declared.[33]

The Tudela incident was bound to happen. In the past, it would have been classified as a common crime gone horribly wrong but, at this time, it took on national proportions because the victim was a Spaniard and the suspects Algerian immigrants. The facts were simple, according to press reports from this prosperous industrial center in northern Spain. Javier Marínez Llort, a thirty-two-year-old technical engineer, was returning home alone at 6:30 am Sunday, after a late night with his fiancée and some friends, when he was accosted by thieves, apparently intent on stealing his cellphone. After beating him severely in the face and on the back of his head with a plank from a park bench, the aggressors fled the scene, taking the cellphone, but not his wallet or watch, and leaving him unconscious in the street. Marínez was found by a passerby an hour later, rushed to the local hospital and then flown by helicopter to Pamplona's hospital, where he died from his injuries that night. Although there were no eyewitnesses or cameras to record the incident, rumors were rife that the Spaniard had been killed by a group of North Africans. Friends of the victim set up a page on Facebook calling for justice, and mourners placed a wreath at the site of the aggression, with a note saying: "Whoever did this, Algerians, South Americans, East Europeans, gypsies or tough guys, what is certain, there's no security in Tudela." Reactions on the web were furious, demanding greater control of immigration and more power for the police. *Minuto Digital* played up the incident as a possible hate crime, noting that "this kind of attack is taking place all over Europe."[34] The Navarran police, backed by the national police, acted swiftly, arresting three Algerian suspects aged thirty-eight, twenty and nineteen, two of them undocumented immigrants. The Muslim community, which was directly affected by the incident, reacted promptly. Both mosques of Tudela and Pamplona held special services with a moment of silence for the Spanish victim. The imam of Tudela, Mourad Bettach Bouali, declared, "All of us Muslims condemn what has happened; if they [the Algerian suspects] are found guilty, Spanish law must be carried out."

There is no doubt that every incident involving immigrants contributes to a growing malaise in Cataluña. But the Cataláns remained ambivalent on the immigration issue. This was evident in a poll published in March

2010 by the Noxa Institute, which found that 52% of Cataláns believed there were too many immigrants in the province but 80% said that immigrants should have equal rights with citizens. And 73% asserted they would never vote for a party with a xenophobic platform.[35]

Naturally, the situation has worsened with the prolongation of the economic crisis. In its grim report on "The State of Racism in Cataluña in 2009," SOS Racismo warned that racist attitudes have spread and immigrants are being used as scapegoats. The study highlighted an increase in xenophobic language in Catalán politics and noted that "arguments of the extreme right were seeping into the discourse of the mainstream parties." The civil rights organization also faulted local authorities for "ambiguity in the fight against racism" and cited the attempt of Vic to limit immigrants' rights.[36]

The surge in immigrant-phobia is not by any means confined to Cataluña but more noticeable there because of the high concentration of immigrants attracted to Spain's most prosperous province. It has become a national problem, and Spain's Socialist government has not attempted to hide the severity of the economic recession and its negative impact on Spanish attitudes. "The crisis has hardened Spanish opinion of immigrants," concluded the Ministry of Labor's report on Racism and Xenophobia in 2009, highlighting figures showing Spaniards think there are too many immigrants and the laws are too lenient. According to this study, 77% think there are too many immigrants, compared to only 28% in 1996, and 42% hold that the laws are too tolerant, up from 24% in 2004. The same report noted that 68% of Spaniards expect immigrants to commit a crime and 60% hold that the Spanish should get preference over immigrants on the job market.[37]

Nevertheless, Celestino Corbacho, the tough-speaking minister of labor and immigration, asserted that xenophobia was being fed by "political interests." He insisted that there were only "isolated" racist incidents in the country and these could be resolved by the official policy of "dialogue and *convivencia*."[38]

Until lately, this policy of tolerance had generally shielded Spain from the wrenching debates over Islamic symbols, like the veil or minaret, which have led to the rise of Islamophobia in France, Belgium, Holland and Switzerland.

In Spain, only two headscarf incidents had received much press attention in 2002 and again in 2007, but both times the authorities insisted on the child's right to education. During that volatile spring of 2010, however, the case of Najwa Malha, barred from school over a head-scarf, stirred national debate over religious freedom. A Spanish citizen of Moroccan parents, Najwa attended the Camilo José Cela Institute in Madrid's suburb of Pozuelo de Alarcón. She was described as an ambi-tious student, a member of the school's hockey team and an aspiring mathematics professor. When she reached sixteen, Najwa donned the Islamic headscarf and soon found herself excluded from classes. According to the institute's internal rules, no kind of head-coverings were allowed in class. At first, Najwa remained in a reception room while sympathetic teachers and students brought her the daily lessons. Najwa's father, Mohamed Malha, head of the local Islamic Center, sup-ported her decision to wear a headscarf and pursue her studies. But the situation reached a climax when the school council voted to enforce the headscarf ban, and anti-Islamic graffiti appeared on the school walls. The Spanish press gave broad coverage to the story, generally favoring the school's decision. Emotional comments on the electronic media pre-sented Najwa's stand as a showdown between Islamic and western val-ues and some spoke of "a second Islamic invasion." The country appeared profoundly divided over the issue. Even members of the Socialist government were at odds with one other. The ministers of jus-tice and education supported the girl's right to education and religious freedom, while the minister of equality expressed distaste for any kind of veil and called for a debate on the subject. The conservative opposi-tion threatened to take the girl's father to court for jeopardizing Najwa's education. The Muslim Federation of Spain declared that this was a clear case of Islamophobia and suggested that the matter be brought before the Constitutional Court. The fiery Islamic leader of Alcalá de Henares, Imam Xavier Colas, said what was on many Mus-lims' minds: "The Muslim head-covering is the same practice as that of nuns, but nobody dares tell them to take off their robes."[39]

Gema Martín Muñoz, head of the Casa Árabe, summed up the case succinctly: "The girl should return to class without becoming an object of discrimination because it is permitted by the law of religious free-dom and she is guaranteed the right to education." Martín Muñoz warned in an interview that failure to let the girl continue her studies "would provoke unnecessary conflicts and feed the extreme right's Islamophobia that is taking place all over Europe."[40]

Even Spain's Roman Catholic episcopate stepped into the debate with a strong defense of the freedom to wear an Islamic headscarf, as well as a crucifix. Monsignor Juan Antonio Martínez Camino, spokes-man for the church, emphasized that Spain's Constitution stipulates "that individuals and institutions have the right to manifest their religious beliefs, limited only by the respect for public order."[41]

Seeking to end the controversy, Madrid's regional government ordered the transfer of Najwa Malha to the San Juan de la Cruz Institute near her old school, and the girl's family agreed. But the question rebounded when San Juan voted to change its rules, barring access to anyone with a head-covering. Embarrassed, the authorities found a place for the outcast at the Gerardo Diego Secondary School, which permits headscarves. The director, Amelia Martín, gave a warm welcome to Najwa and appealed to the large contingent of journalists accompanying her to help the process of normalization and leave the girl alone.

But some Spaniards remained troubled over the implications of the headscarf incident, which showed that part of the country is increasingly intolerant of its Muslim citizens. *El País* columnist, Javier Valenzuela, expressed concern that Spain was moving in the direction of the French model and the turmoil that ensued: the outright ban on headscarves and all religious symbols in the classroom. He noted that in Spain, like the rest of the West, there was a broad coalition opposed to the headscarf. "Feminists consider it a grim sign of discrimination against women; secularists view it as an intolerable demonstration of religiosity; the far right sees more evidence that Spain is being reconquered by Saracens; xenophobes (view it) as proof that immigrants refuse to adopt Spanish customs. Here as elsewhere, the result of such an amalgam is Islamophobia, the successor of what we knew for centuries as anti-Semitism."[42]

His words proved to be eerily prophetic. That spring of 2010, Cataluña would be swept by an anti-burqa-mania, although there were no burqas in sight and the rest of the country seemed largely indifferent to this new crusade. But Catalán attitudes and fashions are often in synch with those of their French neighbors. The French had banned headscarves in schools and were discussing the necessity to ban burqas; it was no accident that Cataluña should take up the cause. Lérida became the first city in Spain to ban burqas and niqabs in municipal buildings by a consensus vote at the end of May. El Vendrell followed with the votes of the Catalán nationalists, the right and far right. The movement culminated with an announcement on 14 June by the Socialist mayor of Barcelona that the burqa, niqab, and any kind of face-covering, including ski masks and motorcycle helmets, would be banned in all municipal establishments.[43]

In a matter of days, the imams of eleven mosques and prayer halls in the region denounced what they called an assault on women's freedom and said they would take the bans to the Constitutional Court. Abdennur Prado, a spokesman for Cataluña's Islamic Junta, blamed election politics for the anti-burqa campaign and warned that the imams "feel under attack and will use the debate to promote burqas and niqabs as a political statement."[44] Other moderate Muslims, who oppose the burqa and niqab, pointed out that the danger of the controversy was that it only strengthened the hand of the far right, which has threatened to move next against headscarves, minarets and Muslim immigrants.

The burqa affair moved out of Catalán politics to the national stage when senator Alicia Sánchez-Camacho, who heads the conservative Catalán People's Party, presented a motion to the senate asking the government for a country-wide ban. It became evident that the ruling Socialist party was itself divided on the issue. Justice minister Francisco Caamaño denounced the full-body veil as a security threat and an infringement on women's dignity and proposed that a ban on burqas should be included in the reform of the Law on Religious Freedom. Most Socialists, however, stressed that there were practically no burqas in Spain and the question was not a national priority, but they acknowledged privately that a ban would be seen as a capitulation to the anti-Islamic, anti-immigrant right.[45] To general surprise, the senate narrowly passed the opposition's motion to prohibit burqas in public places, despite warnings that such a ban might be unconstitutional and a violation of a woman's individual rights.

On the heels of the Spanish vote, a majority of the forty-seven-member Council of Europe (COE) in Strasbourg voted against a general ban on full-body veils like the burqa or niqab, except for reasons of security. Otherwise, Muslim women should be free to dress as they see fit, the ruling said.

Yet it seems cooler heads may still prevail in Spain. In an astonishing about-face, the nationalist Catalán party, Convergencia I Unio (CiU), made a strong appeal for the immigrant vote prior to regional elections at the end of November 2010. The CiU bussed some 2,000 immigrants from all over Cataluña to a pre-election rally at Barcelona's Palace of

Music. Addressing the crowd of Africans, Latin Americans, Pakistanis and Moroccans, some in headscarves, the former anti-immigrant activist Ángel Colom said that at a time of increasing xenophobia in Europe, Cataluña would serve as an example. "We don't want a multicultural Cataluña. Nor ghettos. We want one united people."[46] Pamphlets wooed the potential new voters in Spanish, Catalán, French and Arabic. And perhaps thanks in part to the immigrant vote, the CiU dominated the elections, winning sixty-two seats in the 135-seat Catalán parliament, compared to the ruling Socialists' poor showing of twenty-eight, a loss of nine seats, and eighteen for the conservative Peoples' Party, or an increase of four deputies. While the election showed an expected shift to the right, reflecting the continued economic crisis, the Cataláns did not succumb to the xenophobic rant of the extreme right-wing Plataforma per Cataluña. The blatantly anti-Muslim leader, Josep Anglada, not only did not make it into parliament, but his party lost ground in its two main strongholds; Vic and El Vendrell.

Early in 2011, the Pew Research Center released projections of an 82% rise in Spain's Muslim population over the next two decades, which only fed the budding Islamophobia. By 2030, the number of Muslims would be 1,859,000 or 3.7% of the total population, and then level off, according to the report.[47] Bloggers shouted Islamization of Spain and apparently failed to note that the percentage of Muslims was still relatively low, compared to other European countries like France at 10%.

Then too, angry Muslim youths have fed the incipient Islamophobia by occasional acts of violent protest. In early 2011, the already tense town of Salt was the scene of rampant vandalism by immigrant adolescents. The trouble began when a sixteen-year-old Moroccan boy, pursued by the police for stealing a motorcycle, fell five stories into a courtyard and later died from his injuries. For three nights, youths from the immigrant community expressed their solidarity with the victim, setting fire to cars and motorcycles and trash containers. "What happened in Salt has nothing to do with religion; it's a matter of delinquency," declared the Socialist mayor, Yolanda Pineda.[48] Recalling the 2005 riots of the Paris banlieux, the official said she would do everything to avoid a similar situation. Appealing for calm, the mayor sent in police reinforcements, who arrested two Moroccan minors and a Latino. They also arrested a Spaniard aged thirty-three, known to be a right-wing militant, accused of instigating some fires. A week later, some 3,000 people from 200 Catalán and immigrant associations and six local mosques, joined together in a silent march under the banner of: "We want to live well and in peace." Subsequently, mayor Pineda announced the launching of a one-year pilot project for "social cohesion and *convivencia*" in Salt and four other heavily immigrant towns, with most of the 2.5 million euros funding coming from the European Union.[49] It was no guarantee against new eruptions, but the project was a sign that Cataláns were not ready to succumb to the surge of xenophobia and that the EU believed the fight against exclusion was worthwhile.

Nevertheless, the Council of Europe's watchdog on racism has expressed concern over the deterioration of the situation in Spain, particularly regarding the internet. In its report made public on 8 February 2011, the European Commission against Racism and Intolerance (ECRI) stressed that there are numerous neo-Nazi movements active on the Spanish web. ECRI also criticized the Spanish authorities for insufficient data on racist crimes, discrimination against immigrants and gypsies in schools, and obstacles imposed on Muslim communities to open mosques.

By the end of 2010, thoughtful Spanish writers were warning against the spread of xenophobic discourse in Europe, and even in Spain, from the far right to the mainstream. An editorial in the leading daily *El País* referred to "the xenophobic pull," noting that democratic parties were now contending with populists over an anti-immigration agenda. "The severe effect of the [economic] crisis on the deficit and jobs has brought back the European debate over immigration but the debate has changed; before they were trying to stem the flow of immigrants while now the discussion involves how to deprive them of their rights."[50]

Although political bigots in Spain are less prone to flaunt their views than some European neighbors, the insidious ugliness is here and gaining ground. This is the way Antonio Manuel eloquently put it in *El Día de Córdoba*. "Now it's raining racism and xenophobia all over Spain. The rain is light and invisible because it doesn't appear on the weather maps. Nevertheless, the mobile phones, the network, the television are witness to the messages against the Moor, the Negro, the gypsy and for the territorial and religious unity of the state."[51]

13

THE WAY OF DIALOGUE

The Iberian difference, in my view, is the commitment of political and civil leaders to dialogue with Muslims at the national, European and global levels. Spain and Portugal have been countries of emigration for centuries and for this reason show more empathy than other Europeans to immigrants, including Muslims. Their outreach to Arab countries stems from national interests but also what seems to be an unspoken will to make amends for a long history of prejudice, suspicion and antagonism. The two former leaders of Roman Catholic empire-building are actively engaged in developing relations with the Islamic world as a means to ease international tensions and to assist the integration of their growing Muslim communities. And despite a new surge in Islamophobia, a majority of Spaniards and Portuguese apparently endorse this direction, preferring a dialogue of civilizations to the prophetic clash.

This dialogue is happening through innumerable official, non-governmental and academic channels. I will not attempt to present a comprehensive account of Ibero-Islamic undertakings, but mention only a few of special relevance in recent years. We can begin with the Casa Árabe, Árabe a national institution, founded in Madrid in 2006 by the Spanish Foreign Ministry, with the cooperation of Madrid's city hall and the Autonomous Community. A sister Institute of Arabic and Islamic Studies in Córdoba was established shortly afterwards, with support from Córdoba's city hall and the Junta de Andalucía. The Casa Árabe is not a welcome center for Arab immigrants, but essentially a meeting place for the promotion of Arab and Muslim culture among Spaniards. Ivan Martín, an economist, told me that the aim of the Casa Árabe was twofold: to enhance Spain's relations with Arab countries and to advance the knowledge of Arab culture in Spain. "There's a need for our activities because of the rise of Arabophobia in our society," Martín stressed.[1] Located in the handsome nineteenth century neo-Moorish Aguirre School, near Madrid's Retiro Park, the Casa Árabe presents a year-round program of concerts, films, exhibits, lectures and debates with well known North Africans and Middle East-erners, and Spanish experts on Arab affairs. Under the direction of one of Spain's leading Arabists, Gema Martín Muñoz, the Casa Árabe has become in this short period an important place of reference for special-ists in Islamic and Middle Eastern studies, a research center and a forum for intellectuals and visiting dignitaries from the Islamic world.

Spanish and Portuguese universities are playing an increasingly active role in the effort to promote dialogue with Muslims through a plethora of seminars, forums and publications. Such academic inter-changes with the Islamic world have long taken place in Britain and France but are relatively recent in Iberia. In the spring of 2007, Madrid's Autonomous University invited the controversial Swiss Mus-lim scholar, Tariq Ramadan, to give a course in Mediterranean studies and present a public lecture on "The European Union, the Mediterra-nean and Islam." The urbane Islamist of St. Antony's college Oxford told an enthusiastic audience of mostly young Spaniards and Moroc-cans that Islam has now become "a European religion." Emphasizing that European societies were changing, Ramadan declared: "I have talked to Spanish Muslims and they say: 'We are Spanish citizens.' On the other hand, the French still refer to second generation French North Africans as immigrants." Nevertheless, the speaker noted that the European Union, with the French president, Nicolas Sarkozy, in the lead, has come to the realization that "the future of Europe depends on Africa." He pointed out that in the next twenty years, the fifteen core nations of western Europe will need twenty million work-ers, and praised Spain for its policy of regularizing the status of undoc-umented immigrants "not just for humanitarian reasons but because of the recognition that it needs foreign workers." Discussing the pro-cess of absorbing immigrants, Ramadan said there were five kinds of integration: cultural, legal, social, intellectual and psychological—the latter being the most important. "The young English bombers were integrated on four levels but not psychologically," he said, referring to the attack on the London transportation system on 7 July 2005. "They did not feel that England was their country." Expressing concern over the rise of Islamophobia, he said there was evidence that more young Muslims were willing to speak out and "refuse victimization." The Muslim academic spoke vehemently against "radicals who use Islam" and added that the majority of Muslims felt the same way about radicalization. Responding to my question on how to counter Muslim extremists, Ramadan declared: "There must be a coordinated action against radicals by European governments and by Muslim communities in Europe."[2]

A major event, and the first of its kind in Lisbon, was a two-day seminar on "Muslims in Portugal," organized at the end of 2007 by the University of Lisbon's Institute of Social Sciences in cooperation with the European Muslim Network, the Islamic Community of Lisbon and the Abrahamic Forum of Lisbon. Professor Salman Sayyid, director of the Centre of Ethnicity and Racism Studies at the University of Leeds, gave the keynote address on "Answering the Muslim Question: Euro-Islam and European Dreams." The panel discussion was led by the ubiquitous Tariq Ramadan who, in addition to his academic activities, is president of the European Muslim Network. Prominent Portuguese Jewish and Catholic figures also discussed "Faith in Action, Community and Conviviality." Nina Clara Tiesler, one of the principal organizers of the seminar, told me afterwards, "What could be concluded is that the majority of Muslims with European experience have European values."[3] She said that Ramadan came across as a bridge and conciliator between Europe and Islam and a champion of Euro-Islam, whereas Sayyid rejected the idea of European Islam on the grounds that Islam is universal.

The University of Lisbon and MEL-net, an international research network on Muslims in Portuguese Language Areas, hosted another ground-breaking symposium in May 2010 on Islamophobia, with professors Salman Sayyid and Adoolkarim Vakil, editors of a new book, *Thinking Through Islamophobia*. Professor Sayyid dated the history of the concept of Islamophobia to the end of the Cold War and said it was revealed through a succession of "moral panics" that swept the West: over the Danish cartoons, the murder of cineaste Van Gogh in Holland, the headscarf ban in France, and the burqa ban in Belgium. Professor Vakil of King's College London, son of Abdool Majid Vakil, president of Lisbon's Islamic Community, noted that the first comprehensive survey of Islamophobia was a report by the Runnymede Trust Commission on British Muslims in 1996–97. Emphasizing the global nature of the phenomenon, he traced it back to decolonization and suggested one aim was to demonstrate that "Muslims cannot be assimilated in the West." Although the term Islamophobia remains controversial, Vakil concluded, "It has been legally recognized and therefore allows redress."[4]

An unusual Iberian intercultural event honored two medieval Arab intellectuals in May 2008. The three-day congress was organized by a private Hispano-Moroccan foundation in the southern Portuguese border city of Vila Real de Santo António, with the cooperation of local authorities. Nearly 100 Moroccan, Spanish and Portuguese academics and students gathered to pay homage to the twelfth century Moroccan geographer, Muhammad Al Idrisi, who was also a notable pharmacologist, botanist and historian. The other honoree was a leading poet of Al Andalus, Ibn Darraj al-Qastalli, a native son of the Algarve village of Cacela Velha. After unveiling a plaque in the village square in memory of Ibn Darraj, who straddled the tenth-eleventh centuries, the congress adjourned to the church for a recital of the poet's works in Arabic, Berber, Hebrew, Portuguese, Spanish, French, Italian and English, followed by a concert of Andalucian music.

"The Iberian public has finally begun to be interested in its Muslim past," Ahmed Tahiri, president of the Seville-based Al-Idrisi Foundation, told me in an interview, pointing out that Spanish television was filming the entire congress. Tahiri, a professor of medieval history from Tetuan, said he established the foundation in 1999 around the central figure of Al-Idrisi "as a humanist, scientist, and a unifying Muslim, who had worked for a Christian king." The non-profit organization has received support from the king of Morocco, the Junta de Andalucía, several universities and local municipalities.[5]

One of the more controversial scholarly events was an international seminar on "The state of the Arab World—from North Africa to the Middle East—and the Colonial Legacy," organized by the University of Oporto in the spring of 2008. Academics from Europe, North Africa and the Middle East gathered in the Algarve to answer a basic question: "Are Islamic societies incompatible with the political notion of the nation state or should we look at this scene as the legacy of colonialism?" A poster promoting the seminar showed the photograph of a Saharan guerrilla with a machine gun trained on the enemy. The legend said that the post-colonial Arab world "seems characterized by wars between neighbors, internal strife, masked dictatorships, failed states, widespread illiteracy, delays in science and technology, religious crises and stagnation."[6] Objecting to this grim image of Arabs, the Luso-Arab Center withdrew its sponsorship of the seminar, but the event went ahead as planned. The scholars concurred that the main problems of the region were a direct heritage of the former colonial regimes. And the Saharan guerrilla unapologetically graced the cover of Oporto University's International Journal of African Studies for the first semester of 2009.

At the same time, Iberia's Muslim groups have taken the initiative to communicate with the broader society around them. For example, early in 2010, Madrid saw its first Muslim *feria*, whose twofold aim was to present "the Muslim reality" in Spain and promote Muslim interaction with non-Muslim communities. The three-day fair took place in the multicultural neighborhood of Lavapiés and was organized by the young Muslim Federation of Spain (FEME), with support from the Higher Islamic Council of Valencia, Madrid's city hall and the Movement against Intolerance. Under the theme of "Islam and *Convivencia*", prominent speakers discussed delicate issues facing Spain's Muslims, such as: "Racism, Intolerance and Islamophobia" and "Unity and Diversity in Islam." An important feature of the fair was the first Congress of Muslim Women in Spain, led by Amparo Sánchez Rosell, head of Valencia's Islamic Cultural Center. Laure Rodríguez, president of the Union of Muslim Women in Spain, told the press that the meeting had discussed how to combat media stereotypes of Muslim women "as submissive victims, without the right to speak."[7] Another attraction was the first display of halal gastronomy in the Spanish capital. Organizers also conferred the Prize of Islam and *Convivencia* on figures in culture, politics and civil society, including Madrid's mayor Alberto Ruiz-Gallardón and Valencia's councilor for Solidarity and Citizenship, Rafael Blasco.

While intercultural meetings are occurring with greater frequency all around Iberia, they have been eclipsed to a certain extent by inter-religious events. In Portugal, the National Commission for Religious Freedom, headed by the former president, Mário Soares, has taken the lead in organizing various ecumenical gatherings, such as an interfaith encounter in September 2007 in honor of the Dalai Lama. When the Roman Catholic patriarchate let it be known that it could not host the Buddhist leader, apparently because of pressures from China, the Central Mosque of Lisbon volunteered to receive the controversial guest in a much publicized ceremony.

In the spring of 2008, Soares' Commission held an international conference on "The Contribution of Religions to Peace," which grouped prominent figures from Christianity, Judaism and Islam, as well as Hinduism and Buddhism. As evidence of Portugal's strong interest in interfaith dialogue, the prime minister and other personalities took part in the deliberations. António Costa, newly elected mayor of Lisbon, opened the proceedings recalling one of the ugliest events in Portuguese history, the 1506 Lisbon Massacre, when a Roman Catholic mob slaughtered more than 2,000 Jews. The mayor evoked "a new spirit in Portugal," emphasizing that Lisbon had finally raised a memorial to the Jewish victims of religious fanaticism on São Domingos Square. "There are still risks of fanaticism, stemming from hatred, ignorance, and hunger," Costa noted. "We are conscious of this challenge, but will confront it with a new humanism and respect for differences." Expressing the conviction that the world "can avoid" the shock of civilizations, Grand Rabbi René Samuel Sirat, vice president of the European Conference of Rabbis, singled out Al Andalus as a model of coexistence, in which Iberian peoples had lived "in peace, justice and fraternity." Also hailing medieval Iberia as a positive example was Kuwaiti-born imam Feisal Abdul Rauf, founder of the American Society for Muslim Advancement, the same imam who two years later would become the center of fierce controversy over his plan to build an Islamic Center near Ground Zero in New York City. The sixty-year-old Muslim leader spoke about his "Córdoba Initiative," established in the wake of the 9/11 attacks. He said that in discussions with American Jewish colleagues, there was agreement on the need for "a global multi-faith, multi-cultural, Muslim/non-Muslim partnership to strengthen common values and bridge divides." The Córdoba initiative identifies problem areas fueling international tensions and crafts projects to help resolve them, imam Feisal declared, expressing the hope that Portugal and Spain, located at the intersection of Europe, Africa and the East, would join "in this important work to sustain world peace."[8]

The ultimate experience in interfaith dialogue was convened the summer of 2008 by a most unlikely patron, King Abdullah of Saudi Arabia, a country that practices Wahhabism, an austere school of Islam, and bans the public practice of other faiths within its borders. The venue of the Saudi conference was also unusual, a luxury hotel on the outskirts of Madrid. The king of Spain acted as co-host, and turned over his elegant Pardo Palace for the opening ceremony. Spain's Socialist government appeared somewhat embarrassed by the royal event, and officials told me they had nothing to do with the organization. The prime minister, Zapatero, attended the opening ceremony but pointedly made no statement.

Nevertheless, some 200 spiritual leaders of Islam, Judaism, Christianity and Eastern religions responded positively to the Saudi monarch's invitation to attend the three-day "World Conference on Dialogue." The declared focus was twofold: the role of religion in the struggle against crime, corruption, drugs and terrorism, and in the promotion of a culture of tolerance and understanding.

Of all the interfaith gatherings since 11 September, the Madrid meeting assumed special importance because of the personal commitment of King Abdullah Bin Abdulaziz Al-Saud, whose country is the historic heart of Islam as well as the home of Osama bin Laden and many other Muslim extremists. In his opening address, King Abdullah called on followers of the world's great religions to turn away from extremism and engage in "constructive dialogue." Noting that most dialogues between religions have failed, the Saudi leader stressed: "The tragedies we have experienced throughout history were not the fault of religion but because of the extremism that has been adopted by some followers of all the religions and of all the political systems." He urged believers of different religions "to open a new page for humanity, where reconciliation will substitute disputes. For his part, King Juan Carlos highlighted Spain's "historic tradition as a land enriched by its crossroads of cultures and religions ... a country that has built its democracy on the basis of tolerance, coexistence and mutual respect."[9]

In Saudi tradition, the guest list, media coverage and subject of debates were closely controlled, Guests included celebrities like former the British prime minister, Tony Blair, and American civil rights leader Rev. Jesse Jackson, and Rabbi David Rosen, from Israel but participating as head of the American Jewish Committee's Interreligious Relations. From the outset, the Saudi organizers from the Mecca-based Muslim World League announced: "no politics." Disregarding the blackout on politics, Rabbi Arthur Schneir of New York, who has been engaged in interfaith dialogue for forty years through his Appeal of Conscience Foundation, said it was the role of religious leaders to hasten a solution to what he called "the intractable conflict" in the Middle East between Israelis and

Palestinians. Most delegates emphasized shared values. Cardinal Jean Louis Tauran, who heads the Papal Council for Interfaith Dialogue, declared that "what unites us is faith in God, responsible preservation, and the sacred character of human dignity."[10]

Numerous speakers criticized the conference organizers for the absence of women on the panels. On the final day, to the general surprise, a change of program was announced; Dr. Mekia Nedjar would speak on "The Role of Women in Cultural Dialogue." Thus, my Algerian friend, who was working as a translator for the conference, was drafted at the last minute to bring a feminine voice to that largely male world. Mekia, who just obtained her doctorate in Mediterranean studies at the Autonomous University of Madrid, appeared firmly self-confident in her headscarf and plain coat, as she told the assembly that "the image of Islam has been distorted" by the mass media." In all Muslim-majority countries, the position of women has progressed, she asserted, noting that 80% of the college students are women. After the conference, Mekia told me this was an important "first step" for Saudi Arabia and that it must be followed by "practical developments."

The Saudi conference closed without any major breakthroughs or mishaps, and with a set of principles and recommendations called "The Declaration of Madrid." There was a call "to repulse extremism, fanaticism and terrorism," described as "a global phenomenon that must be confronted by international efforts." Calling for a concerted fight against the premise of an inevitable shock of civilizations, the conference recommended the promotion of "a culture of tolerance and comprehension" through the cooperation of religious, cultural and educational institutions as well as the media.

The Spanish monarchist daily *ABC* stressed that the conference was essentially about "domestic and regional needs of the Saudi monarchy" and "against the influence of the more extremist sectors of the Saudi clergy."[11] Interfaith dialogue will not be easy in Saudi Arabia. Barely ten days after the Madrid conference, a spokesman for Al Qaeda urged Muslims to assassinate the Saudi king for a "betrayal of Islam." In a video aired on an Islamist website, Abu Yahia Al-Libi said the king's appeal for religious dialogue "means renouncing Islam." Whether the Saudi king can use the Madrid Declaration as a lever to pry some kind of opening to other faiths at home remains to be seen. The Madrid conference, however, did produce a reasonable platform for dialogue between the Islamic and non-Islamic worlds.

In Europe, the Iberian nations have been in the vanguard of action to promote political dialogue with the "South" and specifically their Muslim neighbors, as a means of easing world tensions. As early as 1984, the Council of Europe (COE) organized in Portugal its first major conference on European solidarity with the developing world. In June 1988, Spanish king Juan Carlos hosted a major European conference in Madrid, which concluded with an appeal for a North-South partnership against poverty and the abuse of human rights. Then in 1990, the North-South Center opened in Lisbon, with the backing of the COE, and has become a major intercultural forum for the region, involving governments, regional and local authorities, parliaments and non-governmental organizations.

"The North and South do not always share the same values but we can identify common ground," Denis Huber, executive director of the center, told me in an interview in its newly renovated headquarters in Lisbon. "What unites us is far more important than what divides us."[12] Huber said that the North-South Center is composed of nineteen members from Scandinavia and Continental Europe and had working agreements with twelve countries from the Eastern Mediterranean, North Africa and Southern Africa

In May 2010, the North-South Center celebrated its twentieth anniversary. The first non-European states had joined the center, Morocco in 2009 and Cape Verde in 2010, for a total of twenty-two members. One of the main anniversary events was a day-long roundtable discussion on "The twenty-first Century, a Century of Global Interdependence and Solidarity." Egyptian writer, psychiatrist and 2004 North-South Prize laureate, Nawal Al Saadawi, stressed, "Past development concepts have resulted in more poverty, more wars, unimpeded immigration, and more fundamentalists." A precursor of the Arab revolt to come, Al Saadawi, seventy-nine, angrily denounced "the corrupt governments" that dominate her world. "We should use our creativity to develop a new political, economic and social model based on equality, justice and real democracy," she asserted. A year later, there was the indomitable Al Saadawi in the forefront of the Egyptian uprising.

The North-South awards ceremony in the Portuguese parliament attracted attention because the recipients of the 2009 prize were Russian reformer Mikhail Gorbachev (unable to be present for health reasons), and Kuwait's first woman parliamentarian Rola Dashti. Deputy

Dashti declared that Kuwaiti women have made major advances recently, winning the right to vote in 2005 and electing the country's first four female parliamentarians in 2009. "Our experience has started to be taken as an example by neighboring Gulf countries," she said.

But it was through what is known as the Barcelona Process that Europeans and, specifically, Iberians hoped to establish a framework for comprehensive relations with their Muslim neighbors to the south and east. In November 1995, the fifteen members of the European Union met in the Catalán capital with representatives of twelve states from the Southern and Eastern Mediterranean to form a new partnership, whose ambitious aim was "to build together an area of peace, security and shared prosperity."[13] An action plan set out guidelines for the fight against terrorism, cooperation for the social integration of migrants and intercultural dialogue on youth, education and the media.[14]

Lofty ideals notwithstanding, the Barcelona Process was slow to produce meaningful change. The tenth anniversary of the Barcelona Process was a time of critical evaluation. In a severe study, British academic Richard Youngs called the Barcelona Process "a distinctive but so far ineffectual approach to fostering political change in the authoritarian regimes of the southern Mediterranean."[15] It was widely agreed that the Barcelona Process had produced few visible results, aside from enhanced bilateral trade relations. The major obstacles to Mediterranean cooperation were also well known: the worsening of Arab-Israeli relations and the prolonged hostility between Morocco and Algeria over Western Sahara.

Then, out of the blue, Nicolas Sarkozy, campaigning for the French presidency in early 2007, launched his plan for a Mediterranean Union, grouping the countries bordering the sea that has linked, or divided, three continents since antiquity. Once elected president, Sarkozy renewed his proposal. Spain's Zapatero voiced his government's support, declaring: "We want the Mediterranean Union to be a new phase, a new impetus to cooperation between the two shores ... Spain is committed to this process as a country that has always been in the forefront of everything that has to do with the Mediterranean."[16]

In the spring of 2008, the European Commission recognized the achievements of the Barcelona Process on strategic, economic and cultural issues but noted that reforms have been "encouraging but short of initial expectations."[17] Pointing out that the conflict in the Middle East had challenged the Mediterranean partnership "to the limits of its abilities," the Commission's report stressed that "further and faster reforms are needed.'[18] At a summit of forty-three European and Mediterranean nations in Paris on 13 July 2008, the new organization was born, to be known as the Barcelona Process: Union for the Mediterranean, or UpM. In a joint declaration, the co-chairs, Sarkozy and the Egyptian president, Hosni Mubarak, announced that the Union would address common challenges: economic and social development, the world food security crisis, degradation of the environment, energy, migration, terrorism and extremism, and intercultural dialogue. But despite Sarkozy's energy and determination, the Union for the Mediterranean, like its predecessor, found itself bogged down by Arab-Israeli politics.

On my arrival in Barcelona in July of 2010, I was greeted with dire headlines in the leading daily *La Vanguardia*: "A Sea of Difficulties: The Union for the Mediterranean is Sinking on the Shoals of 'very dark' Perspectives."[19] The feature was based on the opinions of 300 experts consulted by the European Institute of the Mediterranean for the European Commission. The European Institute is a Spanish think tank, specialized in Mediterranean relations, and functions independently of the new union. "The UpM will be paralyzed both medium and long-term by the Israeli-Palestinian conflict," the report predicted, adding that this situation would jeopardize all the Union's projects. The study concludes that the huge gap in the income levels between the two shores of the Mediterranean has not been reduced, nor has the disparity in the quality of education and training, which meant a continued brain drain from South to North. It was not surprising that in the wake of this negative publicity, my appointment for a briefing with a staff member of the Mediterranean Union was canceled. Nor was there any surprise when France, Spain and Egypt announced in late November the indefinite postponement of the Mediterranean Summit, until an improvement in the Israeli-Palestinian situation.

The main object of my visit to Barcelona was to attend what is known as the "Olympics of Middle Eastern Studies" at the campus of the Autonomous University of Barcelona (UAB) in a green suburb of the Catalán capital. The UAB, in conjunction with the European Institute of the Mediterranean, had spent the past two years preparing for the World Congress for Middle Eastern Studies or WOCMES, as it is known in academic circles. My friend Laura Feliu, professor at UAB, was academic coordinator for the congress, but I saw little of her in the crush of some 3,000 scholars from seventy-two countries, mainly the United States, the United Kingdom, Spain, Turkey, France, Germany, Japan, Egypt, Iran, Algeria, Morocco and Israel. It was the largest such conference ever held in Europe.

If anything, Barcelona's WOCMES presented a surfeit of knowledge; 500 sessions in one week on everything from "Middle East Politics and Christians in the Muslim World" to Sexuality and Gender Identity in the Muslim World. The 2010 WOCMES Award for Outstanding Contributions to Middle Eastern Studies was given to Josef van Ess of the University of Tübingen, Germany, and Roger Owen of Harvard University. An unstated goal of the congress was evident: Barcelona was determined to reaffirm its role as a bridge to the Islamic world, at least academically, and this time it succeeded.

In a broader context, Iberian leaders have looked primarily to the Alliance of Civilizations as a forum to debate and resolve outstanding problems with the Islamic world. Spanish coordinator for the Alliance, Maximo Cajal López, outlined its history, pointing out that contrary to general opinion, it was the Iranian president, Mohammad Khatami, who first suggested the need for dialogue between Islam and the western world as early as 1998. Then in his address to the UN General Assembly in 2004, Spain's new Socialist prime minister, José Luis Rodríguz Zapatero, called for an alliance of civilizations. "Zapatero pointed out that one wall had just collapsed and it was necessary to prevent the construction of a new wall of hatred," Cajal recalled in an interview over tea in a Madrid hotel.[20] He stressed that it wasn't easy to sell the idea to the Spanish public, coming just six months after the Madrid terrorist attacks and a year after the invasion of Iraq. From the outset, the conservative People's Party has been "strongly opposed to the Alliance," he acknowledged. The Spanish diplomat said that Zapatero persuaded Turkey's prime minister, Tayyip Erdogan, to act as co-sponsor of the Alliance of Civilizations, which was formally launched under the auspices of UN secretary general Kofi Annan on 14 July 2005. The UN chief designated a High Level Group of "eminent persons" to analyze the causes of the current polarization between cultures and recommend practical measures to avert the projected clash of civilizations. Annan's successor, Ban Ki-moon, appointed Jorge Sampaio, former president of Portugal, as his high representative to the Alliance and the visible face of the fledgling agency.

I first met Sampaio in the 1960s, when he was a young lawyer opposed to the dictatorial Salazar regime and later as a two-term president of Portugal, but had not seen him in his new role as international peace-maker. The Lisbon base of the Alliance of Civilizations is the Casa do Regalo, a lemon-colored nineteenth century *palacete*, or little palace, nestled in a cedar forest near the Portuguese Foreign Ministry. "You just missed the Dalai Lama," Sampaio greeted me affably in his professorial British manner. He recalled that when he was president, an "accidental meeting" with the Buddhist leader had been arranged in a museum not to offend Beijing. "Things are much easier now that I don't hold an official position," he said.[21] Indeed, there was a noticeable absence of security around the Casa do Regalo. At the time of our meeting, Sampaio was making preparations for the Alliance's first Forum to be held at Madrid in mid-January 2008. "The Forum will show that our partnership program exists on the ground," he emphasized. The Alliance already boasted sixty-nine members in its Group of Friends, countries and international organizations, including the Council of Europe and the Arab League. The UN envoy said that one of the main problems facing the Alliance was that there were many centers of radical Islam and no single territory, "but we have to deal with them." He stressed that the Palestinian question was "central to any effort at rapprochement between the western world and Islam." Sampaio had to cut short our meeting, but an aide provided me with basic information. The headquarters of the Alliance is located at the United Nations, but it is not another large UN bureaucracy, just a small secretariat of ten people. According to the mission statement, the overall aim of the Alliance is "to improve understanding and cooperative relations among nations and peoples across cultures and religions and to help counter the forces that fuel polarization and extremism." A key objective is the support of projects that "promote understanding and reconciliation among cultures globally and in particular between Muslim and western societies."

The first Forum of the Alliance of Civilizations took place at Madrid's Palace of Congresses in January 2008, with the presence of UN secretary general Ban Ki-Moon and Sampaio, as well as the prime ministers of Turkey and Spain and over a thousand participants. Featured guests included Queen Noor of Jordan, Sheikha Mozah bint Nasser Al Missned of Qatar, Shirin Ebadi Nobel Laureate from Iran, Mary Robinson, former prime minister of Ireland, and Amr Moussa, Arab League secretary general. The United States was conspicuous by the absence of any prominent representative. Spanish sources told me privately that the Bush administration had expressed annoyance over the creation of the Alliance of Civilizations, seen as a Spanish manoeuvre to undermine Washington's Greater Middle East Initiative, which Spain emphatically denied. Nevertheless, the Forum provided fertile ground for cross-cultural discussions. It also produced concrete projects and pledges of funding for two of the Alliance's key concerns: youth and the media. Her highness Mozah announced a $100 million investment in a global youth employment initiative for the Middle East and North Africa aimed at "connecting young people to each other, to capital, to industry, to opportunity." For her part, Queen Noor launched a $10 million Media Fund, which she said would "support the production and distribution of films that entertain as well as enlighten—films, which will enhance the connections that already exist between different societies, but are seldom noted on screen and in popular culture." Another initiative was the creation of the Alliance's online Clearinghouse, involving eighteen universities, which would catalogue developments in media literacy education. A Rapid Response Media Mechanism was set up with an online list of global experts in cross-cultural matters. Finally a Youth Solidarity Fund was established to provide grants for youth-led programs in intercultural and interfaith dialogue worldwide.

As co-founder of the Alliance, Spain presented its two-year National Plan to the Forum, with a list of fifty concrete actions to promote the acceptance of diversity and improve the integration of immigrants, particularly young people. Specific measures included: the teaching of minority religions in public schools; a student exchange program aimed at the Arab world; and the training of Spanish Arabists and Moroccan Hispanists. Among other proposals, there was the translation of classics from Christianity, Judaism and Islam, and the creation of a University of European-Mediterranean cooperation at Tetuan, Morocco.

In the United States, the Alliance of Civilizations was initially met with disinterest, skepticism, and even hostility in some conservative circles, opposed to anything with a United Nations connection. Critics said there was no need for another intercultural organization, that it was too aggressive or too idealistic, too ambitious with too little means. Fox News called it "a questionable initiative" with "a hazy mandate and vague chain of command."[22] The Washington-based Heritage Foundation issued a background paper early in 2007, urging the United States to oppose the UN initiative. Specifically, the foundation attacked the High Level Group's report of November 2006 as being "focused obsessively on the failings of western countries while ignoring the faults of Muslim countries."[23]

The Alliance was also vilified in Spain by conservative politicians and blogs, who rushed to denigrate any initiative by the Socialist government. Nevertheless, the Alliance has since won over a major Spanish critic, Gustavo Arístegui, known as the shadow foreign minister of the opposition People's Party. The conservative parliamentarian, who earlier had called the Alliance "extremely dangerous," told the Chamber of Deputies in the fall of 2009 that the organization had undergone "a positive change," since it was now supported by more than eighty nations.[24]

In fact, the Alliance has caught on internationally. Sampaio has been invited by governments, regional organizations and private groups from Azerbaijan to Buenos Aires, from Strasbourg to Tehran, to talk about the Alliance. At of the end of 2009, there were 105 countries and international organizations in the Group of Friends, although the United States was still missing. In a congratulatory letter to president-elect Barack Obama, Sampaio noted that the United States had failed to join the Alliance for reasons "mostly related with the whole concept of the Bush Administration's war on terrorism." Urging Mr. Obama to change this, Sampaio wrote: "Your election brings new hope to the entire world with your commitment to change, a change that restores America's leadership, America's capacity for dialogue and America's influence!"[25] Sampaio's aide told me later that the United States had attended some Alliance meetings as an observer, and "there are great expectations" that President Obama will bring the US into the Alliance.[26] The United States finally did join the Alliance of Civilizations on 13 May 2010, but the publicity was kept to a minimum, as if trying to avoid a new round of attacks from Fox News and friends. I was in the US at the time and learned of the act through an *Agence France Presse* dispatch in the Spanish press. Sampaio's office confirmed the report and sent me a copy of the Alliance's communiqué from the United Nations. Warmly welcoming the United States as the 100th member country, Sampaio declared this to be a significant opportunity "to expand cross-cultural education, promote dialogue and understanding with a special focus on relations with the Muslim world, and forge the collective political will to address the world's imbalances."[27]

* * *

Throughout my Iberian travels, I have encountered a wide range of Muslims and non-Muslims—political and religious leaders, academics and other opinion makers, social workers, students and ordinary citizens—who believe that Islamic values are not incompatible with modernity and western culture. Most people support the initiatives to promote religious dialogue and cultural interchange as an important contribution to easing world tensions. But conversations invariably conclude that the only way to curb increasing radicalization is to root out the causes for the confrontation between the West and the Islamic world. These are political and economic, and defined as Oil and Gas, Palestine, Gaza, Kashmir, Iraq and Iran ... and beyond the scope of this book. This is the way the UN High Representative for the Alliance of Civilizations put it in his response to the call for interfaith dialogue by the king of Saudi Arabia:

"From Iraq to Afghanistan, from Kashmir to Sri Lanka, from Indonesia to Israel and Palestine, it often seems that religion fuels violence and raises the stakes of war," Sampaio stated. He emphasized that the roots of most conflicts were territorial ambitions, geopolitical interests, political rivalry, competition for natural resources, economic instability, social injustice and inequalities. "Politics and religion should join forces against extremism, totalitarianism and exclusion ... to promote a global alliance for peace through education," he urged.[28]

Independent political analysts generally approved of the Iberian outreach to the Islamic world but pointed out a serious flaw in well-meaning organizations such as the Barcelona Union for the Mediterranean and the Alliance of Civilizations. They were essentially elite, government-driven organizations, without contact to the grassroots militants who must be reached to prevent future conflicts. "The Casa Árabe is preaching to the convinced," stressed Haizam Amirah Fernández, the senior analyst for the Mediterranean and the Arab World at the Elcano Institute. Even the Alliance of Civilizations is flawed because there's no real dialogue, he continued, adding it's the same like-minded people talking to one another. "Frustration may be worse than no policy if governments fail to take concrete steps," he warned.[29]

"Everyone is in favor of inter-religious dialogue," Serge Laurens, spokesperson for the America-Spain Solidarity and Cooperation Association, said, adding that there had to be a response to the threats of an impending clash of civilizations. But he stressed that the Alliance of Civilizations was essentially an elite think tank, structured from top to bottom. "What they need is a regional grassroots structure—something like the rotary clubs to resolve conflicts at the local level."[30]

The question is: where to begin a meaningful dialogue with the dissenters? One suggested avenue is to engage with non-governmental organizations like those which have participated in the Brazil-based World Social Forums, founded in 2000, as an alternative to the World Economic Forum at Davos, Switzerland. Some of these advocacy groups have been involved in demonstrations of solidarity with the Palestinians, protests against the American wars in Iraq and Afghanistan, and gatherings for human rights in general. Some can be found on official blacklists or in the mainstream media's lexicon of "radical" groups, although they are constantly preaching peace and non-violence. These activists know how to communicate with grassroots organizations in Europe, the Americas, Southern Africa, Asia and the Middle East.

An articulate representative of this alternative world, Hussein El Ouariachi is a Moroccan from the northern port of Nador, who obtained his doctorate in history from the University of Granada in 2009. El Ouariachi works with Muslim communities in Cataluña for the Belgium-based Alliance for Freedom and Dignity (AFD), whose mission is to fight against poverty, injustice and inequality. He is also a leader of the Barcelona Consensus, an international group of social activists. He joined the World Social Forum in 2007 and took part in the forum held at Belem, Brazil in 2009.

"The Barcelona Process was doomed at the outset because it was an elite club of governments and did not take into account the real needs of the people, particularly those on the southern shore of the Mediterranean. Worse, it was not egalitarian but rather an effort by the North to impose its policies on the South, namely as a way to control immigration and integrate Israel into the Mediterranean space," El Ouariachi told me over fresh orange juice in a popular café at Barcelona port.[31] Summing up widespread criticism of the Mediterranean initiative, he underlined, "Barcelona should have worked with civil society, supported local NGOs, but there was nothing. It is evident that the process won't work without citizens' participation." He was nearly as hard on the Alliance of Civilizations: "It's a noble idea but everything is at the state level; they're not in contact with the people." Specifically, he suggested there should be more student exchanges, more cooperation among universities, more involvement of senior citizens, more networking with local NGOs.

On the local plane, the Moroccan community advocate said the Alliance for Freedom and Dignity seeks to improve relations between the Moroccan society and the Catalán administration, emphasizing that both sides need to show "more sensitivity." Pointing out that some Moroccan communities have no contact with the government or their neighbors, he said the AFD was working with Islamic and cultural groups to promote dialogue. "We're encouraging democratic training; what we love is organizations like the PTA!" The social mediator said AFD was trying to promote a new Islamic feminism, based on freedom of choice, "We want to free women from the paternalist society." There are between thirty and forty Salafi religious leaders in Cataluña who follow the Saudi Wahabi rite, have no formal education, are misogynist and won't let their women work, he said. But he insisted that these "medieval Muslims" are not radicals and do not advocate violence. "The radicals are young men who learn about violence on the internet, not in the mosques and prayer halls," El Ouariachi affirmed. "They are nourished by inequities and lack of opportunity. The only way to fight radicalization is through anti-violence intercultural associations that can talk to alienated young people about their role in society."

"Europe's reality is multiculturalism and the French policy of assimilation is bound to fail," El Ouariachi concluded, giving Spain credit for adopting an intercultural model which he defined as "a society of equals with cultural differences."

The Muslims I have met generally commend Spain and Portugal for their attempts to work out comprehensive immigration and integration policies, even though these are not always carried out to the letter. The late Mansur Escudero, head of the Islamic Junta and a signatory of Spain's 1992 accord with the Muslim community, emphasized that the accord was still to be fully implemented. "We have freedom of religion and opinion, but we still demand equal rights with other faiths," Escudero said at our last meeting in his home at Almodóvar del Rio.[32] He singled out the problem of Islamic education in public schools; there were only thirty-eight teachers of Islam in Spanish schools, when there should be a thousand for the some 100,000 Muslim school children. Calling Al Andalus a "paradigm for *convivencia*," the Spanish Muslim leader said: "What appeals to Muslims is the model of civilization, the arts and sciences that were developed here under Islamic rule. It has nothing to do with recovery of territory."

Representative of the new generation of Spain's Islamic leaders, Said Ratbi believes that Muslims must participate as citizens in the society where they reside. Moroccan-born Ratbi is president of the Higher Islamic Council of Valencia, established in 2008. "We want to be efficient and beneficial to the multicultural society where we live," Ratbi said in an interview. The aim of the Islamic Council, he said, is "to promote integration and peaceful *convivencia* by transforming Muslims into real citizens of Valencia." Specifically, he spoke of work done in the development of the role of Muslim women in society and the organization of youth camps and plans to train imams to work in social as well as religious areas.[33]

The best measure of Spanish progress on the integration of Muslims is the 2009 report on 767,000 Muslims immigrants in Spain, sponsored by the ministries of justice, interior and labor. The study shows that the majority of Muslim immigrants, or 89%, believe "it's possible to be a good Muslim and a good Spaniard." According to the poll, based on 2,000 interviews, 81% of Muslims feel well adapted to the life and customs of Spain and 70% consider the life good or very good. The findings also reveal that 84% have encountered no obstacles to their religious practice, 87% think Islam is perfectly compatible with democracy and human rights, and 94% say efforts should be made to respect the beliefs of others.[34] Even conservative daily *El Mundo* wrote that the study shows that the Muslim immigrant community in Spain "is tolerant, westernized and liberal, whose opinions don't differ substantially from those of Spanish citizens." Between 4 and 5% of the interviewees indicated radical tendencies, according to Juan José Toharia, the author of the study, who said it was a similar rate in other European countries.[35] Of course there are those who see the glass 95% empty, like the extreme right-wing electronic news site *Minuto Digital*, which gave the same story an alarming headline: "In Spain there are more than 40,000 radical Islamists."[36]

While Lisbon's Sheikh Munir holds that all Muslims have come under suspicion since 11 September, he thinks that Portugal's multicultural society could serve as an example. "We don't have ethnic ghettos although there are social problems and pockets of poverty," the sheikh pointed out in an interview. He noted that Muslims from former Portuguese Africa are well integrated because the Portuguese lived with them as neighbors, "unlike French and English colonies, where the races didn't mix socially." The Muslim cleric applauded Lisbon's multicultural policies but suggested that the authorities could do more to control the prayer halls and ensure that the imams learn Portuguese language and history.[37]

Sources close to the leadership in Spain and Portugal maintain they are determined to develop an Iberian model that guarantees immigrants' rights, including a path to citizenship, and promotes the integration of Muslim communities based on dialogue. At a time when other Europeans were engaged in passionate debate over Switzerland's referendum to ban minarets, right-wing parties in Denmark and Holland called for similar action, and the French were embroiled in controversies over whether to extend the ban on veils, Iberians were going their own way. Spain's ruling Socialist Party publicly apologized for the expulsion of some 300,000 *Moríscos*, or Muslims converted to Christianity, 400 years ago, and the first Muslim political party was created with little ado. The Portuguese celebrated the inauguration of the first mosque on the island of Madeira without public protest; the facilities were provided by the regional government and works financed by the islamic community. Early in 2010, the University of Lisbon organized a course on the history of Islam with a theme that could be seen as revolutionary in the current European context: "Islam at the Origin of Portuguese Identity."

While many Europeans debated the alleged Islamization of Europe and what to do about it, Córdoba marked the 1300th anniversary of the arrival of Muslim forces on the Iberian Peninsula and the establishment of Al Andalus, the fusion of Muslim, Christian and Jewish cultures, lasting several centuries. Arabists, scholars, experts and artists met at Córdoba in February 2011 to debate major issues affecting the Arab-Islamic World and the West. Known as the Averroes Encounters, in honor of the medieval Córdoban philosopher, the meetings were initiated by the Paris Institute of the Arab World in 1994 and held regularly in France and Morocco. This was the first time the event was held in Spain, and the main theme was Córdoba, "a city of *convivencia* and dialogue"[38] The encounters were organized by Madrid's Casa Árabe, Córdoba University and the City of Córdoba, as part of its campaign to be named European Cultural Capital in 2016.

These isolated events do not mean that the Iberians have found the key to understanding their new Muslim communities. After all, the French have been engaged in dialogue with Arabs for years, but relations with their Arab communities are fraught with tension. Nor do these friendly encounters spell an end to anti-Muslim diatribes by far right-wing political groups like the Platform for Cataluña or the outpouring of Islamophobic venom on the internet. They are a demonstration, however, of an Iberian specificity, a strong desire by policy makers to make intercultural *convivencia* work at this gateway to Europe.

At the end of 2010, the former president, Mário Soares, head of the National Commission on Religious Freedom, noted with pride that according to recent international surveys, Portugal is the European country with "the most religious tolerance, dialogue and respect among different religions and between believers and non-believers."[39] Pointing out that this had not always been so, Soares recalled that Catholicism had long been the state religion. and two or three centuries ago, Portugal was "a land of the Inquisition, intolerance, fanaticism, expulsion of Jews, heretics, Muslims and religious persecution against those considered to be non-believers." Everything changed with the 1974 Revolution of Carnations, which led to the establishment of "a secular and democratic State of Law," the Portuguese statesman declared. He said that the Catholic Church still has the most followers and weight in Portuguese society, "but it is today a church open to society, to democracy and geostrategic changes." In conclusion, Soares emphasized: "Today all the great religions are represented by their faithful and worship freely in the temples they have built. Let me repeat: dialogue among the different religions, and between believers and non believers, takes place in mutual respect and in the commitment to multiculturalism. This means an enormous enrichment of Portuguese society as a whole."

One of the foremost authorities on Muslims in contemporary Spain, Professor Bernabé López García, is a firm believer in *convivencia*. "It will happen; there will be a Spanish Islam, a European Islam," asserted the director of international Mediterranean studies at the Autonomous University of Madrid.[40] We met at a café in the strongly multicultural neighborhood of Tirso de Molina that summer of discontent in 2010. Like others, he ascribed the anti-burqa campaign to elections in Cataluña and predicted it would spread when the rest of the country held municipal elections in 2011. But he insisted it was not a rise of Islamophobia. On the contrary, the Spanish public and particularly young people increasingly accept Muslims and the veil. And, he stressed, Moroccans were not leaving but adapting to life in Spain. He gave the example of a family of immigrants from Tangiers he has known for many years. One son was such a strict Muslim that he dropped out of the school at age fourteen because his teacher did not wear a headscarf. Today he has become an imam and holds that Muslims in Spain must follow Spanish law, while observing their religious traditions.

Laila Rattab is a Spanish Muslim and proud of it. She is twenty-five, was born in Madrid and is now studying journalism at Madrid's Complutense University. Her father comes from the Moroccan city of Nador, worked in hotels in Germany many years, and is now employed in a Madrid restaurant. Her mother is from Rabat and works as secretary at the Lebanese embassy. Laila had a "mixed" upbringing, speaking Spanish at home with her parents and five brothers and sisters and studying Arabic at Saudi, Libyan and Iraqi secondary schools in Madrid. She has worn a headscarf since age seventeen and insists "It was my decision," adding that her mother didn't put on the hijab until she was forty-five and her father didn't care what she wore. The family goes to Morocco regularly but she emphasized: "I feel Spanish." Asked if she had problems because of the headscarf, Laila acknowledged there had been several unpleasant incidents after the 11 March 2004 Madrid terrorist attacks. "Twice people called me 'assassin' and once a man in a car spit at me," she recalled. But she stressed there were never any problems at the university.[41]

With the rightward shift in power across northern Europe, the principle of multiculturalism—or the respect for other cultures as long as they do not infringe on national laws and values—has come under fire. After the Madrid and London bombings and Paris riots, European leaders began to question multiculturalism, which had dominated immigration policy—except for the French who still clung to their policy of assimilation. Once-liberal Holland and Scandinavia introduced new immigration rules to placate the far right. Late in 2010, chancellor Angela Merkel proclaimed multiculturalism to be "a complete failure" in Germany. Nicolas Sarkozy also denounced the multiculturalism practiced by the United States and England, as "reinforcing [Islamic] extremism"[42] But the coup de grâce was delivered early in 2011 by the British prime minister, David Cameron, who declared that multiculturalism had encouraged immigrant groups "to live separate lives, apart from each other and the mainstream." Speaking at a conference on European security in Munich, Cameron said that Islamic militants had been left free to radicalize Muslim young people in these "segregated communities." The prime minister then announced plans to bar "preachers of hate" from entering Britain and prevent Muslim groups from spreading views against human rights and democracy in public institutions.

In Madrid, official sources said that Spain was committed to pursuing its model of "intercultural *convivencia*" regardless of declarations by other European leaders. Officials referred me to a policy statement by the new secretary of state for immigration and integration, Anna Terrón i Cusi, at a conference on "European Identity" at the French Institute of Foreign Relations in April 2010. Noting that Spain had only "discovered" immigration in 2000–2001, Terrón recalled that the government had observed the French, British and Dutch models while working out its own plan. Then she spelt out the generous principles of Spain's 2007–2010 Strategic Plan of Citizenship and Integration: equality of rights and duties of natives and immigrants, full participation in civic, political and social life and interculturalism, or the interaction of different communities and respect for diversity.[43]

The Portuguese high commissioner for immigration was even more adamant in defense of her country's policy, in response to my query. "Portugal has chosen the model of interculturalism rather than multiculturalism," Rosário Farmouse wrote in an email message in February 2011. "This means that we encourage migrants to preserve their own culture while learning about the culture of the host country and thereby growing with both [cultures]." Emphasizing that cultures are not static, Farmhouse said, "for this reason, when we speak of interculturalism, both the foreigners and those who welcome them are changed through the meeting of cultures." She pointed out that the Portuguese have always been an enormous mixture of cultures throughout their history. "We are the sons, grandsons and great grandsons of Visigoths, Phoenicians, Barbarians, Moors etc. We don't aim to change anybody but are open to meeting others and the mutual growth that such encounters bring."[44]

The question is still open as to whether Spain and Portugal can achieve what their European partners have failed to do: provide a climate in which Muslim immigrants and their descendants have the sense of belonging. I believe the Iberians have a chance of success because they know what it's like to be an immigrant and can benefit from their northern neighbors' experiences. They can also look to their own past, how for several hundred years Muslims, Christians and Jews created together an advanced and prosperous culture on the Iberian peninsula. And because of the lengthy and brutal period of ethnic cleansing known as the Inquisition, Iberians are aware of the devastating consequences of religious intolerance. Moreover, not so long ago, both societies lived under totalitarian regimes. Perhaps as a result of this long history of intolerance, Iberian leaders appear especially determined to safeguard their young democracies, based on principles of human rights. Spain and Portugal are committed members of the European Union, yet they remain close partners of their former colonies in Latin America and Africa, and are actively engaged in building bridges with the Islamic world. If Iberia succeeds in recapturing the spirit of Al Andalus, it could very well serve as a platform for reconciliation, rather than as a battlefield for any self-destructing conflict of civilizations.

EPILOGUE

From my Iberian balcony, the view of the Arab revolutions spreading across North Africa and the Middle East is much more than apprehension over the supply and price of oil and gas or concern about the flood of immigrants washing up across Europe's southern shores.

Although Portugal and Spain are profoundly preoccupied with their own overwhelming financial and economic crises, they have exhibited spontaneous solidarity with the Arab demands for justice and democracy, and their peaceful protests against autocracy. After all, the Spanish and Portuguese engaged in a similar struggle barely three decades ago, and with support from the European Union, have largely prospered from the fruits of western democracy, as imperfect as it may seem at times. Along with many political leaders, journalists, active citizens, and foreign observers, I recall the heady atmosphere of Portugal's peaceful revolution and Spain's transition, with their reversals, backslidings, and uncertainties, as the peninsular neighbors resolutely engaged on the route to democracy. That euphoria was very much like the recent non-violent demonstrations in Tunisia and Egypt and other North African and Middle Eastern countries, before the ferocious crackdowns by some regimes like Libya and Syria.

While the European Union initially watched in frozen awe as unarmed North African young people took to the streets to defy their entrenched all-powerful rulers, the Spanish and Portuguese were quick to champion the democratic movements on the other side of the Mediterranean. The Spanish prime minister, José Luis Rodríguez Zapatero, hastened to Tunisia to offer the revolutionaries Europe's support. The Spanish foreign secretary was the first foreign dignitary to praise the Moroccan king's pledge to make "global constitutional reforms." The Royal

249

Elcano Institute, an independent Spanish think tank, in February launched a website, "Observatory: Crisis in the Arab World," with the participation of prominent academics, who publish on Facebook in-depth studies on different aspects of the Arab revolution. Spain cooperated with the French-instigated NATO effort to protect the Libyan people from dictator Muammar Qaddafi, and early on made contacts with the Libyan National Transitional Council. When thousands of Africans, fleeing the fighting in Libya, tried to get to Europe, Spain denounced French-Italian moves to reinstate internal European borders to stem the migratory flow. Portuguese Euro-deputies sounded the alarm on the dramatic situation of African refugees, emphasizing: "It's high time Europe concentrates on what is fundamental: saving human lives and helping the democratic transition processes in North Africa."[1] Former Portuguese prime minister, António Guterres, UN high commissioner for refugees, went so far as to take Europe to task for its "grudging and meager" response to the epochal changes in North Africa. "Most of the debate has not been about how to support democracy, but how to keep out those who risk their lives crossing the Mediterranean by boat," Guterres remonstrated in the *International Herald Tribune*.[2]

As relative newcomers to the world's democratic elite, Spain and Portugal are especially well placed to understand the hurdles facing the aspiring Arab democracies to the south. It was no accident that a delegation of Moroccan parliamentarians, including leading socialists, communists, royalists and Islamists, went to Barcelona in the midst of the Arab upheavals to present plans for constitutional reform before the European Institute of the Mediterranean, an official Spanish-Catalán think tank. Another high-powered Moroccan delegation went to Lisbon to explain "the dynamics and perspectives of political reform" a few days after the completion of the new draft constitution. It was, then, only natural that the Arab Forum for Alternatives should invite experts from Portugal and Spain, as well as India, to participate in a conference in Cairo in May 2011, on "Democratic Transition Challenges: Egypt in a Comparative Perspective."

It was Iberian young people, however, who demonstrated forcefully their admiration for the North African revolutionary movement, by emulating it. In Portugal, a group of unemployed college graduates calling themselves "the hardship generation" organized the Twelfth of March Movement, which put half a million people into streets around the country in the biggest demonstration since Portugal's 1974 Revolution. Calling for more and better democracy, organizers said they were inspired by the revolts in North Africa. A few weeks later, a group of Spanish university students organized street protests in the name of "Young people without a future." Their action soon attracted protesters of all ages, and became known as the 15 May Movement, which held mass demonstrations in cities around Spain under the banner of "Real Democracy Now." In their Manifesto, the Spaniards declared: "The Arab world shows us victory is possible."[3]

The Iberian and Arab protest movements stemmed from the same source; a large, educated, disenchanted, jobless youth, who used the same mobilizing techniques of Facebook, Twitter and email. Many protests are similar, against politicians and political parties, corruption, and the lack of jobs. Spain has Europe's highest rate of unemployment at 21.5%, and 45% for young people, figures comparable to those in North Africa. While the Arab struggle is about establishing democracy with basic freedoms and rights, most Spanish and Portuguese don't seek to overthrow their democracies but improve them through greater citizen participation. Although there are no direct links between the two mobilizations as yet, the North Africans are known to have contacts with European and American human rights organizations.

It is not clear to what extent the populist street movements in Spain and Portugal influenced recent elections. But the results were evident: Iberian voters blamed the ruling socialist parties for failure to manage the devastating economic crises and for bowing to European Union and International Monetary Fund demands for drastic social cuts. In an emotional response, Spaniards voted massively for the opposition led by the conservative People's Party in regional and municipal elections, the spring of 2011. Worse, Josep Anglada's anti-Muslim, anti-immigrant Plataforma per Catalunya increased its vote fivefold to 67,000, winning sixty-seven municipal councilors in the northern region. Commenting on his party's stunning defeat, Spain's former prime minister, Felipe González, praised the current Socialist prime minister, Zapatero, for taking the necessary tough decisions for structural reforms while denouncing the People's Party for pursuing "an irresponsible strategy that 'the worse it gets, the better.'"[4] He urged the Socialists to pursue their austerity policies while making efforts to persuade the Spanish public that this is the best route, before legislative elections in March 2012. "We're in a terrible situation," Portuguese statesman Mário Soares, an ardent Europeanist, said in an interview after the Spanish election.

"The present leaders of Europe, particularly France and Germany, are completely absorbed in the defense of the euro and have forgotten about the Europeans. If this drift to the right continues, we are headed for a social explosion, which could be catastrophic. If the conservatives win in Portugal, they will be obliged to carry out austerity measures and would most likely continue our progressive immigration policy because we're a nation of emigrants. But if the right wins in Spanish elections next year, Spain could follow in France's path of confrontation with Muslims and other immigrants. The unknown element is the street movements; we don't know why they voted for the right in Spain or how they'll vote next time. But we have to react to this situation and explain to the people that Europe must save the euro and change the neo-liberal policies that led us to the global crisis."[5]

Snap elections in Portugal at the national level on 5 June followed Spain's swing to the right, as expected. The result was a clear victory for the conservative opposition leader, Pedro Passos Coelho, forty-seven, and his Social Democratic Party, who won 38.6 % of the vote. But it was essentially a vote against the economic crisis, and the international bailout package of 78 billion euros and its stringent austerity measures. The big loser was the incumbent prime minister, José Sócrates, and his Socialist Party, with 28% of the vote and seventy-four deputies, down from 45% and 121 deputies when they came to power in 2005. Assuming responsibility for the defeat, Sócrates resigned before the final votes were tallied, leaving his party floundering for direction. In his sober victory speech, Passos Coelho, a former parliamentarian and investment manager, warned the Portuguese that new sacrifices and patience would be required "to recover the country's credibility." The Social Democratic leader has pledged to defend health benefits for the most vulnerable sectors of society and courted the immigrant vote, claiming to be "the most African of all the candidates" because his wife comes from former Portuguese Guinea. His first political act, however, was to announce plans for a coalition government with the right-wing Christian Democratic Party (CDS), which won nearly 12% of the vote and twenty-four deputies, to build a solid parliamentary majority. In a position to wield considerable influence in such a coalition, CDS leader Paulo Portas has ties with the European right and has taken openly anti-immigrant positions.

Predictably, with an unemployment rate of nearly 22%, zero growth and daunting deficits, Spain's governing Socialist Party suffered a devastating defeat in national elections late 2011. The conservative People's Party (PP) won an absolute majority, with 44.62% of the vote or

186 seats in the 350-member lower chamber of Parliament, compared to 28.73% for the Socialists or 110 seats, with a similar score for the 208-member senate. A leftwing coalition and small nationalist Catalán and Basque parties also made gains at the expense of the Socialists. The far-right parties, which had come to the fore in Cataluña recently, fared poorly, ostensibly because the local PP and Catalán nationalists have embraced some of their anti-immigration and anti-Muslim rhetoric, like calling for the deportation of undocumented immigrants and a ban on the *burqa* in public places. Spain's Muslim leaders and immigrant advocates did not hide their dismay over the PP victory, recalling tensions under the party's previous rule from 1996 to 2004. But in fact, immigration and "Islamization" rarely came up in the election campaign, which focused almost entirely on the disastrous state of the economy. During the campaign, PP leader Mariano Rajoy, a former cabinet minister, declared his main goals were economic growth and job creation, but was short on specifics. Pledging to overhaul the country's cumbersome labor legislation, the 56-year-old Rajoy stressed however that he would not cut pensions, healthcare or education. This was seen as a move to reassure los *indignados*, the national protest movement, believed to have helped oust the incumbent socialists, and potentially the main opposition to the new center-right government.

An unstated concern in some political circles is that a rightward trend, particularly in Spain, would mean a more aggressive stance on homeland security, with further loss of basic human rights. Thus far, the Iberian administrations have been careful to avoid targeting Muslim communities in counterterrorism operations. Even after the devastating attacks by Muslim extremists in Madrid in 2004, the official response was decisive but moderate, on the premise that more could be gained through cooperation with the Muslim community than treating it as an enemy.

There were no celebrations in Madrid or Lisbon for the death of Osama bin Laden, although Al Qaeda was believed to be behind the Madrid bombings and Bin Laden had personally threatened to "recover" Al Andalus. Officials and analysts expressed satisfaction over the coup against the most dangerous terrorist organization in recent times, but no one thought the problem was resolved. And a number of voices, including Lisbon's Patriarch Dom José Policarpo and Spanish magistrate Baltasar Garzón, regretted the manner in which Bin Laden was killed. Admitting he was glad Bin Laden is gone, *El País* columnist Josep Ramoneda noted, however: "In a democratic culture, you detain criminals and turn them over to the court to be tried." He went on to emphasize: "If this absent icon can be considered the end of an epoch, we must give thanks to the citizens of the Arab and Muslim countries, in particular the new generations, who have defeated Islamic fundamentalism."[6]

Above all, the Arab Spring has served to validate the Iberian policies of approximation with their Muslim neighbors and the Arab and Muslim world in general, policies observed by governments of the right and left. The Arab revolutionary movements underway, while only at their inception, have demonstrated that Muslims not only share democratic values but are willing to die for them. Almost overnight, Arab youth have earned a new image, as courageous, technically astute people, who have turned their backs on virulently anti-western radicalism in favor of democracy.

It is the young rebels of North Africa and Iberia, fired by common frustrations and the demand for social and economic justice, who could provide the grassroots networks essential to establish a genuine Mediterranean dialogue between Muslims and the non-Islamic worlds. These new voices on both sides of the Mediterranean must be heard.

NOTES

1. GATE CRASHERS

1. Pro-Human Rights Association of Andalucía, "Human Rights on the Southern Border," report of 30 January 2007.
2. María Vallejo Nágera, *Luna negra: La luz del Padre Pateras,* Barcelona: Belacqva, 2004.
3. Interview with María José Hernández Velázquez, coordinator of the Red Cross in Andalucía, 22 July 2009.
4. Conversation with Aziz Darai, 28 July 2006.
5. Interview with Encarna Márquez, 28 July 2006.
6. Marisa Ortún Rubio, "Are the Spanish For or Against Immigration?" Opinion poll, Centro de Investigaciones Sociológicas, eds, Michel Korinman and John Laughland, *The Long March to the West,* London: Vallentine Mitchell Academic, 2007.
7. Pew Global Attitudes Project, "Survey Finds Growing European Negativity Toward Muslims and Jews," *Pakistan Daily Times,* 18 September 2008.
8. "De la Vega Savages Italian Clampdown on Immigrants," *El País,* English edition, 17 May 2008, p. 3.
9. Conversations with *Padre Pateras,* 11 and 15 August 2008.
10. Ibid.
11. Interview with Encarna Márquez, 11 August 2008.
12. Santiago Gimeno, "España recibe la cifra mas baja de inmigrantes de los últimos tres anos," *El País,* 17 January 2010.
13. Interview with Dr. Fernando de la Vieter Nobre, president of AMI, 14 September 2006.
14. Paulo Moura, *Passaporte para o Céu,* Lisbon: Dom Quixote, 2006.
15. Elise Vincent, "Boat People Looking for New Ways in," *AFP, Le Monde,* 24 June 2010.
16. "Rubalcaba: 'Hay riesgo de que llegue un grupo–no pequeño–de inmigrantes a Europa,'" *El País,* 24 February 2011.

17. EFE, "Rubalcaba anuncia firmeza "en la defensa de nuestras fronteras" ante el conflicto en el norte de África," *La Vanguardia*, 26 February 2011.

2. MOORISH LEGACY

1. Miguel de Unamuno and Ángel Ganivet, *El Porvenir de España*, Madrid, 1912, p. 53.
2. José Ortega y Gasset, tr. Mildred Adams, *Invertebrate Spain*, New York: W.W. Norton, 1937, p. 95.
3. Washington Irving, "Spanish Romance," *The Alhambra*, Vol. XIV, Boston, p. 248.
4. Américo Castro, *España en su Historia: Cristianos Moros y Judíos*, Buenos Aires: Losada, 1948.
5. Henry Kamen, *The Disinherited: Exile and the Making of Spanish Culture, 1492–1975*, New York: HarperCollins, 2007, p. 49.
6. Ibid., p. 92–3.
7. Miguel Hernando de Larramendi and Barbara Azaola, "Studies in Spain of the Contemporary Arab World and the Mediterranean," British Council workshop, Barcelona, 10–11 March 2006, p. 2.
8. Ibid.
9. Ibid., p. 97.
10. Interview with Professor Bernabé López García, 24 May 2006.
11. Serafín Fanjul, interview with the political review, *El Catoblepas*, issue 30, online: August 2004.
12. Gustavo de Arístegui, *La Yihad en España: La Obsesión por la reconquista de Al-Andalus*, Madrid: La Esfera de los Libros, 3rd edition, 2005, p. 16.
13. Maria Rosa Menocal, *Ornament of the World*, New York: Little, Brown and Company, 2002, p. 11.
14. Gema Martín Muñoz, director, *Muslims in Spain: A Reference Guide*, Madrid: Casa Árabe-IEAM 2009, p. 7.
15. Interview with Adriano Moreira, the former minister of overseas territories and president of the Portuguese Academy of Sciences, 10 September 2009.
16. A.H. de Oliveira Marques, *History of Portugal*, Vol. I., New York: Columbia University, 1972, pp. 13–19.
17. Ibid., p. 73.
18. Ibid., p. 11.
19. Interview with Professor António Dias Farinha, 16 September 2006.
20. Interview with Professor Adalberto Alves, 28 May 2008.
21. Interview with Claudio Torres, 11 April 2006.
22. Jesús Riosalido, *Guía de Al-Andalus*, Madrid: Sapere Aude Foundation, 2004, p. 13.
23. Calahorra Tower, *Welcome*, Córdoba: Fundación Roger Garaudy, 2006. p. 3.

24. Interview with Darío Marimón García, Foundation for Three Cultures, 19 July 2006.
25. P.H. "Todas las mezquitas de Valencia se oponen a la propuesta de Herrero para suprimir la fiesta de moros y cristianos," Las Provincias Webislam, 6 October 2006.
26. Ofelia Mármol, "La fiesta de 'Moros y Cristianos' en la localidad valenciana de Bocairent cambia la tradición para no ofender a los musulmanes," Webislam—antena3.com, 2 February 2007.
27. Gema Martín Muñoz, Expulsados de su patria, Madrid: El País, 30 April 2009.
28. Mariano Calleja, "Asombro en el congreso por la iniciativa del PSOE sobre los Moríscos," Madrid: ABC, 25 November 2009.

3. THE EARLY NEWCOMERS

1. Interview with Bernabé López García, head of Mediterranean studies at the Autonomous University of Madrid, 24 May 2006.
2. Conversation with Abdeljalil Reklaoui, 28 July 2006.
3. Conversation with Abdeljalil Reklaoui, 10 August 2008.
4. Conversation with Mohamed Azaf, 18 June 2006.
5. Conversation with Ali Lmrabet, 3 June 2006.
6. Interview with Abdool Majid Vakil, 15 September 2006.
7. Interview with Faranz Keshavjee, 14 September 2006.
8. Interview with José Amara Queta, 27 April 2007.
9. Conversation with Abdel Almountazir, 31 May 2006.
10. Tomás Bárbulo, "Moroccans in Spain: A Business of Half a Million People," Atlas de la inmigración marroquí en España II, Madrid: UAM cd, 2005.
11. Conversation with Abdel Rahman Essadi, former Moroccan migrant, 21 July 2006.
12. Interview with Braima Djalo, construction worker, 26 August 2006.
13. Conversation with Taslim Rana, Bangladeshi entrepreneur, 6 September 2006.

4. SPAIN'S 11 SEPTEMBER

1. Ambassador J. Cofer Black, coordinator of the Office for Counterterrorism, US Department of State, "The Effects of the Madrid Terrorist Attacks on U.S.-European Cooperation in the War on Terrorism," Hearing before Senate Subcommittee on European Affairs, Transcript, Washington: 31 March 2004, p. 8.
2. Cambio 16, 19 April, p. 6.
3. Interview with Fernando Reinares, Cambio16, 29 March 2004, p. 4.

4. Interview with Said Kirhlani, Moroccan PhD student at Madrid's Autonomous University, 27 May 2006.

5. A copy of the *fatwa* obtained from Mansur Escudero during an interview at Almodóvar del Rio, 12 June 2006.

6. These diplomatic sources, based in Madrid, Lisbon and Rabat, are leading experts in counterterrorism and have access to a broad range of intelligence on subversive movements in the area. They requested anonymity because of the ongoing nature of their work.

7. Evan Kohlmann, Global Terror Alert, www.globalterroralert.com, 11 July 2005.

8. Ibid.

9. Craig Whitlock, "Architect of a New War on the West: Writings Lay Out Post-9/11 Strategy of Isolated Cells Joined in Jihad," *The Washington Post*, 22 May 2006, p. A01.

10. Haizam Amirah Fernández, "Does Al-Qaeda have a Global Strategy?" Madrid: *ARI*, Vol. 74, 2004.

11. Ibid.

12. Interview with Haizam Amirah Fernández, senior analyst with Elcano Royal Institute, 19 June 2006.

13. Interview with Mohamed Azaf, municipal social worker, 18 June 2006.

14. Interview with Mohamed Saleh, secretary of the Islamic Center in Madrid, 16 June 2006.

15. Interview with Helal-Jamal Abboshi, secretary of the Abu Bakr Mosque in Madrid, 16 June 2006.

16. José María Irujo. "Averting the Clash of Civilizations," *El País*, 20 April 2006, p. 4.

17. Bruce Hoffman. "Terrorism has become extremely politicized in Spain," *El País*, English edition, 20 March 2007, p. 3.

18. Interview with the Portuguese minister of internal administration, António Costa, 18 September 2006.

19. Interview with Sheikh David Munir, 12 May 2008.

5. IBERIAN OUTREACH

1. Conversation with Sérgio Tréfaut, 25 April 2006.

2. Conversation with Alexandra Prado Coelho, 7 September 2006.

3. Interview with Portuguese high commissioner for immigration, Rui Marques, 11 August 2006

4. Rosa Aparicio Goméz lecture at seminar on "Descendents of Immigrants: Among Three Worlds," Fundação Oriente, Arrábida, 13 July 2006.

5. Anabela Rodrigues, comment during debate on "Descendents of Immigrants" at Arrábida Monastery, 13 July 2006.

6. Interview with Portugal's high commissioner for immigration, Rui Marques, 11 August 2006.

7. Interview with Francesca Teixeira, head of ACIME's National Support Centers, 22 August 2006.
8. Interview with Sister Mafalda, 19 September 2006.
9. Interview with Rosário Farmhouse, head of the Jesuit Refugee Service, 7 September 2006.
10. Interview with Timoteo Macedo, director of Solidaridade Imigrante, 18 August 2006.
11. Conversation with Portuguese journalist Diana Andringa, 22 August 2006.
12. Interview with César Mogo Zaro, director of the Secretariat of State for Immigration and Emigration, 13 April 2007.
13. Interview with Mercedes Rico, director general of the Spanish Ministry of Justice, 12 April 2007.
14. Interview with José Miguel Morales, spokesman for Andalucía Acoge, 20 July 2006.
15. Interview with Sara Verdú Vila head of CEAR in Valencia, 8 June 2006.
16. Interview with Francisco Javier Edo Ausach, head of AVAR in Valencia, 7 June 2006.
17. Interview with Ghassan Saliba Zeghondi, secretary of immigration, National Workers Commission of Cataluña, 1 July 2006.

6. MUSLIM SOLIDARITY

1. Conversation with Hanan Taibi and Saida Diouri, members of the Moroccan University Students Association of Spain, 23 May 2006.
2. Interview with Khalid Shakroun, head of El Atlas, a volunteer group working with street children, 18 April 2007.
3. Interview with Hassan al Arabi, head of ASSISI, an association for Moroccan immigrants in Spain, 20 April 2007.
4. Interview with Kamal Rahmouni, leader of ATIME, Moroccan Workers' Association, 18 April 2007.
5. Interviews with Mohammed Chaib, Socialist deputy in Catalán parliament, 31 May and 1 June 2006.
6. Interview with Mercés Amor, Spanish teacher at Ibn Batuta social center, 2 June 2006.
7. Interview with Dr. Huma Jamshed, president of the Pakistani women's organization, ACESOP, 20 July 2010.
8. Meritexell M. Paume, "Mujeres musulmanas pedirán mezquitas más grandes para poder ir a rezar," *La Vanguardia*, 22 November 2010.
9. Interview with Laure Rodríguez Quiroga, president of the Union for Muslim Women in Spain, 22 November 2010.
10. Abdool Majid Vakil, address for commemorations of 40th anniversary of CIL, 22 June 2008.
11. Interview with Nazir Sacoor, CEO of the Aga Kahn Foundation's Development Network in Portugal, 21 September 2006.

12. Interview with Sheikh Bubacar Baldé, 13 September 2006.
13. Ibid., 17 September 2006.
14. Interview with Mamadou Ba, delegate of SOS Racismo in Portugal, 30 March 2007.
15. Interview with ambassador of Morocco to Lisbon, Karima Benyaïch, 31 July 2009.
16. Interview with Hamou Amgoun, president of Essalam–Oporto, 22 August 2009.

7. PORTUGAL'S CENTRAL MOSQUE AND ASSOCIATES

1. Margarida Mota, "*Xeque Munir entre os 500 mais influentes,*" Lisbon: *Expresso*, 22 November 2009.
2. Interview with Sheikh Munir at the Central Mosque, 12 August 2006.
3. Conversation with Esmael Loonat, 11 September 2006.
4. Alexandra Prado Coelho, "We are Missionaries of Islam," *Público*, 30 May 2004.
5. Interview with Zakir Karim, a leader of Lisbon Islamic Community's Youth Association, 17 May 2008.
6. Nina Clara Tiesler and David Cairns, *Islam en Lusophonies*, Vol. XIV (1), Brill, 2007, pp. 223–238.
7. Interview with Raúl Braga Pires, graduate student at the University of Oporto, 23 September 2008.
8. Interview with Sheikh Rizwan, headmaster of the Islamic School at Palmela, 20 September 2006.
9. Sermon in the Bangladeshi mosque, recorded by Sérgio Tréfaut in the film, *Os Lisboetas*, 2006.
10. Alexandra Prado Coelho, "*Muçulmanos em Portugal, Público,*" *Publico*, June 2005, p. 118.
11. Interview with Moulana Zabir, 26 April 2007.

8. SPAIN'S MULTIPLE MUSLIM VOICES

1. Interview with Mercedes Rico Carabias, director general of religious affairs, Ministry of Justice, 12 April 2007.
2. Interview with Helal-Jamal Abboshi, secretary general of UCIDE, 17 June 2006.
3. Interview with Mohammed Saleh, secretary of the Islamic Centre of Madrid, 16 June 2006.
4. Interview with Sheikh Moneir Mahmoud, imam of the M-30 mosque, 16 June 2006.
5. Conversation with Amparo Sánchez Rosell, Spanish convert and a leader of the Islamic Cultural Center of Valencia, 7 June 2006.

6. Conclusions of the International Congress on the Alliance for Civilizations, pp. 7–8.
7. Mohammed Ziane, caretaker of the Grand Mosque of Granada, 10 June 2006.
8. Conversation with restaurateur Mustafa Akalay, 10 June 2006.
9. Sheikh Dr. Abdalqadir as-Sufi's website, retrieved from http://en.wikipedia.org/wiki/Murabitun.
10. Denis Campbell, "Revealed: He Leads an Extreme and Anti-Semitic Islamic Sect, He Believes Hitler was a Great Man—and Now He's Back in Scotland," *Scotland on Sunday*, 4 November 1995, p. 1.
11. Denis Campbell, "Shadowy World of a Sect," *Scotland on Sunday*, 12 November 1995, p. 4.
12. My first interview with Mansur Escudero, head of the Islamic Junta, 12 June 2008.
13. J. Cabrera, "*El nuevo obispo de Córdoba afirma que 'no es posible' el uso conjunto de la Mezquita,*" *El Día de Córdoba*, 23 March 2010.
14. Rachel Donadio, "Name Debate Echoes an Old Clash of Faiths," *The New York Times*, 4 November 2010.
15. Jesus García, "Barcelona promete a los ulemas de Marruecos acoger una gran mesquite," *El País, WebIslam*, 28 December 2010.
16. Interview with Catalán anthropologist, Jordi Moreras, 2 June 2006.
17. Interview with Mohamed Kharchich, secretary general of FEERI, 17 April 2007.
18. Josep Playa Maset, "El Islam se reorganiza en Cataluña," Barcelona: *La Vanguardia*, 14 February 2010.
19. C. Moran and Q. Chirino, "Musulmanes de Granada impulsan la creación de un partido político nacional," *El Ideal de Granada*, 16 February 2009.
20. EFE, "Lideres de la comunidad islámica de Granada escépticos con la creación del nuevo partido," *Webislam*, 16 February 2009.
21. J. Pagola, "*Un partido islámico se moviliza para conquistar os municipios claves in 2011,*" *ABC*, 10 November 2009.
22. "Constituido en Granada el PRUNE, un partido nacional dirigido a las minorías," *Europa Press*, 21 January 2010.
23. CDPI, *Condolencias de la Casa Real Española, Webislam*, 8 October 2010.
24. "Justicia dice que se pierde al impulsor 'de un Islam más Moderno,'" *Webislam, Europa Press*, 5 October 2010.
25. Juan José Tamayo, *Manuel Escudero, el San Francisco de Asis del Islam, Webislam, El País*, 5 Octobre 2010.
26. Amparo Sánchez Rosell, "*La muerte de Manuel Escudero. Algo se muere en el alma,*" *Webislam, Periodista Digital*, 5 October 2010.
27. Abdul Haqq Salaberria, "*El Islam Español no quiere árbitros,*" *Webislam*, 15 February 2011.
28. Ibid.

9. THE RADICAL FRINGE

1. Gustavo de Arístegui, *La Yihad en España: La obsesión por reconquistar Al-Andalus*, Madrid: La Esfera de los Libros, 2005, p. 16.
2. Interview with António da Costa, then Portuguese minister of interior, 18 September 2006.
3. Paul Gallis, coordinator, "Muslims in Europe: Integration Policies in Selected Countries," Congressional Research Service, 18 November 2005.
4. Antonio Baquero, "Una Red de españoles conversos al Islam ultra crece en internet," *El Periódico*, 12 May 2008, pp. 22–23.
5. Interview with a senior official in Spain's counterterrorism unit, Madrid, 19 September 2007.
6. Fernando Reinares interview by Antonio Baquero, *El Periódico*, 22 January, pp. 16–17.
7. Interview with Jorje Silva Carvalho, 22 April 2008.
8. Interview with the same senior official in Spain's counterterrorism unit, Madrid, mentioned above, 14 July 2008.
9. Conversation with Said Kirhlani, president of Moroccan Students Association, and other graduate students at Autonomous University of Madrid, 18 September 2007.
10. Interview with Mansur Escudero, leader of the Islamic Junta, at Almodóvar del Rio, 18 August 2008.
11. Interview with graduate student, Raúl Braga Pires, of the University of Oporto, 23 September 2008.
12. Interview with Sheikh Munir at Lison's Central Mosque, 12 May 2008.
13. Pol. Co. Kathy Fitzpatrick, "Spain an Active Front in the War on terror," US embassy, 5 September 2005, released by Wikileaks, December 2010.
14. Chargé Hugo Llorens, "Proposal to Create a Southern European Law Enforcement Counterterrorism and Regional Intelligence Hub in Barcelona," US embassy Madrid, 2 October 2007, released by Wikileaks December 2010.
15. José María Irujo, "EU considera Cataluña el 'mayor centro Mediterráneo del yihadismo,'" *El País*, 10 December 2010.
16. Ibid.
17. Miguel González, "Rubalcaba dice que la principal amenaza para España viene del Sahel," *El País*, 22 December 2010.
18. D. Martínez and J. Pagola, "Al Qaida implanta su 'jihad' ideológica en más de cien mezquitas," *ABC*, 27 December 2010.

10. JEWISH ROOTS

1. Stanley G. Payne, *A History of Spain and Portugal*, Madison: University of Wisconsin, 1973, p. 17.
2. Kamen, *The Disinherited: Exile and the Making of Spanish Culture*, 1492–1975, New York: HarperCollins, 2007, p. 215.

3. Ibid., p. 24.
4. Edward Burman, *The Inquisition*, Wellingborough, Northamptonshire: Aquarian Press, 1984, p. 155.
5. Ibid., p. 156.
6. Stanley Payne, op. cit., p. 230.
7. Francois Soyer, *The Persecution of the Jews and Muslims of Portugal*, Leiden/Boston: Brill, 2007, p. 3.
8. Interview with Samuel Levy, former president of Lisbon's Jewish Community, 24 April 2007.
9. Interview with Esther Mucznik, vice president of the Lisbon Jewish Community, 1 June 2007.
10. Interview with Mery Ruah, a founder of the Portuguese Association of Jewish Studies, 13 June 2007.
11. Laura Cesana, *Jewish Vestiges in Portugal,* Lisbon: Printer Portuguesa, 1997.
12. Interview with Abílio Henriques, leader of the Jewish Community in Belmonte, 14 June 2007.
13. Job 16–18, *The New Oxford Annotated Bible with the Apocrypha*, eds, Herbert G. May and Bruce Metzger, Oxford University, New York: 1977, p. 628.
14. Interview with António Mendes, new head of Belmonte's Jewish Community, 2 November 2010.
15. Interview with Jacobo Israel Garzón, president of the Federation of Jewish Communities of Spain, 20 April 2007.
16. Jacobo Israel Garzón, *Escrito en Sefarad*, Madrid: Hebraica Ediciones, 2005.
17. Interview with Mercedes Rico Carabias, director general of religious affairs in the Justice Ministry, 12 April 2007.

11. THE IBERIAN MODEL

1. Interview with Federico Mayor Zaragoza, head of the Foundation for a Culture of Peace, 23 May 2006.
2. Interview with former Portuguese president, Mário Soares, 18 May 2006.
3. Mário Soares and Federico Mayor Zaragoza, *Um Diálogo Ibérico no Contexto Europeu e Mundial, Temas e Debates*, Lisbon, 2006, p. 121.
4. Ibid., p. 124.
5. Carmen González Enriquez, "Spain," ed., Anna Triandafyllidou, *European Immigration: A Source Book*, Burlington, Vt.: Ashgate, 2007, p. 323.
6. Declaration by the Portuguese prime minister, José Sócrates, at Gulbenkian Immigration Forum, March 6, 2007.
7. Declaration by Manuel Marín González, Socialist chairman of the Spanish Congress of Deputies at the Gulbenkian Immigration Forum, 6 March 2007.

8. Statement by André Azoulay, counselor of King Mohammed VI of Morocco at the Immigration Forum, 6 March 2007.

9. Interview with António Vitorino, commissioner of Gulbenkian Immigration Forum, 6 September 2007.

10. Interview with António Costa, Portuguese minister of interior, 18 September 2006.

11. "Immigration in Europe: An Iberian Vision," Seminarios Palhava, embassy of Spain, 14 May 2007.

12. Ibid., p. 7.

13. Ibid.

14. Spanish minister of foreign affairs and cooperation, Miguel Ángel Moratinos Cuyaube, "Introduction," *Plan Africa 2006–2008*, Office of Foreign Communications, 2007, p. 6.

15. Interview with Manuel Gómez-Acebo, head of North African desk, Spain's Ministry of Foreign Affairs and Cooperation, 13 April 2007.

16. Interview with ambassador Sánchez Benedito, director general of The Africa Plan, Spain's Ministry of Foreign Affairs and Cooperation, 13 April 2007.

17. Agence France Presse, "Gadhafi Demands Compensation for Colonial Rule," 8 December 2007.

18. Peru Egurbide, "Zapatero propone para Africa mas educación, empleo y infraestructuras," *El País*, 9 December 2007.

19. Ana Carbajosa/Miguel Mora, "Un grupo de países africanos rechaza los acuerdos comerciales con Europa," *El País*, 10 December 2007.

20. Interview with Portuguese secretary of state for foreign affairs and cooperation, João Gomes Cravinho, 29 April 2008.

21. Natalia Junquera, "Government Proposal to Pay Immigrants to Leave Spain Garners Few Returns," *El País* English edition, 23 September 2008.

22. Andrew Eatwell, "Ministers Go Back on Foreign Worker Freeze," *El País*, English edition, 6 September 2008.

23. News Agencies, "Los Trabajadores de la construcción afectados por expediente de regulación se multiplican un 399%," *El País*, 4 September 2008.

24. Editorial, "Locking the Doors," *El País*, English edition, 6 September 2008.

25. Tomás Bárbulo, "*El 'cambiazo' en inmigración*," *El País*, 20 July 2008.

26. Council of European Union, Presidency "European Pact on Immigration and Asylum," Brussels, 24 September 2008, p. 7.

27. Elizabeth Collett, "The European Union Immigration Pact—from Hague to Stockholm via Paris," European policy brief, October 2008.

28. Ibid., "European Pact on Immigration and Asylum."

29. Briefing from David Chico Zamanillo, adviser to Spain's secretary of state for immigration, 22 May 2009.

30. Conversation with Estrella Rodríguez Pardo, general director of the Integration of Immigrants, 22 May 2009.

31. Interview with José Manuel López Rodrigo, director of the Foundation for Pluralism and Coexistence, 22 May 2009.

32. Declarations at the Course for Imams organized by the Foundation for Pluralism and Coexistence, 23 May 2009.

33. Conversation with the Mayor of Lisbon, António da Costa, 23 June 2008.

34. Interview with Rosário Farmhouse, high commissioner for immigration and intercultural dialogue, 11 May 2009.

35. Interview with Monica Goracci, director of the International Organization for Migrations in Portugal, 14 May 2009.

36. Farmhouse interview, 11 May 2009.

37. ACIDI's Anti-violence campaign at Basic School #1 in Cova da Moura, 13 May 2009.

38. President of the Social Solidarity Association, Alto Cova da Moura, 13 May 2009.

39. Interview with Ana Gomes, Portuguese Socialist Euro-deputy, 27 June 2009.

40. Europa Press, "Corbacho sostiene que Europa debe de apostar por una inmigración 'con control,'" Brussels: *La Vanguardia*, 26 January 2010.

41. Interview by email with a senior policy maker in Madrid, who asked not to be named.

42. Interview with Oriol Amorós, secretary of immigration in the government of Cataluña, 21 July 2010.

43. Interview with José María Contreras, head of Spain's Department for Religious Affairs in Ministry of Justice, 9 July 2010.

44. Interview with José Manuel López Rodrigo, director of the Foundation for Pluralism and Coexistence, 9 July 2010.

45. Luis Benvenuty, Raúl Montilla, "Los alcaldes piden más control de la inmigración," *La Vanguardia*, 22 December 2010.

46. Oscar Muñoz, "Barcelona pierde 7,609 habitantes en un ano," *La Vanguardia*, 24 January 2011.

47. Pablo Ximénez de Sandoval, "Los inmigrantes retornados tendrán prioridad para regresar a España," *El País*, 3 February 2011.

48. Interview with Rosário Farmhouse, Portugal's high commissioner for immigration, 26 July 2010.

12. WRESTLING WITH PHOBIAS

1. Pew Forum on Religion and Public Life, "How Many Muslims," 16 September 2008.

2. "Spain to host OSCE Conference on Muslim Discrimination," *AFP*, Madrid: 24 September 2007.

3. "Cathedral Controversy," *Catholic News Agency*, Madrid: 11 October 2007.

4. Elizabeth Nash, "Spain's Bishops Fear Rebirth of Islamic Kingdom," *The Independent*, 5 January 2007.

5. Javier Noya, "Spaniards and Islam," Elcano Royal Institute Barometer Survey, 28 November 2007.

6. European Network against Racism, Shadow Report Spain 2007, issued October 2008, p. 3.

7. Ibid., pp. 15–16.

8. Ibid., pp. 19–21.

9. Soeren Kern, "Spain prefers Islam over Roman Catholicism," *Euro-News*, Brussels: 22 September 2008.

10. *Earth Times*, 26 June 2008.

11. Ruiz del Árbol, "Racism in Schools Preys on Muslims," *El País*, 8 December 2008.

12. Email message from Professor Bernabé López García.

13. Conversation with Mustafa Snabi Himri, vice president of the Federation of Muslim Communities of Castilla-La Mancha, 23 May 2009.

14. Conversation with Mekia Nedjar, Algerian professor of Arabic in Madrid, 21 September 2007.

15. Juan González, "El Día de la Toma de Granada," *Minuto Digital*, 29 December 2010.

16. Belen Rico, "La plataforma contra la Toma pide que se cree una Fiscalía de Delitos de Odio," *Granada Hoy/Webislam*, 4 January 2011.

17. Casa Árabe-IEAM, *Muslims in Spain: A reference guide*, Madrid: OSCE's Office for Democratic Institutions and Human Rights, 2009, pp. 6–7.

18. Ibid., pp. 72–77.

19. Interview with José María Contreras, director general of religious affairs, Ministry of Justice, 20 May 2009.

20. European Network Against Racism, "Shadow Report Portugal 2006," issued October 2007, p. 5.

21. Tiago Santos, ed., *Research Survey on Migrants' Experiences of Racism and Discrimination in Portugal*, Lisbon: Numena. 2009, pp. 47–69.

22. Interview with Sheikh David Munir, 12 May 2008.

23. "'Cautela com os amores' com muçulmanos, avisou D. José Policarpo," *Jornal de Notícias*, 14 January 2009.

24. Ibid., "Conferência Episcopal concord com advertência D. José Policarpo."

25. Ibid., "Islámicos 'magodos' com D. José Policarpo."

26. Alexandra Prado Coelho, "Senhor cardeal 'nao tem que se preocupar connosco,'" *Público*, 15 January 2009.

27. Europa Press, "Una mujer denuncia al iman de la principal mezquita de Lleida por poligamia y malos tratos," *La Vanguardia*, 12 March 2010.

28. "Comunicado sobre las declaraciones del Sr. Ángel Colom," *Webislam*, Feb. 14, 2010.

29. "El Gobierno catalán rechaza la deportación de imanes," *Minuto Digital*, 13 February 2010.

30. Jordi Ribalaygue, "Vecinos de Badalona se quejan de los rezos musulmanes en la calle," *El Mundo*, 7 February 2010.

31. "Los musulmanes se hacen con las calles en Cataluña," *Minuto Digital*, 14 February 2010.

32. "Anglada: 'La Guerra étnica ha comenzado!'" *Minuto Digital*, 19 February 2010.

33. Ferran Cosculluela, "Pacto por la convivencia entre los inmigrantes y la alcaldesa de Salt," *El Periódico*, 3 March 2010.

34. "Tres magrebíes apalean hasta la muerte a un vecino de Tudela," *Minuto Digital*, 13 April 2010.

35. "La mayoría rechaza que los Catalanes tengan mas derechos que los extranjeros," *La Vanguardia*, 15 March 2010. xlix Jesús García, "SOS Racismo alerta del auge de mensajes xenófobos en los partidos políticos," *El País*, 26 March 2010.

36. Jesús García, "SOS Racismo alerta del auge de mensajes xenófobos en los partidos políticos," *El País*, 26 March 2010

37. Tomás Bárbulo, "La crisis económica radicaliza a la sociedad en contra de la inmigración," *El País*, 3 March 2010.

38. Efe, "Corbacho dice que no hay un sentimiento Xenófobo," *El País*, 3 March 2010.

39. Xavier Colas, "El líder musulman de Alcalá de Henares justifica la lapidación de mujeres," *Minuto Digital-Diario de Alcalá*, 29 April 2010.

40. Gema Martín Muñoz, "Entrevista: la escuela multicultural," *El País*, 27 April 2010.

41. Laura Daniele, "Los obispos recuerdan que la Constitución ampara el uso del velo," *ABC*, 24 April 2010.

42. Javier Valenzuela, "Cabellos velados, miradas veladas," *El País*, 27 April 2010.

43. Agencies, "El Vendrell Segundo municipio Catalán en prohibirr el uso del burka y el niqab en los equipamientos municipales," *La Vanguardia*, 11 June 2010.

44. Jesús García and Ferrán Balsells, "Imames en pie de Guerra por el derecho al "burka", *El País*, 10 June 2010.

45. Pablo X de Sandoval, "Senate to Stop Short of Calling for Burqa Ban," *El País*, English edition, 23 June 2010.

46. Ángels Piñol, "CiU 'enseña' a 2.000 inmigrantes como deben ejercer el voto el 28-N," *El País*, 21 November 2010.

47. N.G., "La población Musulman aumentara um 82% en España hasta 2030," *El País*, 28 January 2011.

48. "Los inmigrantes de Salt continuan quemando coches," *El País*, 17 January 2011.

49. EFE, "Salt recivira inversions de la UE para reforzar la cohesion y la convivencia," *La Vanguardia*, 31 January 2011.
50. Editorial, "Arrastre xenófobo," *El País*, 19 December 2010.
51. Antonio Manuel, "Obedencia preventiva," *El Dia de Córdoba*, accessed on *Webislam*, 14 December 2010.

13. THE WAY OF DIALOGUE

1. Interview with Ivan Martín, a senior official with the Casa Árabe, 16 April 2007.
2. Tariq Ramadan, lecturer at the Autonomous University of Madrid, 19 May 2007.
3. Interview with Nina Clara Tiesler, Senior Research Fellow, University of Lisbon, Institute of Social Sciences, 29 May 2008.
4. Abdoolkarim Vakil and S. Sayyid, co-editors of, *Thinking Through Islamophobia* (London: Hurst, 2010), and speakers at a symposium on Islamophobia at University of Lisbon, Institute of Social Sciences, 28 May 2010.
5. Interview with Dr. Ahmed Tahiri, president of the *Fundación al-Idrisi Hispano Marroquí*, 3 May 2008.
6. Seminar on "Arab States from Maghreb to Machrek—a Colonial Legacy?," sponsored by Oporto University's Center for African Studies, at Vila Real de Santo António, 27–28 June 2008.
7. AmecoPress, "Más allá de los tópicos sobre las mujeres musulmanes," *Webislam*, 21 February 2010.
8. Declarations at the Lisbon conference on "The Contribution of Religions to Peace," 23–24 June 2008.
9. Declarations at World Conference on Dialogue, called by King Abdullah Bin Abdulaziz Al Saud of Saudi Arabia and co-hosted by King Juan Carlos of Spain, Madrid, 16–18 July 2008.
10. Ibid.
11. Borja Bergareche, "Madrid's Religious Summit Responds to the Saudi Battle with Fundamentalism," *ABC*, 19 July 2008.
12. Interview with Denis Huber, executive director of the North-South Centre in Lisbon, 18 September 2008.
13. "Barcelona Declaration," Europa bulletin of EU, 27–28 November 1995.
14. Valencia Action Plan, Europa bulletin of EU, 22–23 April 2002.
15. Richard Youngs, "Ten Years of the Barcelona Process: a Model for Supporting Arab Reform?" FRIDE, Madrid, January 2005, summary.
16. Peru Egurbide, "La Unión por el Mediterráneo toma el relevo del Proceso de Barcelona," *El País*, 22 December 2007.
17. Commission of the European Communities, "Barcelona Process: Union for the Mediterranean," Brussels, 20 May 2008. pp. 2–3.
18. Ibid.

19. Xavier Mas e Xaxas, "Um mar de dificultades," *La Vanguardia*, 19 July 2010.
20. Interview with Maximo Cajal López, Spanish coordinator for the Alliance of Civilizations, 17 July 2008.
21. Interview with Jorge Sampaio, UN high representative to the Alliance of Civilizations, 14 September 2007.
22. Claudia Rosett and George Russell, "New UN Scheme Alliance of Civilizations," *Fox News online*, 22 November 2005.
23. Brett D. Schaefer, "The U.S. Should Oppose the Proposed UN Alliance of Civilizations," 22 February 2007.
24. Javier Monjas, "Arístegui y el PP, 'Now and Then,'" Madrid: *Nuevo Digital*, 26 October 2009.
25. Jorge Sampaio, Letter to president-elect Barack Obama, 5 November 2008.
26. Helena Barroco, aide to Jorge Sampaio, Alliance of Civilizations office in Lisbon, email message, 4 January 2009.
27. Jorge Sampaio, press statement welcoming the United States as 100th member of the Alliance of Civilizations, United Nations Alliance of Civilizations, New York, 13 May 2010.
28. Jorge Sampaio, UN high representative for the Alliance of Civilizations, "Message to the World Conference on Dialogue," Madrid, 18 July 2008.
29. Interview with Haizam Amirah Fernández, senior analyst, Royal Institute Elcano, 6 July 2010.
30. Interview with Serge Laurens, spokesperson for the America-Spain Solidarity Cooperation Association (AESCO), 6 July 2010.
31. Interview with Hussein El Ouariachi, Barcelona representative of the Alliance for Freedom and Dignity, 21 July 2010.
32. Interview with Mansur Escudero, president of the Islamic Junta, 18 August 2008.
33. Maribel Amoriza, "Más allá delas mesquitas," *El Periódico Mediterráneo.com*, 22 March 2010.
34. "*El 81 por ciento de los inmigrantes musulmanes se siente adaptado a las costumbres españolas*," Spanish Ministry of Interior, 7 April 2010.
35. Olga R. Sanmartín, "El 5% de los musulmanes residentes en España es radical, según un sondeo del Gobierno," *El Mundo*, 7 April 2010.
36. "En España ya hay más de 40.000 islamistas radicales," *Minuto Digital*, 7 April 2010.
37. Ibid., Interview with Sheikh David Munir, 12 May 2008.
38. "Expertos exploran el valor de Córdoba como paradigma de interculturalidad,"*El Dia de Córdoba accessed on Webislam*, 1 February 2011.
39. Mário Soares, president of Portugal's Commission on Religious Freedom, "A Pausa do Natal," *Diário de Notícias*, 28 December 2010.
40. Interview with Bernabé López García, professor of the history of contemporary Islam at the Autonomous University of Madrid, 5 July 2010.

41. Interview with Laila Rattab, journalism student at Madrid's Complutense University, 13 July 2010.
42. "Sarkozy afirma que el 'multiculturalismo es un fracaso,'" *Islam España/ noticia.terra.com.pe*, 10 February 2011.
43. Anna Terrón i Cusí, "L'Immigration et la construction des politiques d'integration en Espagne," *IFRI*, 8 April 2010.
44. Email statement by Dr. Rosário Farmhouse, Portuguese high commissioner for immigration, 15 February 2011.

EPILOGUE

1. Ana Gomes and Rui Tavares, "Eurodeputados portugueses alertam para a situação de refugiados no Mediterrâneo: Responsabilidade de proteger," *Expresso*, 14 May 2011.
2. António Guterres, "Look Who's Coming to Europe," *International Herald Tribune*, 10 May 2011.
3. Juventud Sin Futuro, Manifesto, juventudsinfuturo.net, 7 April 2011.
4. Felipe González, "Y ahora?," *El País*, 27 May 2011.
5. Mário Soares, interview, Lisbon, 27 May 2011.
6. Josep Ramoneda, "Sensibilidad Democrática," *El País*, 5 May 2011.

BIBLIOGRAPHY

Ablal, Ayad. *L'Emigration Clandestine:Approche Sociologique*, Fez: Info-Print, 2002.

Alves, Adalberto *Em busca da Lisboa Arabe*, Lisbon: CTTCorreios de Portugal, 2007.

Arango, E. Ramon, *Spain; From Repression to Renewal*, Boulder: Westview Press, 1986.

Bakkach, Mohammed Mohammed, *La Inmigración Clandestina (Historias Cortas)*, Tangier: Aliyra, 2008.

Baganha, Maria Joannis, Maria Lucinda Fonseca, eds. *New Waves: Migration from Eastern to Southern Europe*, Luso-American Foundation. Lisbon: 2004.

Brenan, Gerald. *The Spanish Labyrinth*, Cambridge, GB: Cambridge University, 1944.

Bruce, Neil. *Portugal The last Empire*. New York: John Wiley and Sons, 1975.

Caldwell, Christopher. *Reflections on the Revolution in Europe: Immigration, Islam, and the West*, New York: Doubleday, 2009.

Castro, Américo. *España en su Historia: Cristianos Moros y Judíos*, Buenos Aires: Losada, 1948.

—— Edmund L. King tr. *The Structure of Spanish History*. Princeton: University of Princeton, 1954.

—— *The Spaniards*, Berkeley: University of California, 1971.

Cesana, Laura, *Jewish Vestiges in Portugal: Travels of a Painter*, author's edition. Lisbon, 1997.

Chejne, Anwar G., *Islam and the West: The Moriscos*, Albany: State University of New York, 1983.

Coelho, Antonio Borges. *Portugal na Espanha Arabe*, 5 vols. Lisbon: Sea Nova, 1972-75.

Cohen, Robin. Ed. *The Cambridge Survey of World Migration*. Cambrid GB: Cambridge University, 1995.

Constable, Olivia Remie, ed. Medieval Iberia: *Readings from Christian, M lim, and Jewish Sources*. Philadelphia: University of Pennsylvania, 199

De Madriaga, Salvador, *Spain: A Modern History*, New York: Praeger, 1958.

Epps, Bradley S., Significant *Violence: Oppression and Resistance in the Narratives of Juan Goytisolo, 1970–1990*, Oxford: Clarendon Press, 1996.

Felner, Ricardo Dias. *Voltar a ser médico: Médicos Imigrantes Bolseiros da Fundação Calouste Gulbenkian*. Lisbon: Calouste Gulbenkian Foundation, 2005.

Fletcher, Richard, *Moorish Spain*, New York: Henry Holt, 1992.

Ginio, Alisa Meyuhas, ed. *Jews, Christians, and Muslims in the Mediterranean world after 1492*. London: Frank Cass, 1992.

Glick, Thomas F. *Islamic and Christian Spain in the Early Middle Ages*. Leiden, Netherlands: Brill, 2005.

Goytisolo, Juan, *Makbara*, Barcelona: Galaxia Gutenberg, 1980.

Hernando de Larramendi, Miguel and Puerto García Ortiz, eds. *religión.es: Minorías religiosas en Castilla-La Mancha*. Icaria Pluralismo y Convivencia, Barcelona: 2009.

Henke, Holger, ed. *Crossing Over: Comparing Recent Migration in the United States and Europe*. Lanham, MD: Lexington Books, 2005.

Harris, Max. *Aztecs, Moors and* Christians: *Festivals of Reconquest in Mexico and Spain*. Austin: University of Texas, 2000.

Haik, Kaoutar and Virtu Morón. *La Niña de la Calle*. Barcelona: Debolsillo, 2009.

Ibn Khaldun. Franz Rosenthal tr.*The Muqaddimah: An Introduction to History*. New York: Bollingen Foundation, 1958.

Irving, Washington, eds. William T. Lenehan, Andrew B. Myers. *The Alhambra: The Complete Works of Washington Irving*, vol. XIV, Boston: Twayne Publishers, 1983.

Irwin, Robert. *The Alhambra*, Cambridge: Harvard University, 2004.

Jayyusi, Salma Khadra, ed. *The Legacy of Muslim Spain*, 2 vols. Leiden: E.J. Brill, 1994.

Kamen, Henry. *The Disinherited: Exile and the Making of Spanish Culture, 1492–1975*. New York: HarperCollins, 2007.

———— *The Spanish Inquisition: A Historical Review*, New Haven: Yale, 1999.

Kennedy, Hugh. *Muslim Spain and Portugal: a Political History of al-Andalus*. London: Longman, 1996.

Korinman, Michel and John Laughland, eds. *The Long March to the West: Twenty-First Century Migration in Europe and the Greater Mediterranean Area*. Edgware, Middlesex: Valentine Mitchell Academic, 2007.

Levi-Provençal, *Histoire de l'Espagne Musulmane: Le Siècle du Califat de Cordoue*, Vol. III, Paris: G.P. Maisonneuve and Cie., 1953.

———— *Histoire de l'Espagne Musulmane: La Conquête et L'Emirat Hispano-Umaiyade (710–912)*, Vol. I, Paris: G.P. Maisonneuve and Cie., 1950.

López García, Bernabé and Miguel Hernando de Larramendi, eds. *Historia y Memoria de las Relaciones Hispano-Marroquíes*. Madrid: Oriente y Mediterráneo, 2009.

——— Ángeles Ramírez Fernández, Eva Herrero Galiano, Said Kirhlani, Mariana Tello Weiss, *Arraigados: Minorías religiosas en la Comunidad de Madrid*. Madrid: Fundación Pluralismo y Convivencia, 2007.

Lowney, Christopher. *A Vanished World*. New York: Free Press, 2005.

Macagno, Lorenzo. *Outros Muçulmanos: Islão e narrativas coloniais*, Lisbon: Imprensa de Ciencias Sociais, 2006

Madariaga, Salvador de. *España: Ensayo de historia contemporánea*. Madrid: Espasa-Calpe, 1979. Martin Muñoz, Gema, ed. *Muslims in Spain: A reference guide*. Madrid: Casa Árabe, 2009. ... *Marroquíes en España: Estudio sobre su integración*. Madrid: Fundación Repsol YPF, 2003.

Martins, Jorge, *Breve História dos Judeus em Portugal*. 2nd edition. Lisbon: Nova Vega, 2010.

Menocal, Maria Rosa, *The Ornament of the World*, Boston, New York, London: Little Brown and Company, 2002.

Monroe, James T. *Islam and the Arabs in Spanish Scholarship*. Leiden: E.J. Brill, 1970.

Moura, Paulo. *Passaporte Para O Céu*. Lisbon: Dom Quixote, 2006.

Oliveira Marques, António Henriques de. *History of Portugal*, vol. I. New York: Columbia University, 1972.

Ortega y Gasset, José. *Invertebrate Spain*. New York: W. W. Norton, 1937.

Payne, Stanley G. *A History of Spain and Portugal*. 2 vols. Madison: University of Wisconsin, 1973. ... *The Franco Regime 1936–1975*. Madison: University of Wisconsin, 1987.

Porch, Douglas. *The Portuguese Armed Forces and the Revolution*. London: Croon Helm, 1977.

Prado Coelho, Alexandra and Daniel Rocha. *Muçulmanes em Portugal*. Lisbon: Público, 2005.

Read, Jan. *The Moors in Spain and Portugal*. Totowa, N.J.: Rowman and Littlefield, 1975.

Riosalido, Jesús. *Guia de Al-Andalus*. Madrid: Fundación Sapere Aude, 2004.

Romero Salvado, Francisco J. *Twentieth-Century Spain: Politics and Society in Spain, 1898–1998*. New York: St. Martin's Press, 1999.

Royo, Sebastian, ed. *Portugal, Espanha e a Integração Europeia: Um Balanço*. Lisbon: Institute of Social Sciences, 2005.

Sánchez Nogales, José Luis. *El Islam entre Nosotros: Cristianismo e Islam en España*. Madrid: Biblioteca de Autores Cristianos, 2004.

Santos, Maciel, Dir. *Os Estados Nacionais entre o Maghreb e o Machrek: Uma herança do Colonialismo?* Oporto: University of Oporto African Studies Center, 2009.

Santos, Tiago, ed. *Research Survey on Migrants' Experiences of Racism and Discrimination in Portugal*. Porto Salvo: Numena, 2009

Settle, Mary Lee. *Spanish Recognitions: The Roads to the Present*. New York: W.W. Norton and Company, 2004.

Soares, Mário and Federico Mayor Zaragoza. *Um Diálogo Ibérico no Contexto Europeu e Mundial*, Lisbon: Temas e Debates, 2006.

BIBLIOGRAPHY

Soyer, Francois. *The Persecution of the Jews and Muslims of Portugal.* Leiden/Boston: Brill, 2007.

Torres, Claudio and Santiago Macias. *O legado islámico em Portugal,* Lisbon: Círculo de Leitores, 1998.

Torres, Claudio, Santiago Macias and Susana Gomez. *Terras da Moura Encantada,* Oporto: Livraria Civilização, 1999.

Tremlett, Giles. *Ghosts of Spain: Travels through Spain and its Silent Past,* New York: Walker and Company, 2006.

Vallejo-Nacera, María *Luna negra: La luz del Padre Pateras.* 4th ed., Barcelona: Belacqva, 2005.

Triandafyllidou, Anna, Ruby Gropas eds. *European Immigration: A Sourcebook.* Hampshire, England: Ashgate Publishing, 2007.

Wiarda, Howard J., ed. *The Iberian-Latin American Connection: Implications for U.S. Foreign Policy.* Boulder: Westview, 1986.

Welles, Benjamin, *Spain, The Gentle Anarchy,* New York: Praeger, 1965.

INDEX

Abd al Rahman: defeat of Emir of Córdoba (756), 18; role in creation of Al Andalus, 18

Abd al Rahman III: family of, 26; proclaimed Caliph (929), 18

Abu Hafs Al-Masri Brigade: blaming of Al Qaeda for Madrid train bombing (2004), 53

Acebes, Ángel: Spanish Interior Minister, 52, 55

Acoge: 6, 83; concept of, 4–5; personnel of, 11, 46; services offered by, 7, 83

Afghanistan: 57, 59, 142–3, 151, 179, 240; Al Ghuraba training camp, 57; borders of, 58; cultural role of burqa in, 96; immigrants from, 75; NATO presence in, 54; Operation Enduring Freedom, 53, 57–8, 128, 142, 148, 204, 241; Soviet Invasion of (1979–89), 57

Africa: 1, 7, 24, 30, 37, 75, 112; AIDS crisis in, 185; development aid provided to, 9; Kabylie, 25; Rif, 25; sub-Saharan, 35, 101–2

African Party for the Independence of Guinea and Cape Verde (PAIGC): opponents of, 42

Aga Khan, Karim: 40; background of, 118; veneration of, 118

Aga Khan Foundation: 119; Development Network, 97–8, 119; establishment of (1983), 98; personnel of, 97

Ahmed, Rabei Osman el Sayed: acquittal of (2007), 66; background of, 66

Ahmidan, Jamal: leader of GICM, 55; suicide of (2004), 55, 65

Al Andalus: 1, 17–18, 25, 27, 43, 62, 115, 135, 140, 230, 248; Jewish community of, 158; political use of image of, 51, 63, 90, 138–9, 242, 253; population of, 19, 141; rulers of, 19

Al Jazeera; personnel of, 60

Al Mansur: destruction of shrine of Santiago (997), 29

Al Qaeda: 53, 58, 61, 64–7, 90, 108, 119, 139–41, 146, 154, 177, 253; implication in Madrid train bombings (2004), 53; leaders of, 1, 51; members of, 57, 142, 147, 150; presence in Europe, 55, 57, 64, 142, 150; propaganda of, 144; sympathizers of, 52

Al Qaeda in Islamic Maghreb: 143, 150

Alfonso II, King: construction of church on grave of St James, 29

Alfonso the Wise: 28

Colonialism: Portuguese, 24–5, 33, 37, 97, 107, 109, 118, 176

Columbus, Christopher: 80; discovery of Americas (1492), 43

Commission on Religious Freedom (2004): delegates in attendance, 40

Committee for Help to Refugees (CEAR): 14

Communism: 37

Conde, José Antonio: *Historia de la denominación de los Árabes en España*, 20

Contreras, José María: director of religious affairs at Spanish Ministry of Justice, 137

Convergence and Union of Cataluña: members of, 215

Convergencia I Union (CiU): 221; electoral performance of, 222

Consortium for Applied Research on International Migration (CARIM): 2

Corbacho, Celestino: background of, 186; Spanish Minister of Labor and Immigration, 186

da Costa, António: background of, 180; Mayor of Lisbon, 27, 191, 230; Portuguese Interior Minister, 67, 140, 180

Costa Rica: street children of, 95

Council of Europe (COE): 233, 237; Inter-cultural Dialogue, Issues and Perspectives (2007) 119; voting on wearing of burqa or niqab, 221

Cravinho, João Gomes: Portuguese Secretary of State for Foreign Affairs, 185

Cuba: 75, 161; refugees from, 3

Cultural, Educational, Social Operation Association of Pakistani Women (ACESOP): aims of, 94; founding of (2005), 94; members of, 93

Czechoslovakia: Prague, 25

Dashti, Rola: first female parliamentarian of Kuwait, 233–4

de la Vega, María Teresa Fernández: Spanish Deputy Prime Minister, 187

Denmark: 144

Deobandism: 146

deVries, Gijs: named as EU counter-terrorism coordinator, 54

Dhikr: concept of, 29

Dominican Republic: immigrants from, 71

Don João VI, Regent: 160

Don Pedro, King: palaces of, 169–70

Ebadi, Shirin: Nobel Laureate, 237

Egypt: 57, 116, 148, 170, 235–6; borders of, 15; Cairo, 250; immigrants from, 122; Revolution (2011–12), 233, 249

El Atlas: 90; aims of, 89

Engineering Financial Company Ltd (EFISA): 39; personnel of, 38

Enriquez, Carmen González: report on immigration in Spain, 176–7

Erdogan, Tayyip: Turkish Prime Minister, 236

Escudero, Mansur: 130–2, 152, 242; background of, 129; conversion to Islam (1979), 129; death of, 137; head of FEERI, 130

European Commission against Racism and Intolerance (ECRI): observations of neo-Nazi movements on Spanish websites (2011), 223

European Conference of Rabbis: members of, 230

European Council: 184; Brussels meeting (2004), 54

European Economic Community: Treaty of Schengen (1990), 34–5

Judaism: 80–1, 110, 124, 157, 177, 202, 230–1, 238; Kabbalah, 160; Marranos, 163–5; persecution by Spanish Inquisition, 158–9; presence in Al Andalus, 158; presence in Morocco, 171; presence in Portugal, 159–60, 162–7; presence in Spain, 157–8, 169–71; Sephardic, 131, 158, 169, 173; Yom Kippur, 165

Jum'ah, Ali: Mufti of Egypt, 13

Junta of Andalucía: 83, 95, 225, 228

Kashmir: 240

Kazakhstan: immigrants from, 76

Ki-moon, Ban: UN Secretary General, 236–7

Kuwait: 233–4; oil reserves of, 152

Lashcar e Tayyba: 150

Lebanon: 106, 128, 143; July War (2006), 171

Libya: 15, 249; Civil War (2011), 250; Libyan National Transitional Council, 250

Machado, Mário: imprisonment of (2008), 212; leader of National Front, 212

Macías, Father Isidoro: *Padre Pateras*, 3, 10–11

Madrasa: 105; examples of, 115

de Magalhães, José: Portuguese Secretary of State for Interior, 147

Mahmoud, Sheikh Moneir: hate mail received by, 63

Maimonides, Moses: 28

Mali: 14; refugees from, 4; Spanish Embassy in, 183

Malta: coast of, 15; undocumented immigrants coming to, 8

Manuel, Antonio: *El Día de Córdoba*, 223

Manuel I, King: expulsion of Jews and Muslims from Portugal (1496), 158, 160, 164; role in Lisbon Massacre (1506), 162

Marques, Rui: High Commissioner of ACIME, 72, 74

Mauritania: 8–10, 47, 175; refugees from, 4, 8

Menocal, María Rosa: *Ornament of the World*, 22

Merkel, Angela: German Chancellor, 246

Mexico: 161

Al Missned, Sheikha Mozah bint Nasser: 237

Mohammed, Prophet: 28–9, 39, 107, 116, 130; descendants of, 118; insults against, 105

Mohammed VI, King: granting of royal pardon to political prisoners (2004), 36

Moldova: 44; immigrants from, 75

Montávez, Pedro Martínez: head of Department of Arab and Islamic Studies and Oriental Studies at Madrid's Autonomous University, 21

Moors: 29; architecture of, 25–6

Moratinas, Miguel Ángel: Spanish Foreign Minister, 182, 202

Moreira, Adriano: Portuguese Minister of Overseas Territories, 24

Moriscos: expulsion from Spain (1608–14), 30–1

Moroccan Association of Education for Young People: personnel of, 46

Moroccan Islamic Combatant Group (GICM): 149–50, 154; implication in Madrid train bombings (2004), 54–5; members of, 64

Morocco: 1–2, 7–8, 11, 14, 18, 20, 22, 28, 44, 60, 80, 155, 159, 163, 166, 170, 175, 226, 234,

7; Lisbon, 13, 18, 27, 40–4, 47–9, 67–8, 70–7, 96–102, 105, 107, 113, 116, 118, 140, 146, 153, 160, 180, 192, 227, 230, 243; Lisbon Central Mosque, 49, 68, 97, 99–100, 105–15, 117–19, 121, 153, 230; Lisbon Massacre (1506), 162, 230; Lusitania, 23; Mértola, 25–7; Madrasa Ahle Sunny Jamat, 115; Martim Moniz Mosque, 117; member of EU, 248; military of, 148; Ministry of Education, 114; Ministry of Foreign Affairs, 237; Ministry of Health, 75; Ministry of Interior, 140; Ministry of Labor, 98; Mozambican community of, 114; Muslim community of, 38–40, 42, 68, 96, 98–9, 112–14, 117, 119, 145, 192, 202; navy of, 12; Network of Portuguese Jewish Sites, 168; Nigerian community in, 69; Odivelas, 116; Oporto, 72, 75, 103; Pakistani community in, 69, 114; Palmela, 97, 113–14, 116–17; Penal Code (2007), 211; Plan for Integration of Immigrants, 181; Roma of, 211; Russian community in, 69; Sacavém, 42; Salamanca, 167; Santarém, 29; Senegalese community in, 69, 107, 117; Social Democratic Party, 200, 252; Strategic Defense Intelligence, 146; Tagus River, 113, 115; UEFA Euro Football Championship host (2004), 44, 66–7; Ukrainian community in, 69, 211

Portuguese Commission for Religious Freedom: representatives of, 118

Portuguese Research Center of Arabic-Pulaar and Islamic Culture: offices of, 99; personnel of, 99–100

Protestantism: 80–1, 177; Spanish, 82

Qaddafi, Muammar: 184–5, 250
Qatar: 237

Rajoy, Mariano: leader of PP, 195, 253
Rauf, Feisal Abdul: founder of American Society for Muslim Advancement, 230
Real, Baltasar Garzón: 149, 253; call for extradition of Augusto Pinochet, 59; investigation of Islamic radicals, 58–61
Rebirth and Union Party of Spain (PRUNE): ideology of, 136
Reinares, Fernando: *El Nuevo Terrorismo Islamista: Del 11-M al 11-S*, 141
Retornados: 193; concept of, 38
Rif War (1920–6): 36; Battle of Annoual (1921), 24
Riosalido, Jesús: *Guía de Al-Andalus*, 26–7
Robinson, Mary: Icelandic Prime Minister, 237
Roman Empire: conquest of Jerusalem (70 AD), 157
Romania: 11, 44, 85; undocumented immigrants from, 7
Rosen, Rabbi David: 231
Rubalcaba, Alfredo Pérez: Spanish Interior Minister, 12, 15–16, 155; Spanish Vice President, 155
Ruis, Josep Anglada I: leader of Platform for Cataluña, 216
Runnymede Trust Commission: Survey of Islamophobia (1996–7), 228
Russian Federation: immigrants from, 69, 75, 192

Said, Edward: 28
Salafism: 96, 142, 144; Moroccan, 153

joz, 46; Baena, 4; Barcelona, 22, 34, 37, 43–4, 58–9, 83, 85, 92–4, 119, 132–3, 144–6, 153–4, 168, 172, 199, 209, 215, 221–2, 234; borders of, 2; Burgos, 143; Cádiz, 10, 13; Cataluña, 44, 52, 63, 85, 92, 95–6, 132–3, 154–5, 197, 199, 215, 217, 220–2; coast of, 30; Congress of Deputies, 178, 239; Constitution of, 220; Córdoba, 3, 23, 26, 29, 128–32, 168–9, 202–3, 225, 243; Costa del Sol, 1–3, 8, 12, 46, 170; Department of Pluralism and Coexistence, 177; Dominican community of, 71; economy of, 185, 188, 199; El Algar Mosque, 214; El Ejido incident (2001), 45–6, 216; El Vendrell incident (2010), 216; Girona, 168–9; government of, 3, 9, 56, 62, 88, 92, 130, 190, 219; Granada, 5, 7, 17, 19, 27, 127, 136, 203, 208; Great Mosque of Córdoba, 23, 29, 131–3, 141, 203; Guardia Civil, 2, 143–4, 147, 215; Huelva, 46; Islamophobia in, 138, 201, 203–6, 208–10, 219–20, 222, 225; Jaén, 46; Jewish community of, 82, 157, 169–71; La Línea de la Concepción, 7; Law of Universal Justice, 59; Law on Foreigners, 176; Leganés, 55, 64–5; Lerida, 46; M/11 trial (2007), 63, 65–6; M-30 Mosque, 123, 131, 133–4; Madrid, 5, 7–8, 11, 20–1, 26, 35, 43, 54–6, 59, 65, 80, 82–3, 87, 89–90, 93–4, 124, 129, 137, 139–40, 142–3, 145, 165, 169, 172–3, 182, 200, 206, 209, 219, 225–6, 229, 233, 237, 246; Madrid train bombings (2004), 21, 30, 37, 47, 51–6, 58, 60–4, 66–8, 81, 87, 89, 91, 106, 122–6, 131, 133, 139, 143, 146,

149, 152, 154, 190, 202, 206, 236, 246, 253; Málaga, 5, 123, 129; Mallorca, 15; Marbella, 58; Medina Zahra, 203; member of EU, 248; military of, 53, 61, 143; Ministry of Education and Culture, 83, 172; Ministry of Foreign Affairs, 20, 79, 126, 173, 182–3, 225; Ministry of Interior, 79, 81, 90, 136, 142, 146, 190, 209; Ministry of Justice, 79, 134, 137, 189, 198, 209; Ministry of Labor and Social Affairs, 79, 91–2, 189, 199–200, 204, 218; Moroccan community of, 71, 88–9, 133–4; Murcia, 15, 82; Muslim community of, 63, 81, 124, 129–30, 133, 136, 202, 242–3, 245, 253; National Anti-Terrorist Center, 140; National Intelligence Center (CNI), 147; Pakistani community of, 133; per capita income, 34; Peruvian community of, 71; Protestant community of, 82; Reconquista, 18, 28–9, 139; Routes of Sepharad, 168; Salt incident (2010), 216–17, 222; Seville, 5, 28, 54, 83, 168, 203; Strategic Plan for Citizenship and Integration (2007–10), 79–80, 189, 247; Strategic Plan for Citizenship and Integration (2011–14), 196; Summer Olympics (1992), 43; Tarifa, 2–3, 5, 7, 10; Tarragona, 59, 216; teaching of Islam in education system of, 81–2; Toledo, 18, 168–70, 173; Union Mosque, 123; Valencia, 18, 46, 63, 83–5, 124–7, 137; Vic, 195, 218, 222, 229; Vila Joiosa, 207–8; views of Muslims, 9; Vitoria, 46; Zaragoza, 46, 168

Spanish Commission for Help to Refugees (CEAR): branches of, 84

Spanish Federation of Islamic Religious Entities (FEERI): 121, 128–30; members of, 122–3, 134–5, 137

Spanish Red Cross: 4; personnel of, 3; preparations for *patera* crisis, 3

Spanish Socialist Worker's Party: 31, 53, 83, 186; electoral performance of (2011), 252

Spiritual Foundation of India: founding of Madrasa Ahle Sunny Jamat (1996), 115

Sri Lanka: 240

Sufism: 29, 115, 127–8, 130; music of, 87

Sunnism: 40, 106; presence in Portugal, 111

Al Suri, Mohammed: role in development of European Al Qaeda cells, 149–50

Sweden: 144

Switzerland: 4, 6; Davos, 241; Geneva, 118

Syria: 57, 75–6, 249; Aleppo, 57; Damascus, 18; immigrants from, 122; Islamophobia in, 218; military of, 76

Tabligh Jamaat: 144–5; alleged connection to Barcelona terrorist plot (2008), 119; *Itjimah*, 146; members of, 153

Tariq ben Ziyad: military campaigns of, 18

Tauran, Cardinal Jean Louis: head of Papal Council for Interfaith Dialogue, 232

Toledo International Centre for Peace: founded by FRIDE (2004), 170

Trashorras, José Emilio Suarez: imprisonment of (2007), 65

Tréfaut, Sérgio: *Os Lisboetas* (The Lisboners), 69–70

Tunisia: 2; borders of, 15; Revolution (2011), 15, 249

Turkey: 236–7; decorations provided for Lisbon Central Mosque, 108; Istanbul, 163, 204; undocumented immigrants arriving in, 15

Ukraine: 44, 75–6, 192, 211; undocumented immigrants from, 7, 69

Umayyads: fall of, 18

Umma: concept of, 146

Union for Muslim Women in Spain: founding of (2008), 95; members of, 95

Union for the Mediterranean (UpM): proposals for, 234–5

Union of Islamic Communities of Spain (UCIDE): 82, 121, 134, 137; funding of, 122; members of, 122

United Kingdom (UK): 148, 192, 236; 7/7 bombings, 58, 68, 140, 227, 246; anti-Semitism in, 205; British National Party (BNP), 195; immigration policy model of, 247; Islamophobia in, 205; Ismaili presence in, 41; Labour Party, 194; London, 39, 41, 55, 160, 203; Manchester, 113, 116; Muslim community of, 202; Norwich, 129

United Nations (UN): 125–6, 143, 237, 239; Educational, Scientific and Cultural Organization (UNESCO), 132, 175, 184; Forum of Alliance of Civilizations (2008), 237–8; General Assembly, 236; High Commission for Refugees, 15; personnel of, 119, 179, 240, 250

United States of America (USA): 33, 49, 104, 142, 144, 146, 150, 161, 166, 236–7; 9/11 attacks, 21, 25, 35, 40, 51, 53, 58–60, 76, 98, 106, 109, 111, 133, 143,